AF531367

TOWARDS ECONOMIC DEVELOPMENT

TOWARDS ECONOMIC DEVELOPMENT

By

B. L. MATHUR
Faculty Member
Department of
Economic Administration & Financial Management
University of Rajasthan
Jaipur – 3020001

2001

Discovery Publishing House

New Delhi–110002

First Published–2001

ISBN 81-7141-592-X

© Author

Published by :
DISCOVERY PUBLISHING HOUSE
4831/24, Ansari Road, Prahlad Street,
Darya Ganj, New Delhi-110002 (INDIA)
☎ : 3279245 • Fax : 91-11-3253475
E-mail : dphtemp@indiatimes.com

Printed at : Tarun Offset

Preface

Indian Economy from the eve of independence marched towards, depended economy to self-sustained economy. Five decades after independence, Indian economy tried best to develop important sector of nation's economy viz, agriculture, industry, trade and transport. No doubt development have taken place in all the aforesaid sector of economy. But it is also true that fast growth of population has created the problems of inequality poverty etc. and hence posed obstacles in the way of economic development. In the presence of all these factors and circumstance, Indian economy marched towards development.

In the present book efforts have been made by the author to discuss in detailed trends of Indian economy Towards Development. No originality is claimed about the subject matter in the book. I drawn liberally informations, facts, figures and texts from various Government publications as well from others. I thankfully acknowledge to all the sources from which I have taken assistance in bringing-out the book in its present shape.

While no effort has been spared to remove printing and other mistakes, I sincerely hope and trust that my readers will favour me by pointing out errors that might have crept in due to over-sight. I shall consider my efforts amply rewarded if those for whom the book is intended are benefited by it. Suggestions for improvement may be highly appreciated and gladly adhered to. Finally, I wish to thank My publisher for this efforts in quality printing.

B.L.Mathur

Contents

1

Introduction

UNDER DEVELOPMENT

Economic Development has now become the cherished goal in world economies. Economies are striving to boost the process of economic development. World economies on the basis of level of economic development can broadly be classified into two categories -developed and under-developed. It will be proper before the study of development to know what does mean under-developmentDifferent economists and different agencies like the U.N. and Planning Commission in India have defined ' underdevelopment ' in different ways. In general, all low income countries whose per capital income is less than U.S. $ 500 per year are said to be underdeveloped economies.

Prof. Ragnar Nurkse defines underdeveloped economies as those which when compared with the advanced countries "are under-equipped with capital in relation to the population and national resource."

According to Samuelson, " An underdeveloped nation in simply one with real per capita income low relative to the present day per capita incomes of such nations as Canada, the United States, Great Britain, France and Western Europe, generally. Usually an underdeveloped nation is one regarded as being capable of substantial improvements in its income level."

According to the U.N. experts, the term ' underdevelopment ' refers to the state of economy of a country in which the per capita real income is low when compared with the per capita real incomes of countries such as United States of America , Australia, Canada and Western Europe. This definition mainly highlights one of the important features of underdevelopment i.e, poverty. Hence this definition can not be taken as a comprehensive one.

A definition given by the Indian Planning Commission states that existence of idle resources is the feature of underdevelopment. This definition too can not be taken as one which gives the true picture. Because, there are some developed countries in which resources remain idle. Similarly, the above definition does not spell out the causes for the existence of idle resources . Moreover , existence of idle capacity may also be due to the following reasons :

a) Lack of Technical Know How

b) Inadequate Capital Resources .

From the above, it becomes clear that it is very difficult to define the term ' underdevelopment in its true sense. For this purpose, one has to understand the various characteristics of an underdeveloped economy .

Characteristics of an Underdeveloped Economy

Before we discuss charactristics of developed economy, it will be proper to study charactristics of underdeveloped. A developed country is one which has fully utilised the existing natural resources and thereby attained the maximum level of economic development. A developing country is one, which is utilising the existing natural resources and thereby tries to attain economic maturity. An underdeveloped country is one which has plenty of human and natural resources with it but unable to utilise them or is underutilising them.

Some of the important characteristics of an underdeveloped economy are as under ;

1. *Predominance of Agriculture* - Generally, an underdeveloped economy would mainly depend on agriculture. Agriculture would be the main source of employment .Nearly 70 to 85 per cent of the population of such economies gets its living from agriculture. The economy will be dependent upon the agricultural production. Agriculture would contribute a major share to the national income. About 50 per cent of the gross domestic production in underdeveloped countries come from

agriculture whereas its percentage is Just 2 to 4 per cent in developed countries. The industries would also be mainly agro based. There are some exceptions to these phenomena e.g., Denmark, Netherlands. The exports of an under-developed economy largely consist of agricultural product and agricultural raw material. Despite of pre-dominance of agriculture the agriculture sector in under-developed countries has been growing at a miserably lower rate. The productivity in the agriculture sector has tends to remained low. The rising pressure of population on agricultural productivity is caused by varieties of factors such as small holdings, low capital investment, old techniques, indebtedness of the farmers etc. But in most of the cases economic development of such countries depends to a great extent upon agriculture.

India is predominantly an agricultural country. It provides employment to around 72% of the population. Around 50% of the country's income is contributed by agriculture. Many of our industries are agro based. The concentration of population on agriculture is too heavy. But the recent technological progress has led to country towards a substantial increase in agricultural production knows as green revolution. However, this too has remained counted to few crops and few regions. The overall situation in agriculture is still backward as prevailed in other under-developed countries.

2. *Over Population and Unemployment* - Underdeveloped countries are generally over populated. The increase in population will be more than the economic development made. The problem of unemployment would be serious . In almost all the under-developed countries, there is tendencies of very high birth rate and quite lower death rates are found because of expansion of medical facilities. The existence of wide gap between high birth rate and law death rate has been main cause of rapid population growth. Table-1 clearly reveals the trend of growth rate of population in developed and under-developed countries. The growth rate of population in under-developed countries is quite high as compared to developed countries.

Table-1

Growth Rate of Population (%)

Developed Countries	*Growth Rate*	*Under-developed Countries*	*Growth Rate*
England	0.3	India	1.8
U.S.A.	0.9	Pakistan	2.8
Japn	0.6	Kenya	2.5

3. *Inequalities in Income and Wealth* - In under-developed countries there exists a widespread inequalities in distribution income. In underdeveloped countries, a major portion of the country's economy is controlled by very few individuals or business houses. This smaller group accrues a large part of the national income. The larger part of population in under-developed countries have to be satisfied with the smaller part of the income. Therefore, in such economies concentration of income or wealth in the hands of few would be more . As a result , there is a wide gap between the rich and the poor.

This tendency is found in almost all the under developed country including in India. The disparities in the distribution of income in developed countries is quite low. There is inverse relationship found between the level of economic development and income-disparity. According to this relationship higher the level of development, lower will the inequality of income. In India top 20 per cent of countries population obtain 55 per cent of national income whereas the poorest 60 per cent of the population obtain only 28 per cent of national income.

4. *Low Income and Poor Savings* - In underdeveloped countries , the per capita income will be very low and as a result , there will be a situation of little savings or there will be no savings . Due to vicious circle of poverty , the saving is very little or no savings in the country.

5. *Low Capital Formation* - Capital is a crucial determinant of economic development. Underdeveloped countries have a very low rate of capital formation. In view of

this, such countries have to depend on foreign countries for the inflow of capital. In advanced countries like U.S.A. a nd Canada , around 20 -25 % of the national income constitutes capital and it is used for investment purposes. In underdeveloped countries , the inducement to invest and capacity to save will be either absent or very less.

6. Lack of Technical Know -how - In underdeveloped countries , sufficient technical exertise will not be available and as a result, the production methods will be based on traditional system only. Therefore, the level of production in both industrial and agricultural sectors will be very low. In underdeveloped countries, in the absence of higher advanced education and training , the quality of products will be very poor. There will be lack of entrepreneur ship also.

7. Excessive Dependence on Exports - The economy of many underdeveloped countries depend primarily on their exports . The items generally exported are traditional items such as raw materials, minerals, etc. They , in turn import machinery and consumer items. Too much of dependence on export is not conducive for an economy as it is likely to be affected by many external factors like frequent changes in international prices of export commodities. Moreover in such economies importance would be given to export sectors only and thereby other sectors will be neglected.

8. Under Utilisation of Natural Resources - Generally, natural resources, such as fertile land, water, minerals, etc. will be available in plenty in underdeveloped economies. But the basic problem is how to use it. These resources are either improperly used or not at all used . The main reasons for under utilisation is lack of education , capital , and market.

9. Lack of Socio Economic Set -Up - Socio - economic set-up plays an important role in the economic development of a country. In many underdeveloped countries people are still governed by caste system, superstitions etc. These factors, coupled with poverty and illiteracy stand in the way of economic development. For this , we should not blame the people. This problem is existent mainly because of the narrow mindedness of petty politicians. A country which could effectively utilise the available socio-economic .Set ups will make progress steadily and gradually. England can be cited as an example in this regard,.

Some Special Problems of Underdeveloped Economy

The steady of characteristics of underdeveloped economy indices some special problem which are normally faced by these economy. The following are the some of the special problems faced by underdeveloped economy :

1. *Greater dependence on agriculture.* One criterion for classification of countries as developed or underdeveloped is the ratio of the agricultural population to total population. It is commonly agreed that in an underdeveloped economy a major portion of population is engaged in agricultural sector. This greater dependence on agriculture is due to the fact that manufacturing sector (or industrial sector) and the services sector remain underdeveloped. Further because of the higher rate of growth of population in the past few years the pressure of population on land has increaed. As a result of it the agricultural holdings have become very small and uneconomical. Thus we cannot use the modern methods of cultivation. For example, India has less than 10 acres of standard land for each man in agriculture, China six acres, Egypt 2 to 4 acres. These small holdings do not permit the use of mechanised methods of production.

Thus in underdeveloped economies as compared to developed economies like U.S.A. there is low productivity per man in the agricultural sector. According to 1961 census 137 million people are engaged in agriculture but these 137 million are unable to produce sufficient food for the entire Indian population. In U.S.A. where population is roughly one half of India, less than 8 million people are engaged in agriculture. These 8 million agriculturists in U.S.A. not only feed the entire population of U.S.A. but also give a surplus for export.

2. *Scarcity of Capital and Low Per Capita Income.* Availability of capital is another criterion for judging whether a country is developed or underdeveloped. The scarcity or insufficiency of capital is taken as a sign that there is underdevelopment. One indication of capital deficiency is the high rate of interest on capital. However, this alone cannot be a decisive test. In underdeveloped countries rate of capital formation is very low. It is between 5% to 8% of the national income whereas in developed countries like U.S.A., Canada etc. It is between 15% to 18%.

The cause of low rate of capital formation in an underdeveloped economy are :

(a) low inducement to invest; and

(b) low propensity and capacity to save.

Let us explain both these causes.

(a) There is a low level of per capita income in underdeveloped countries. Because of low level of per capita income the demand for manufactured goods or size of the market for demand for manufactured output is very limited and hence the inducement to invest is low.

(b) Savings give birth to capital but unfortunately both the propensity and capacity to save (will and power to save) in underdeveloped countries are low. Since the level of per capita income is low, almost all the earnings of the people are spent in satisfying their necessities of life. Thus, sometimes very little or even nothing is left with the people to save and hence the rate of accumulation of capital is very low.

It is argued that even if there is an increase in the level of per capita income in these countries the rate of capital formation does not increase. It is due to the reason that people in these countries also have a tendency to have the same level of consumption as prevailing in the developed economies. Nurkse has named this tendency as 'demonstration effect.'

3. *Unutilization or underutilisation of productive resources.* Another characteristics of underdeveloped economies is that the productive resources in these economies are either underutilized, or unutilized . Infact, these economies are not

deficient in land, water minerals, forests etc. The real problem with them is that these resources are not fully exploited or utilized due to many obstacles as inaccessibility of these resources, lack of capital, lack of technical know how and primitive methods of production. For the same reason, India is described as a rich country with poor people'. India is endowed with rich natural resources and huge manpower but due to lack of capital and technical knowledge, these resources, remain unexploted or unutilized and as such account for India's poverty. The same is true of most of the underdeveloped economies of the world.

4. *High net rate of population increase and disguised unemployment.* A high net rate of population increase is generally considered to be a characteristic of underdeveloped economies. The problem of high net rate of population is more serious in countries like Latin America, Africa, Middle East and some but not all of the countries of South East Asia where resources of land are limited. In recent years the rate has been rising still more and so there is poverty amidst plenty. There is unemployment as well as 'disguised unemployment which is a clear indication of underutilisation of manpower.

By disguised unemployment we mean "that part of the manpower pool that does almost nothing because there is nothing to do. Such people may not be counted in the census of unemployment, but they can be scarcely called employed. They live with their kinfolk and when a boom or a development plan comes along sweeping them into productive city jobs, there is almost no reduction in the production back on the farm."Briefly, 'disguised unemployment' means that there are more people engaged in agriculture than are actually required and as such their withdrawal from land will not lower production.

Mere growth in numbers does not necessarily mean development. Indeed since writers as Malthus have warned,

"Unbridled increase in number is likely to invoke th law of diminishing rturns and to work against increases in per capita living standards. Admitedly we do find many underdeveloped countries repeating the pattern of the eighteenth and nineteenth century developing economies. Improved technology (e.g. sanitation and in our day cheap D.D.T.) first reduces the death rate, and with birth rates remaining high, population grows rapidly."

"Puerto Rico, Java and numerous other modern examples underline the twin lessons, first, that much of the increase in output made possible by technological advances may be spent on duplication of numbers and second, that modern science, conquering disease faster than it operates on food supply, might in the future keep people from dying from germs — only to threaten them with death from famine as they die with each other for insufficient food.

5. *Backwardness of the people.* Economic backwardness of the people is another important characteristic kof underdeveloped countries. By backward people, we mean people who are not successful in the economic struggle to earn their livelihood. These people have not been able to adapt themselves to the environments. Thus economic backwardness of the people means that labour in these countries is less efficient, almost immobile ignorant, lacking in specializatiion in occupation and trade and other entrepreneurship.

The Indian economy also possesses many of the features of underdeveloped economies which have been discussed at the end of this chapter.

Definitions of Economic Development

The term economic development is normally used in number of synonymous terms such as economic growth, economic welfare, secular change, social justice and economic progress. In such a situation, it is not easy to give any precise and clear definition of economic development. But in view of its scientific study and its popularity, a working definition of the term seems to be quite essential.

Economic development as it is now generally understood includes the development of agriculture, industry, trade, transport, means of irrigation, power resources, etc. It, thus, indicates a process of development. The sectoral improvement is the part of the process of development which refers to the economic development. Broadly speaking economic development has been defined in three ways :

Firstly , economic development is " an increase in the economy's real national income over a long period of time. " But it may not be accepted as a complete and satisfactory definition. The term : real national income : has been used here simply for the country's total production of goods and services in real sense and not in terms of money. Thus the calculation of real national income will not consider the effect of price changes. But it is not practicable in a development economy where price changes are inevitable. In this definition, economic , development implies a sustained and continuous increase in real national income over a long period of time. A short period increase in national income for one or the other reasons does not constitute economic development .

As a matter or fact , the above definition does not consider the changes in the growth of population. If a degree of increase in the real national income is followed by a rapid growth in population, economic development may be neutralised or even negative. But this indicator of economic development should consider the changes in real national income due to cyclical swings, variations in the growth of population and the value of money.

Secondly, economic development implies, an increase in the per capita real income of the economy over the long period."Economists generally recognise this concept unanimously and define economic development as an increase in per capita real income or output. According to *Meir,* economic development is " the process whereby the real percapita income of a country increases over a long period of time. " *Buchanan* and *Ellis defines* , " Development means developing the real income potentialities of the underdeveloped areas by using investment to effect those changes and to augment those productive resources which promise to raise real income per person. " *Prof. Baran* defines economic development as " an increase over a time in per capita output of material goods." These definitions point out clearly that the rate of rise in the real national income should be more than the growth rate of population for economic development.

Here the difficulty arise is that a rise in per capita income does not secure a rise in the real standard of living of the masses. It is quite possible that an increased per capita income may adversely affect per capita consumption in the society , because people may increase the rate of their savings or the state may use the increased income for defensive or other purposes. It is, further, possible that the gap between the poor and the rich may increase i.e. the rich may be more richer and masses may remain poor despite an increase in the real national income . Moreover , such a perimeter or indicator of economic development may be related with the facts like " the structure of the society the size and composition of its population its institutions and culture, the resource patterns and even distribution of output among the society;s members ".

Thirdly, some economists define economic development in terms of economic welfare . According to *Okun and Richardson,* economic development is a sustained secular improvement in material well-being which we may consider to be reflected in an increasing flow of goods and services. "

This definition has also the following limitations as mentioned on next page:

(i) *Growth in Income and Economic welfare* - Sustained and constant growth in real national income does not essentially reflect an improvement in economic welfare. In the same way, a mere increase in economic welfare cannot be real indicator of economic development till there is just and fair distribution of national real income amongst the members of the society;

(ii) *Measurement of Output* - The main difficulty comes in the way while measuring the value of output on which the economic welfare depends. However, the output may be measured at market prices whereas economic welfare may be measured by an increase in real national income;

(iii) *Measurement of Economic Welfare* - The economic welfare should be measured not only by an increase in the real national output , but also in the way it is produced. It is quite possible that the real and social cost (pain and sacrifice) would have enhanced; and

(iv) *Lack of Real Indicator* - It is difficult to equate the economic welfare with an increase in per capita real income, and hence, it cannot be a real indicator of economic development. It is for these difficultires that the economists recognise the per capita real national income as the correct perimeter of economic development.

Thus it can conclude that economic development is a process rather than the result of it which results in a rise in real national income, and the net national product must have a sustained increase i.e. it must be over a long period of time.

ECONOMIC DEVELOPMENT & ECONOMIC GROWTH

As have been already expressed earlier, the terms ' economic development ; economic growth and economic progress are commonly used in day-to-day life. But in economics these terms have been defined in quite a different way with separate meanings. First, we shall discuss here the difference between economic development and economic growth and later between economic development and economic progress.

Economic growth refers to as a steady and continuous increase in the agreagate real national product of an economy over a sufficient long period of time. Every nation all over the world, either advanced or backward anxious to maintain an adequate level of its annual growth rate. Of course, backward economies would like to overcome their backwardness and poverty and to ensure fuller use of their natural and human resources. In modern time growth has become a necessity for every nation of the world. The advanced countries seems to be more anxious to maintain high levels of employment as well as high standard of living. These nations have to continue to grow at a satisfactory rate. The target of backward nations have to achieve at a much higher rate of growth so as to provide ever risiing standard of living to large number of people by providing more employment opportunities. In fact, in anticipations to achieve high rate of economic growth to advanced countries need to have much higher rate of growth per annum.

Economic growth may also be explain as the process through which an under developed economy is transformed into a high level of economic achievement welfare of the citizens of that country also increased.

When a country is said to be economically growing , it means that the production potential of that country is increasing. This is generally reflected in ' National Income :. We are aware that the term ' National Income ' refers to the aggregate money value of goods and services of a country during a year. If we say that the national income is growing , it means that the production is increasing. In this sense the national income growth is considered to be the important measure of economic growth.

Economic growth can also be measured either in terms of increase in economic welfare or in terms of increase in per capita income. Economists who consider standard of living as the best index of economic growth prefer per capita income criterion to other criteria mentioned above. They are also of the view that only with the per capita income criterion, distinction could be made between developing and developed economies.

However, both national income and per capita income criteria require necessary adjustment to price level changes for the purpose of arriving at real growth rate.

These two terms are used as synonyans or interchangeable . On some occasion this use is entirely acceptable, but when two related term exists, there must be some scope af distiction between the two . Hence some economists have made slight distiction between two. Schumpter and Mrs. Ursula Hicks have distinguished economic development from economic growth. In brief economic development deals with the problems of underdeveloped countries and economic growth with those of advanced and rich countries. In the world of Schumpeter. " Development is a discontinuous and spontaneous change in the satistionary state which for ever alters and displaces the equilibrium state previously existing ; while growth is a gradual and steady change in the long run which comes about by a general increase in the rate of savings and population. " In his simple words, A . Maddison observes, " The raising of income levels is generally called economic growth in rich countries and in poor ones it is called economic development. " Mrs. Hicks has also expressed almost the same views and said that economic development refers to the problems of underdeveloped countries and economic growth to those of advanced countries. She points out that the problems of underdeveloped countries are concerned with development of unused resources, even though their uses are well-known; while those of advanced countries are related to growth, most of their resources being already known and developed to a considerable extent.

More elaborately, economic development may be defined as " a progress whereby an economy's real national income increase". Thus, economic development refers to both process as well as an increase in the real national income. A rise in the real national income is the growth of the economy . Economic development is, thus, the cause or process whereas economic growth is its effect or result. It may be said that economic development includes variations in the supply of factors of production on the one hand and in demand for products based on economic and non-economic factors on the other. But economic growth is the outcome of this long process of development. Economic growth, in short is the result of economic development, which in itself is expressed as a long-run change in an economy's national product or national income.

The difference between economic development and economic growth may also be explain in a tabular form is illustrated below.

Economic Growth	Economic Development
1. This is used with reference to advanced countries	1.This is used with reference to underdeveloped countries
2. Growth is unidimensional in nature - (i.e.) more output in quantitative terms. Growth refers to increase in income - both national and per capita income	2.Development is multi-dimensional in nature. Development refers to not only increase in income but also increase in savings, investment etc. It also involves fundamental changes in technology, structure of the economy , even changes in the attitute of the people etc.
3.Growth is almost automatic . It is a process of change	3.Development is a difficult phenomenon. It needs planning or some form of government action.
4.Growth refers to consolidation of gains already achieved .	4.Development refers to starting from the fundamentals.

ECONOMIC DEVELOPMENT AND ECONOMIC PROGRESS

Economic development and economic progress have the same meaning . If there is rise in the national product (or real national income) of the country and the growth of population is lesser than the national income, the economic welfare, being synonym of economic progress will be comparatively higher, and the country will gradually head towards prosperity and economic betterment. Thus, the higher economic welfare will register economic progress in the country.

Economic development refers to an increase in the real national income which is an important feature for economic welfare or economic progress . In this way, economic development becomes an essential condition for the economic welfare of the country. If the major part of the increased national income goes to the rich, the rich become richer and the poor become poorer. Such a case of affairs can hardly be recognised as the economic progress . Economic progress , thus means the betterment of the masses and not of a few. So, economic development and economic progress have quite a different meaning and cannot be treated as synonymous.

Economic welfare also depends on the composition of the national output. If the national output consists largely of military equipment or it consists largely of capital goods, as it has happened in Russia in the early stages of economic development, this type of economic development cannot support the economic welfare in the country. It is rather against the economic progress. Besides the composition of output it is also essential for the economic welfare to consider the process of production. If the process of production involves the exploitation of working force, and it is not given its due share out of the total production, the economic welfare of the masses will be adversely affected. In such a matter of affairs, the violence or labour movements may rise against such exploitation, which would increase the economic welfare of the masses in the society. Further, economic welfare is not positively sure to lead to social welfare in general. The process of development has vast influence upon social institutions (habits, customs, beliefs and attitudes) on the one hand and they also impress economic development largely on the other . The old traditions may influence the entire process of development which may cause serious discontentment. Thus, economic welfare may not necessarity raise social welfare.

ECONOMIC GROWTH & WELFARE

Under certain situations economic growth and welfare mean the same thing and on other occasions they do not. Increase in national income will be helpful to provide increased welfare to the people. But it is not automatic. Before coming to any conclusion on the increase in economic growth and welfare, we must see that the national income figures are quoted after adjusting to the price level changes. If an increase in GNP is due to inflationary prices , and there is no increase in real GNP in terms of goods and services, it can not signify any increase in welfare of the people. Hence an increase in GNP does not necessarily imply an increase in general welfare of the people . It will depend upon the following factors.

a) The composition of economic growth and (b) The distribution of GNP among the different sections of community. When we closely analyse the composition of economic growth measured in terms of GNP we find that an increase in national income, due to increased activities of defence production may not increase the welfare of the people. If the GNP increases on account of production of war materials ammunitions and so on, the welfare of the common man may further decline even though GNP increase.

With uneven distribution of resources among different sectors and priority to heavy industry and low priority to agriculture, in a predominantly agriculture country like ours. The poverty of the farmers will continue even when high growth rate is registered in the GNP through growth in industrial sector.

BASIC CHARACTERISTICS OF INDIAN ECONOMY

The world economy on the basis of their level of economic development have been categorised by the economist into two broad groups– (i) Developed Economies and (ii) Under-developed Economies. Developed economy refers to that state of affair where there is high standard of production, consumption, saving and investment and where there no exists of involuntary unemployment. Thus developed economies are characterised by higher level of aggregate output followed by higher level of consumption standard. These economies accounts for nearly 85 per cent of the world supply. Underdeveloped economies are those which are characterised by mass poverty, illiteracy, hunger, disease and thus miserably low standard of living of the population.

INDIAN ECONOMY– NATURE AND CHARACTERISTICS

Indian economy is an under-developed economy as it has almost all the characteristics of an under-developed country. despite of these inherent characteristics of the economy, it will not be fair to call Indian economy as under-developed economy. There has been remarkable transformation took place in the economic, social and other spheres during last four and half decades of economic planning. Therefore it would be correct to call Indian economy a *developing economy.*

Indian Economy–A Developing Economy

Samuelson and *Nordhaus* defines, 'A developing country is one with real per capita income that is low relative to that in industrialized countries like the United States, Japan, and those in Western Europe. In human terms, developing countries typically have populations with poor health, low levels of literacy, inadequate dwellings, and meager diets.'[1]. According to this definition a developing country is one whose per capita income is low as compared to the industrially developed nations of the world and the low standard of people found in the developing nation only because lower income.

There are some economists who believe that low level of saving is the main characteristic of a developing economy As defined in the *Collins Dictionary of Economics*, 'developing country or less developed country or underdeveloped country or Third World country as a country in which the level of Gross Domestic Product and income per head is presently inadequate to generate the savings necessary to embark upon substantial agricultural and industrial investment programmes.'[2] This definition of developing economies points out the fact that because of inadequate saving developing economies deprived from making large scale investment out of domestic savings for the development of agriculture and industries. Hence developing economies mostly relies on foreign capital for raising the levels of investment.

---

1. Paul A. Samuelson and William D. Nordhaus, with the assistance of Michael J. Mandel, Economics, Fifteenth Edition, 1955, p. 702.

World economies are also classified on the basis of income. On this basis economies are recognised as low-income economies[3]. Middle-income economies and high income economies[4] Middle income economies are further classified as lower-middle[5] group and upper-middle group economies.[6]The various nations of the worl are compared on the basis of per capita GNP which shows that there exists wide gap among the per capita real income of India and some of the advanced countries of the world. Though Indian economy has shown several positive sign of progress during the planning era, yet it is considered as a developing economy.

The economy of India has possess all the potentials for further development. The shape of the nation's economy at present has significantly changed from what is was in 1947. With the help of selected indicator, the performance of Indian economy can be analysed.

Net National Product at constant prices (1980-81) has gone-up from Rs. 40,454 crores in 1950-51 to Rs 2,52,838 crores in 1996-97. The per capita net national product during the aforesaid period increased from Rs. 1,126.9 to Rs. 2,701. The rate of gross domestic capital formation which was only 10.66 per cent during the period 1951-56 has gone-up to 26.2 per cent in 1995-96 at current prices.

Some upper-middle group economies of the world are Malaysia,

The other sector, in which Indian economy has registered substantial progress are summarised below:

---

2 Wrold Development Report, 1997. p. 207.

3. Some low-income economies of the world are Vietnam, Nepal, Bangladesh, India, Pakistan, China and Sri Lanka.
4. Some high income economies of the world are New Zealand, Israel, Australia, U.K., France, Germany, United State, Japan, Switzerland etc.
5. Some low-middle economies of the world are Indonesia, Philippines, Romania, Thailand, Poland etc.
6. Some upper-middle group economies of the world are Malaysia,Oman..

(a) A break through has been achieved in the field of agriculture with the use of modern technology. Foodgrain production which was mere 107 million tonnes in 1971-72 has gone up to 198.2 M. T. in 1996-97.

(b) The country emerged as a leading industrialized country. The country has developed the capacity to producing the most sophisticated consumer and capital goods by making use of modern technology.

(c) The country could able to developed a viable infrastructure consisting of social overhead capital.

Notable development have taken place in the field of communication, transport, banking, insurance, health care, education, science & technology etc.

(d) The volume of India's Foreign Trade has increased from 1214 crores in 1950-51 to Rs. 2,52,369 crores in 1996-97.

It is clear from the aforesaid explanation that the performance of the Indian economy has been commendable in almost all sector during the era of planned economic development. It has emerged as a self-reliant economy. Thus, it will not be fair to call Indian economy and under-developed economy, it would be correct to call Indian economy a developing economy.

BASIC CHARACTERISTICS OF INDIAN ECONOMY – A DEVELOPING ECONOMY

Like other economies of the world, Indian economy too possesses some basic features which distinguish it from rest of the economies of the world in terms of natural resources, infrastructure, technology, social and cultural environment etc. The basic characteristics or principal features of the Indian economy are summarised as follows:

(1) Mass Poverty and Low Per Capita Income– The most important feature of Indian economy is low per capita income. Per capita income in India is estimated at about Rs. 2,701 in 1996-97 which is one of the lowest in the world. One can easily visualise that how a large proportion of the country's population can live with such a low income. As estimated by the Planning Commission, about 28 per cent of India's population lives below the poverty line. One can easily judge the extent of poverty from the poor quality of food, clothing, housing, education medical and health facilities inadequately available to the common citizen of the country.

(2) Inequalities in Income Distribution– There exists gross inequalities in India. The alarming situation of inequalities of income distribution can be observed both in the rural as well as in urban areas. So far as rural areas are concerned, about 10 per cent holding belongs to medium and large group (*i.e.* upto 4 hectares and 10 hectare and above respectively), held 49.2 per cent of land whereas 90 per cent holding held only 50.8 per cent of land. Likewise, the assets of the top 20 big business houses is over Rs. 80,000 crores which is about 70 per cent of the total assets held by the private sector industries.

According to the World Development Report 1997, in 1995, the lowest 20 per cent household had only 8.5 per cent in the household income, whereas the highest 20 per cent households had 42.6 per cent.

(3) Pre-dominance of Agriculture– It is a paradox that agriculture occupies a pre-dominate place in the Indian economy. Despite of pre-dominance, agriculture in the country is backward. Nearly 65 per cent of the national population gets its living from agriculture. The agriculture and allied activities contributes about 28.8 percent in the national income of India. Agricultural commodities accounts about 80 per cent of the total consumer expenditure, out of which 63 per cent is exclusively spent on food articles. Agricultural product in the country of about Rs. 21,000 crores which represents 19.8 per cent in the total export earnings.

Despite of the aforesaid contribution of agriculture in the Indian economy. The productivity of agriculture is miserably low. Per hectare yield of agriculture in India is also very low as compared with the yield of agriculture production obtained in the developed countries.

(4) Un-explored Natural Resources–The country is rich by availability in plenty of varieties of renewable and non-renewable resources. Among the non-renewable resources, the most important are mineral deposits.

A large part of the natural resources available to India still remains un-explored either because of lack of financial resources or technical know-how. As estimated by U.N. in 1988, the per head production of crude steel in India was 11 kg. as against 528 kg. in the U.S.A. Similarly the production of electricity per head in U.S.A. was 8,297 kwh. which was 75 times greater than that of India.

World Bank estimates for 1995 points out the fact that the per capita consumption measured in thousand of kilogram of oil was 237 in India as compared to 7,918 in the U.S.A. 7,821 in Canada, and 3,718 in the United Kingdom.

(5) Demographic Peculiarities– The Indian economy is also faced with the problem of population explosion. The population has risen at an average rate of about 2.11 per annum during the last decade 1980-81. As what generally found in underdeveloped countries, in India too, the birth rate which was 49.2 per thousand in 1921 has come down to about 28.0 per thousand in 1977. The death rate has also sharply declined from 48.6 per thousand to about 9.0 per thousand between 1921-97. If the this trend of population growth is continue, it is likely to reach 1,000 million by the end of present century. Not only the size of Indian population is quite large, but a large part of population are unemployed and under-employed. Moreover the quality of population is also poor which is sufficient cause for keeping the per capita productivity at low level.

(6) Wide Spread Unemployment– The economy of the country is characterised by the large mass of unemployment and under employment. In March 1997, the total number of unemployed was estimated at 185 lakhs. A disheartening feature of the pattern of employment is that only 10 to 11 per cent of increase in the labour force find employment in the organised sector. There also exists disguised unemployment in the rural sector of India. This is situation under which more persons are working in a job than actually required. However, such type of situation is hidden and cannot openly be seen.

(7) Quality of Human Capital– The poor quality of human capital in India can be estimated by the rate of illiteracy, malnutrition, inadequate medical and health care facilities etc. The number of hospital beds available in the country was only 6.42,000 for a population of over 920 million. The doctor-population ratio was 1 : 3,000 and only 1.6 per cent of the total expenditure incurred on health services whereas it is 16.0 per cent of total population in the U.S.A. About 30 per cent of India's population has not been provided even safe drinking water.

(8) Dualistic Economy– Dualism is found in all the sectors of the Indian economy. The term implies the existence of two different segments in the economy. In the two segments, *One*, is fully developed and organised in which market oriented modern techniques of production are used. The *Other* segment seems to be un-organised and underdeveloped in which old and outdated techniques of production are used. The second segment of economy poses varieties of growth barrier to the growth in the market economy and tends to keep an economy most backward. In developing economies, such type of dualism is found both in the urban as well as in rural sector of the economy. For example, In Indian agriculture, one can find latest technology at work alongwith the primitive techniques. Most modern industries and primitive handicraft have co-existence in the Indian economy.

(9) Technological Backwardness– Underdeveloped countries adhere to the outdated techniques of production. The main causes responsible for such a sorry affairs are lack of education and paucity of capital resources forced to use of outdated technology. Low productivity of Indian agriculture and industry may be attributed to the backward technology.

(10) Backward Infrastructure–Infrastructure refers to those basic economic and social institutions which are inevitable for initiating the process of development. Indian economy does not have a well-developed infrastructure. Social infrastructure, which consists of education, training, research, health, housing, civic amenities, etc., available in India is rather backward. Similarly, economic infrastructure, which comprises the network of transport and communication system, irrigation, power, banking and insurance institutions, etc., is also not fully developed. Backward infrastructure hinders economic development.

(11) Backward Foreign Trade– An underdeveloped economy is generally foreign trade oriented. Traditionally, these countries export primary products, *i.e.* products of agricultural origin and minerals. Their imports consist of foodgrains, consumer and capital goods, technical know-how, etc. The most unfortunate thing about the foreign trade is that the underdeveloped economies have unfavourable balance of payments and the deficit in foreign trade is continuously on the increase. The deficit in India's foreign trade which was only Rs. 2 crores in 1950-51 had gone up to Rs. 10,643 crores in 1990-91. According to the quick estimates for 1996-97 the trade balance has gone up to Rs. 19,319 crores.

****

2

Development of Human Resources

The task of human resource development in India is a complex net. There are acute shortage as well as excess supply of manpower in many categories which posses a net set of priorities to the man power planners and managers in the country. Uneven development of the various sectors of the economy from the point of view of absorbing the available supply and to maintain a balance between the demand and supply of manpower resources is yet another special feature to be taken into consideration . Still one more short-coming is that the manpower development is mainly concentrated on high level manpower requirements which has resulted in lowering of quality. At the same time the neglect of middle level and lower-level personnel has led to the emergence of artificial and uneconomic structure ; a case in point is that we have more trained executives than workers. Such a situation leads to all kinds of distortions, lop-sided development and under-utilisation of available resources. Instead detailed statistics in respect of working force of different categories in industrial sectors is not available due to weak data base. The estimation of manpower requirements both qualitative and quantitative is , therefore, a crucial phase of human resource development from the point of view of drawing up appropriate human resource development programme to meet the existing manpower requirements and to avoid redundancies in future.

Although the country has now become the tenth industrially developed country in the world , but it is a sad commentry that this development has made little change in the fate of masses which continue to be living below powerty line and facing unemployment. Today, "the number of unemployed in India is about 26 millions which comes to about 12 per cent of the total labour force. This ratio is 5.2 percent in the U.S., 3.3. per cent in the U.K. and 1.3 per cent in Japan". The number of job seekers on the live register of Employment Exchanges which gives an idea about urban unemployment rose from 0.33 million in 1950 to 14.4 millions in 1980. The situation in rural areas is worse. There is precisely no workable estimate of rural employment basically due to weak data base. Roughly , the rural and semi-rural joblessness, taking into account the incidence of seasonal and disguised unemployment recorded at different Employment Exchanges all over the country taken together. The Planning Commission's estimate of population below poverty line in 1977-78 was 48 percent for rural areas, and 41 per cent for urban areas, the average for the country being 46 percent. According to the World Development Report, 1981, Indiawith per capita GNP of $ 190 is the 15th poorest country of the world.

Despite the decades of focus on non-human variables in development planning, with the hope that these would contribute to the development, the country stood disillusioned and this could well be a reason for the economic stagnation of the country. The cause of this dismal performance lies in the implementation of right type of development planning. Human resource development has been looked upon as a by product of economic growth or regarded, as a corollary of development rather than a direct objective. The strategy has so far been based on the notion of what is called to be the spread effect of overall growth . It cannot be denied that development of industries on modern lines will generate employment opportunities and that there is a correlation between the increase in the growth of industrial production and expansion of employment opportunities. But, the result of such a strategy in the country has been discouraging to absorb the past, the present and the growing number of unemployed and under-employed.

The problem of unemployment and poverty in the country should be regarded as a direct objective of development planning not a by product of economic growth which would disappear as development proceeds. Thus, without exploring the new avenues and that is human resource development, the economic, financial , environmental, energy planning--- all these would turn to be an exercise in futility. Appropriate human resource development programme is , therefore, the need of the hour.

However, the emphasis on human resource development in India is of recent origin. As a matter of fact, the stress on human resource development has been properly laid in the 7th Plan (1985-90) . Realising the importance of human factor in the national economy, the Government of India has also created a separate Ministry for human resource development under the control of a Cabinet Minister. Policies and programmes in education, health and welfare etc. are also being restructured for the purpose .

Developing nations need a wide variety of human skills to bring about economic and social development. It is assumed to be the leadership role of educational institutions to anticipate national manpower needs and meet these demands through tailored educational offerings. This leadership role is however, not fulfilled in developing nations. Whereas, in developed countries, education is treated as an end in itself. "The developing countries are producing a large number of graduates with the general education, but without the specialised knowledge in some field of technology the nation requires."[7] The educational offerings should, therefore be concentrated to develop knowledge and skills and attitudes and values among the people to bring about changes in a meaningful manner. For instance , an electrician should be provided theoritical knowledge with safety procedures as well as practical training. Alongwith it, efforts should also be made to eliminate work thinking in this mind about the job of an electrician.

The basic questions related to human resource development are: How to make people more efficient ? How to improve their performance ? How to utilise their talents ? How to keep them satisfied ? How to train them for a change ? How to motivate them to work in a changed atmosphere ? The answer of all these questions lies in an effective human resource development programme. So such an effective programme should include :

(a) Proper human resource development strategy;

(b) Adequate manpower development procedures; and

(c) A specialised motivational plan.

Role of Human Resources in Economic Development

Human resourtes has its own importance in economic development of any country. The construction and fall of world civilisation in every era depends on human being. According to scripture if it is true that this earth has been created by the God of heaven, then it is also true that the existence of this world and its changed structure are depends on the God of this earth, who is no doubt a human being. To demolish and reconstruct are two artistic activities of human. Man is the author and hero both of the world history.

Like this, human resources are the most important sources of economic and industrial development of any country.

That is why Dr. V.K.R.V. Row has explained that human is not only a important means of production, but a practicable too. Economic development and human resources are so related that generally they called complimentary to each other. Because the object of economic development is to increase the living standard of human efforts. It is no doubt that economic development of any country depends up to most extent on natural resources and quantity of capital of that country but human resources are that strength which mobilise these physical resources. New invention, construction of sky-touching building and grand factories, to break mountain, conquest on sea, construction of dam to control the water of rivers and bring out large minerals from the earth are the result of human activities and effort no doubt. Prof. Richard T. Gill has said that economic development is not a mechanical process. It is human enterprise and like all human enterprises its outcome will depend finally on the skill quality and attitudes of the men who under takes it.

According to Lipson the actual property of any country depends on its inhabitant's ability. That country will be poorer which has huge natural resources but people are idle and conventional there than countries who have very few natural resource but people are labourious, devoted and active.

Essential Elements of Development of Human Resources

Prof. T. V. Schultz has mentioned four methods four methods of development of human resources.

1. Availability of that kind of medical facilities which influences anticipated life, energy, enthusiasm and workmanship.
2. Extention of training.

3. To organise education on primary, secondary and higher stages.
4. Availability of educational facilities to adult workers.

In broder approach there are three most important factors in process of human investment or skill of construction, such as follow:

1. Present generation should know the standard of that knowledge which are being applied by the previous generation.
2. People should be taught how to enforce the current knowledge of present time in new direction by new approach.
3. But to teach people that how to modernise the traditional thought will not be the last task, they should also come to know the new invention, new thought, modern goods, new process of production and they should be encouraged also to adopt these factors.

Utilization of Human Resources in Economic Development

According to approach of economic development various developing economists have advised the utilization of human resources. The final aim of these optionals are to gain desired economic development through the best utilisation of available man power. In this connection Prof. Ragner Nurkse, Prof. Harney Leibenstein, Prof. Arthur Lewis, Prof. Mahalanobish and Thomson and Notestin are mentioned specially, as follow :

1. *Prof. Ragnar Nurkse* : In developing countries approximately twentyfive percent people are victim of disguised unemployment. Mostly these unemployment are persist in agriculture. So it will be better to divert these labour power from agriculture sector to construction and industrial sector for utilisation of capital formation and in another hand there will be no loss in agricultural production. In another words if population shiefted from villages.

(1) pressure of population at one place will be lower
(2) Increase in Industrial production
(3) disguised unemployment will be lower.
(4) New Industries and construction work will be developed
(5) Probable saving will be increased
(6) Formation of capital formation will be strengthen
(7) Immediate possibility of economic and industrial development of the country.

It means there is hardly any need to stress the obvious point that it is enough to get labour released from agriculture, that 'saved'. The labour must at once be employed for productive capital formation that is invested. Otherwise the man-power released wil be wasted and the advantages derived from the increase in productivity lost.

2. Prof. *Harney Leigenstin's* Thought

The Thought of Prof. Leibenstein depends on the recognition that the reproduction rate in society is reduces if income increases. Though this thought is just against the thought of Malthus. Malthus says that in developing countries where population is huge, established there. Exactly so in preliminary stage of developing countries huge quantity is needed for investment for the rapid expansion of national income. This effort has two benefits

(a) Fall of population rate
(b) As a result of this work of economic development will be easier.

In the own word of Prof. Leibenstein's "In sum, the initial stimulant has to be sufficiently large to cover temporary losses and generated income-depressing forces, and also to provide a surplus growth." He clearly says that econmies are under-developed because of the efforts to ascape from economic backwardness be they spontaneous or forced are below the recitical minimum required for persistent growth.

3. Prof. *Arthur Levis's* **hypothesis**

On the basis of a model, Prof. Levis has tried to clear that acute economic development is possible if there is unlimited supply of labour, due to manpower is cheeper in developing countries and desired quantity is available in easy way. So it is required to get more and more power from rural sector and transferred them to industrial sector by giving them incentive of handsom wages. This will give them standard of libe up because of increased production.

But utility of disguised unemployment has not been discussed by Prof. Lewis. He has only three conditions, namely

(1) Rate of wages must be fixed in industrial sector than rural sector, though it may be high;

(2) Investment must be more in industrial sector;

(3) cost of training of labourers must be constant in whole period.

The hypothesis of Mr. Lewis are based on abundent of sources. But because there is always lack ofsources in developing countries . This modle of Mr. Lewies is not applicable in these countries.

4. Transition theory of *Waren Thamson* and *Frank Notestein* Transition theory has been patronised. This theory actually does not discussed the utility of increased population, but it clears the effect of increased popultion on economic development. According to this theory population of any country passes through three conditions as a result of economic development.

First Stage — is the condition of stagnant in the eyes of increased population. In this condition economic and social approach of people is narrow. There are lack of education, balanced food, health and medical facilities . So rate of birth and death both are excess but actual increase of population remains constant.

Second Stage — is the stage of population eruption. In this stage economic activities are expanded, and incomes are increased. Field of Bank, Insurance, transport, Education, inefficient , uneducated and conservative population of India, Pakistan and Bangladesh has been a great obstacle in the path of their economic development. Thus, the population of a country plays a significant role in the economic progress.

Population of a country is closely related to its economic development. After the destruction caused by Second World War in Germany and Japan, the efficient, hardworking, educated and healthy population of these countries has contributed to a large extent to the rapid economic development and reconstruction of these countries . In sharp contrast to it, the inefficient , uneducated and conservative population of India, Pakistan and Bangladesh has been a great obstacle in the path of their economic development. Thus, the population of a country plays a significant role in the economic progress.

MAIN FEATURES OF INDIA'S POPULATION

(1) Size of Population–India is the country has a large population. India's population, as on March 1, 1991 stood at 846.30 million (439.23 million males and 407.07 million female. India has the largest population in the world next to China. The second largest populous country India is the home of 16 per cent of world's population. The country, however accounts for 2.42 per cent of the total world area. As depicted in Table-1, the population of India as recorded at each decadial census from 1901 has grown stadily except for a decrease during 1911- 21.

Table- 1

Decadial Growth of India's Population (1901-91)

Year	*Population*[1] *(in crore)*	*Decade growth rate (per cent)*[1]	*Average Annual exponential growth rate (Per cent)*	*Progressive growth rate over 1901*
1901	23.8	–	–	–
1911	25.2	+ 5.75	0.56	+ 5.75
1921	25.1	– 0.31	– 0.03	+ 5.42
1931	27.9	+ 11.00	1.04	+ 17.02
1941	31.9	+ 14.22	1.33	+ 33.67
1951	36.1	+ 13.31	1.25	+ 51.47
1961	43.9	+ 21.51	1.96	+ 84.25
1971	54.8	+ 24.80	2.20	+ 129.94
1981	63.4	+ 24.66	2.22	+ 186.64
1991	84.6	+ 23.85	2.14	+ 255.00

1. Census of India 1991 Series 1 India, Paper 2 of 1992 Final Population Totals.

The size of India's population is not only large but also at continuous to go fast. The population of India has been continuously rising since 1921. Presently, Indias population is growing 2.1 per cent per year. In most states the growth rate declined during the decade. However, Andhra Pradesh, Arunachal pradesh, Madhya Pradesh, Maharashtra, Nagaland, Triura, West Bengal, Daman and Diu, Lakshadweep and Pondicherry which account for one-third of the country's population, recorded increase in growth rate. Nagaland registered the highest growth rate of 56.08 per cent while Kerala the lowest 14.32 per cent.

Mumbai metropolis continued to be the most populated city of the country with urban population of 12.60 million, Calcutta taking the second place having 11.02 million. Delhi ranks third with a population (urban) of 8.42 million followed by Chennai 5.42 million.

(2) Birth Rate and Death Rate– The death rate in India has declined sharply (particularly since 1951) but on the other hand declined in birth rate has been very slow. As a consequence of aforesaid dilema, the growth rate of population in India has been very high since 1951 as depicted in Table-2.

Table 2

Birth Rate and Death Rate in India

Year	*Birth rate (Per thousand)*	*Death rate (Per thousand)*
1911	49.2	42.6
1921	48.1	47.2
1931	46.4	36.2
1941	45.2	37.2
1951	39.9	27.4
1961	41.7	22.8
1971	41.2	18.9
1981	37.2	15.0
1991	30.9	10.8

(3) Density of Population– One of the important indicator which shows concentration of population in India is the density of population. It refers the average number of person living in per square kilometre of area. The densty of population be claculated by dividing the total population of a country by the total area. It is one of the important indices to know whether a particular country, region or state is thickly populated or thinly populated. The density of population in India since 1921 is shown in Table-3.

The 10 heavily populated districts of the country are Calcutta, Chennai, Greater Mumbai, Hyderabad, Delhi, Chandigarh, Mahe, Howrah, Kanpur City and Bangalore. All of them have density of above 2,000 persons per square kilometre and 5.01 per cent of the country's populationlives in these districts. The average density of these districts is 6,888.

Table-3

Density of Population in India

Year	*Density of Population (Per Sq. Kilometre)*
1921	81
1931	90
1941	103
1951	117
1961	142
1971	173
1981	216
1991	267

Delhi has the highest density of population in the country (It is 6352 persons per sq. km.) and Arunachal pradesh has the lowest density of population in the country which is 10 person per sq. kilometre.

Table 4
Selected States and Union Territories
By Density 1991

	1981	*1991*
Delhi	4,194	6,352
West Bengal	615	676
Kerla	655	749
Madhya Pradesh	118	149
Himachal Pradesh	77	93
Rajasthan	100	129
Mizoram	23	33
Arunachal pradesh	8	10

(4) Sex Ratio– Sex ratio refers to the number of females per thousand male. In India the position of sex ratio is quite different in comparison to other countries. In other countries number of women is more then men. In India, it has generally been adverse to women where main are more than women. In 1971 census there were 930 females per 1000 of males in India. As per 1981 census, there were 935 females per thousand of males in India. In 1991 census sex ratio were 927 females per 1000 males. Taking the country as a whole, there has been a steady decline in the number of female per thousand males. Table -5 illustrates this fact clearly.

Table 5

Sex Ratio in India

Thousand Males

Year	*Sex Ratio (Number of females per)*
1901	972
1911	964
1921	955
1931	950
1941	945
1951	946
1961	941
1971	930
1981	934
1991	927

The ratio has declined over the years except in 1981 when it slightly improved to 934 from 927. In 1991 , there has been a fall by seven points to 927 per thousand males. But kerala represented a different spectrum. The State has a higher number of females than males, 1036 females for 1000 males. In the Indian context a sex ratio of 950 and above can be considered as favourable to females.

(5) **Age Composition** - Age Composition is yet another important feature in determining the proportion working population . In any country's population persons belongs to too young group (in the age groups 0-14 years) cannot work to earn their living. They prove mere dependent on the earning members of their families. Age structure projection of India's population is shown in Table -6

Table - 6

Age Structure Projection

(As on 1st March)

(per cent)

Age Group	*1980*	*1985*	*1990*	*2000*
0-4	14.18	13.91	12.85	10.66
5-14	25.54	24.34	23.15	20.95
15-59	54.07	55.51	57.51	60.80
60 Plus	6,21	6.24	6.49	7.59
Total	100.00	100.00	100.00	100.00

Source : Seventh Five Year Plan 1985-1990.

Table -6 shows that working population in India (15-59 age group) is 57.15 per cent. The ratio of working population in the country's total population is only 35 per cent . Howevers all the working population is not engaged or employed in income earning activities . This shown that small proportion of population (i.e. 35 per cent) has to bear the burden of large proportion of country's population.

(6) **Life Expectancy** - Life expectancy refers to the number of years on average, a new born child is expected to live. Table -7 illustrates the fact that life expectancy in India has been steadly rising.

Table -7

Life Expentency in India

YEAR	*Life Expectancy (In years)*
1921	19.4
1931	26.9
1941	32.0
1951	33.0
1961	41.0
1971	52.0
1981	54.0
1991	59.0

Table -7 shows that average age in India has increased over the years. This has happened because of (i) decrease in infant mortality rate and (ii) sufficient improvement in medical and health facilities.

(7) **Literacy** - For the purpose of census, a person is deemed as literate if he or she can read and write any language with understanding. The rate of literacy determines the quality of population of a country. According to 1971 census., the rate of literacy in India was 29.45% . According to 1981 census, literacy rate in India is 36.17 per cent. According to the population census of 1991 , 52.21 per cent of the total population is literate. As compared with other countries, percentage of literacy in India is quite low. In U.K., U.S.A. and France about 90 to 95 per cent people are literate. However, literacy percentage in India is steadily increasing . For example in 1901 it was 5.35 per cent, increased to 18.3 per cent in 1951 and 52.21 per cent in 1991. The steady improvement in literacy rate is also apparent from Table -8 . Spread of education has increased the pace of economic development in India.

Table -8

Literacy Rate -1951-1991

Year	*Persons*	*Males*	*Females*
1951	18.33	27.16	8.86
1961	28.31	40.40	15.34
1971	34.45	45.95	21.97
1981	43.56	56.37	29.75
1991	52.21	64.13	39.29

According to 1991 census , Kerala retained its position by being on top with a 89.91 per cent literacy rate in the country. Bihar stood at the bottom with a literacy rate of 38.48 per cent with Rajasthan being close to it having 38.55 per cent literacy per centage

POPULATION POLICY

The government of India has always shown its grave concern over the stupendous growth of country's population. The policy of the Government has been one of reducing the birth rate to slow down the growth of population. The policy of family planning was officially adopted in 1952. Since then variety of efforts has been done in this direction.

Salient Features

The salient features of the National Population Policy 1976 are summarised below:

(1) Age of Marriage– Through legislation the age of marriage raised to 18 years for girls and 21 years for boys.

(2) Female Education– Several measures in the policy have been suggested with regard to raise the level of female education.

(3) Monetary Incentive– The policy proposed for the monetary incentives for the couples accepting family planning ranging from Rs. 70 to Rs. 150.

(4) Population Study Curriculum– The policy proposed to introduce the study of population as a part of the school/college curriculum.

(5) Professional Group Incentive– The policy also advocated for suitable group incentives to medical professionals, Zila Parishads, Panchayat Samities, teachers, trade unions etc.

(6) Family Planning Legislation– The policy discouraged for any central legislation of compulsory family planning. The Central Government would not, however, object to any particular state opting for compulsory sterilisation.

No doubt, the National Population policy was formulated with the right spirit. However its wrong implementation by the over-zealous administrative staff led to a distortion of the programme in various ways.

FAMILY WELFARE PLANNING POLICY IN INDIA

The family planning programme in India emphasises the need of limiting the size of family. It also includes proper spacing of children. The different aspect of government family welfare planning policy may be described as follows:

Approach of the Policy

The approach of the policy has marked two elements.

First, by and large, family planning in the country is to be practised on a voluntary basis. Accordingly, the government mainly confined its measures to the provision of birth-control devices. The policy propagated the need and adoption of the norm of small family. Though incentives were announced to popularise the programme but the actual practice was left to the people themselves.

Second, the approach of the policy emphasised to treat it as a mere technical problem of limiting birth. But since Fourth Five Year Plan, it began to looked upon in a wider context. Family Planning Programme has been integrated with health, maternity and child welfare and nutritional programmes. At present it has become a family welfare programme which leads to an increase in the survival rate of children.

Provision in the Plans

Family Welfare Planning and Five-Year Plans–As pointed earlier that, the family planning programme emphasises the need of limiting the size of family. It also includes proper spacing of children.

During the *First Plan* a sum of Rs. 65 lakhs was allocated for family planning out of which only Rs. 18 lakhs was actually spent. During the *Second Plan,* Rs. 5 crores were allocated for family planning. Research institutes were set up in Bombay, Calcutta, Delhi and Tiruvanthapuram to study the usefulness of family planning. During the *Third Plan,* Rs. 27 crores were allocated for family planning out of which Rs. 25 crores were spent. The *Fourth Plan* laid special emphasis on family planning programmes. Central Family Planning Council was set up. In the *Fifth Plan,* Rs. 681.66 crores were allocated for these programmes. The Plan proposed to bring down the birth rate at 30 per thousand by the end of 1979. The *Sixth Plan* accorded high priority to the family welfare. The Plan allocated Rs. 2,831 crores for family welfare programmes.

Evaluation– The Family Welfare programme has not succeeded in achieving the desired goal, *i.e.,* containing the rapidly growing population. The failure of the programmes is attributed to the following:

(i) Acceptance of the family welfare is voluntary.

(ii) The Government's role is confined only up to the spreading of awareness, information, education and incentives for adopting family planning.

(iii) The programme has suffered on account of centralised planning and target setting from the top.

(iv) Both pre-service and in-service training of programme personnel is poor because of lack of the emphasis, at all levels of training programmes for family welfare.

(v) Community's active involvement in the programme has been marginal.

Measures

The Family Welfare Programme adopted by the Government includes a variety of measures. In these measures some relates to the education of population with regard to the need for population control. Efforts have also been made to spread information and knowledge about family planning methods. Further, devices for birth-control are also made available through various agencies. Incentives have also been provided for those who voluntary adopt family planning. The age of marriage has been raised 18 years in case of girls and 21 years in case of boys. With a view to encourage research to discover new device, easy and safe methods of family planning, workers have also been trained for the propagation of birth control measures. During 1996-97, 38.16 lakh sterlisations were performed in the country. The number of IUD insertion during the same period was 57.12 lakh. Besides, there were 171.11 lakh condom users and 51.68 lakh OP users. It is estimated that 45.4 per cent of 16.47 crore eligible couples were protected by one or the other approved family planning methods as on 31 March 1997 averting 21.22 crore births, since inception of the programme.

Social Marketing of Contraceptives

Social Marketing of Contraceptives aims at making contraceptives available to that segment of population who can afford to buy the same from the market at a lower cost. Under the scheme of Social Marketing of Contraceptives, condoms and Oral Pills are currently being sold at subsidised prices through the distribution network of private marketing companies and NGOs. Subsidy ranging from 55-88 per cent on the procurement cost in being provided by the Government.

Medical Termination of Pregnancy

It is estimated that about one-fourth of the maternal morbidity and mortality are due to illegal abortions. In order to prevent these health hazards to women, the Medical Termination of Pregnancy Act, 1971 was promulgated. Under this Act medical termination of pregnancy can be done in pregnant women upto 20 weeks, if pregnancy is likely to result in birth of a congenitally malformed child or continuation of pregnancy is likely to harm the mother in the existing circumstances and in case of contraceptive failure. Since inception of the programme in April 1972, 107.07 lakh terminations upto December 1996 were conducted under MTP Act.

Organisation

For the success of the programme, organisational arrangements have also been made for its implementation. The set-up of the programme at present exists at the centre, state, urban and village levels. The set-up has been designed caters to the programme of family planning as a part of the normal health services. In order to popularize this programme popular advertising media *i.e.* posts, newspaper, radio, T.V. etc. are being extensively used. A great number of institutions have been set-up for undertaking research on family planning. With a view of to evaluate the progress made under the Family Planning Programme, population evaluation centres have also been established at the states level. Besides voluntary organisations and private medical practitioners have also been associated with the programme.

Implementation Machinery

Family Welfare Programme is implemented through the state governments with hundred per cent Central assistance. In rural areas, services are provided through the network of sub-centres, primary health centres and community health centres. Establishment of sub-centres has been made hundred per cent Centrally-sponsored scheme (except the salary of male health worker and construction of sub-centre building) from April 1981. Against the requirement of 1.34 lakh sub-centres, there are 1.33 lakh sub-centres functioning as on 31 December 1996.

Evaluation

The different elements of the Population Policy outlined above shows that the Government has adopted comprehensive measure to exercises effective control over rapid rise of population in the country. The policy covers almost all the important aspects of the problem. But it is equally true that much still remains to be achieved because the success achieved so far has been quite disappointing. This is evident from the fact that the country's population continues to grow at a fast rate. The targets reducing the birth-rate also remained unfulfilled.

The Family Welfare Programme has not succeeded in achieving the desired goals *i.e.,* containing the rapidly growing population. The failures of the programme is attributed to the following:

(1) Voluntary Nature– The acceptance of the family welfare in India is voluntary.

(2) Role of the Government– The role of the Government in our country is confined only to the spreading of awareness, information, education and incentive for adopting family planning. It seems quite inadequate. Therefore, there is urgent need for active participation of the government in this regard.

(3) Lack of Planning– The Family Planning Programme in India also suffered because of lack of centralised planning and target setting from the top.

(4) Inadequacy of Training Programme– At all the levels of training programmes for family welfare, both pre-service and in-service training programme remained poor because of lack of the emphasis in proper direction.

Strategy for the Eight Plan– The Government is much aware about the fast rising population growth in the country. This is evident from the fact that containing population growth has been accepted as one of the important objective of Eight Plan. The strategy to achieve this objective emphasises upon the following:

(i) Convergence of services provided by various social services, *e.g.*, welfare, human resource development, nutrition, etc.

(ii) Decentralised planning and implementation of the programme. Panchayati Raj institutions to play significant role in planning.

(iii) The young couples, who are reproductively most active, will be the focus of attention with necessarily a greater emphasis on spacing methods, although the terminal methods would continue to remain the important means of birth control.

(iv) The targetted reduction in the birth rate will be the basis of designing, implementing and monitoring the programme against the current method of couple protection rate.

(v) Child survival and safe motherhood initiatives will be rigorously pursued.

(vi) The entire package of incentives and awards will be restructured to make it more purposeful.

(vii) Involvement of practitioners of all systems of medicine in population control programme.

(viii) Providing short-term re-orientation courses to the practising doctors.

(ix) Providing incentives and recognition for exhibiting initiative and leadership in population control activities.

(x) Involvement of voluntary organisations and corporate sector.

(xi) Information, Education and Communication, which are critical inputs, will be further strengthened and expanded.

(xii) A new thrust in the research and development of methods aimed at regulation of fertility in the male, and of vaccines for fertility regulation, both in the male and female, will be given.

(xiii) Continuous monitoring and review of the progress of the programme.

****

3

Agriculture Development

Agriculture is the backbone of Indian economy and at the same time that it is the most back ward sector of the economy. All the economists have recognised the dominant role of agriculture in the development economies and have also concluded that economic development requires a big shift in our of agriculture. This means employment in industries. Industrial development requires capital which can be made available through efficient and better farming. Thus it is very clear that agricultural development is a prerequisite for industrial development. We can analyse the contribution of agriculture to the process of economic development under five prepositions as discussed in the following paragraphs :

1. *Exapanding Supply of Food Items.* Due to increasing population and per capita income demand for foodgrains is also bound to increas. In India the growth rate of population is around 2.2 % per annum. Income elasticity of demand for food is also higher comparing with the developed countries of the West. A scarcity in food supplies creates two types of imbalances : (a) A scarcity of food pushes its prices upward. This is a good justification for a demand for higher wages-higher wages lead to cost escalations and thus the vicious circle goes on and on. (b) It may be possible to meet the

deficiency of food items through imports. But it is easier said than done. But India has not abundance of foreign exchange and food imports may further aggravate its balance of payments position. Food imports thus come into the way of imports of capital goods, technical know-how, etc. In short any of the two imbalance can slow down the process of growth.

2. *Enlarged exports.* In the initial stages industry earns little foreign exchange but creates a strong demand for it. If the agriculture does not provide foreign exchange through export sales of primary products, the country's balance of payments position will further deteriorate thereby retarding the process of industrialisation. However, in the long-run the exclusive reliance only on such products will be a blunder and the country must diversify its exports of manufactured goods also.

3. *Greater Capital Formation* . India's needs for capital are inevitable and formidable in the context of creation of further productive assets and social services. For this purpose the largest contribution can come from agriculture sector because of its size. There is considerable scope to raise productivity in agriculture through greater use of fertilisers better seeds and conservation and use of water, which require moderate capital but can contribute a lot to the capital requirements of development : Japan's economic development is lively example to it. In its initial stage of development its agriculture was too much backward but through agriculture development it has become a great industrial power of the world.

4. *Providing employment* . Ultimately it is the industrialisation of a country that can provide adequate and better employment opportunities. In fact , agriculture will be a source of labour for industries of tomorrow. However, there is the immediate problem of providing more productive work to those dependent upon this sector. An increase in productivity and production in this sector will provide more, jobs and raise the volume of work to be done . Agro -based industries will also get a philip resulting in expansion of employment opportunities

5. *Stimulating well- developed Market.* For industry to operate and function efficiently it needs a strong and well developed market. There are many industries to adopt latest technology to get advantages of large scale. Such a scheme is to produce in bulk thereby also demanding a large market and this can be provided by those people directly engaged in agriculture. If there is not improvement in the incomes of this sector wherefrom the market for industrial goods will come from.

Thus it is quite clear that there is an urgent need for agriculture development to overcome its backwardness but also because its progress is the only stimulant factor to the total process of development.

DEVELOPMENT DURING PLANS

The economic condition on the eve of the First Plan was quite unfavourable. There was severe food shortage and deficit of raw material . Industrial production was below par. The occupational pattern was very defective-as many as 64% people were dependent on agriculture . Due to partition the country had suffered severely. India was left with 82% of the total population of undivided India but with only 69% of land under rice , 65% under wheat , 75% under cereals; and 70 % area under irrigation. The cultivators were under heavy debt of the moneylenders and the holdings were quite uneconomic .

Objectives and Strategy

The major objectives of agricultural development in India's successive Five Year Plans have been as under:

(a) To achieve self sufficiency in foodgrains.

(b) To increase agricultural production to meet the needs of growing industries and exports to earn foreign exchange for accelerating industrial development.

(c) To diversify the rural economy with stress on animal husbandry 'dairying, fisheries and forestry.

(d) To improve the levels of living of the farming community (including small cultivators , the farmèrs in dry areas and the agricultural labourer) who form the bulk of the population.

In every Five Year Plan, the Planning Commission fixed specific targets for each crop and commodity. It also specified the various programmes for increasing agricultural production like irrigation, soil conservation dry farming and land reclamation, supply fo fertilizers , ploughs and improved agricultural implements, adoption of scientific practices, etc. The Government has also given considerable attention to institutional changes like setting up of the community development programme and agricultural extension services, implementing land reforms , expanding transport, power, marketing and other facilities. From the Third Plan ownwards the Government, is laying emphasis on Intensive Agricultural District Programme and High Yielding Varieties Programes, multiple cropping raising land productivity , etc.

Production of Major Crops

There are three main crop seasons observed in India namely kharif, rabi and summer.

Kharif - Major kharif crops are rice, jawar, bajra, maize, cotton, sugercane, sayabean and groundnut.

Rabi - Major rabi crops are wheat, jawar, barley, gram, lingeed, rapeseed and mustard.

Summer - Rice Maize and groundnut are grown is summer season also.

It has been estimated that growth in agriculture production would be about 3.9 per cent in 1998-99 against a drop of 6 per cent in 1997-98 as depicted in table -1

Table -1

Annual Growth in Agriculture Production

Year	*Index*	*% change*
1994-95	165.2	5.0
1995-96	160.7	(-)2.7
1996-97	175.4	9.1
1997-98(P)	164.9	(-)6.0
1998-99 (P)	171.3	3.9

* Index of Agricultural Production (46 principal crops) with triennium ending 1981-82 = 100 .

P = Provisional

Source : Economic Survey 1998-99 P .115.

Compound growth rate in agriculture production during the period 1949-50 to 1995-96 is 2.67 per cent per annum. The index of agricultural production , base .150.4 in 1995-96 (India 303). Production Major Crop is depicted in table -2

GROWTH IN FOODGRAINS PRODUCTION

It has been realised that there are limits to increasing the foodgrains production through increase in area under cultivation because the country has almost reached a plateau in so far as cultivable land is concerned . The contribution of high yielding varieties which has been the basis of green revolution in Seventies has now plateaued and there is hardly any fresh contribution to growth in yields. There is a new awareness that a substantial proportion of food crop output is lost after harvest. A grain saved is grain produced should be India's motto as ten per cent of the foodgrains produced in the country is lost before it reaches the consumer.

Table -2

Production of Major Crops

(All in Million Units Cotton in Bales).

Group Commodity	*1960-61*	*1970-71*	*1980-81*	*1990-91*	*1997-98*
Foodgrain	82.0	108.4	129.6	176.4	192.4
Cereals	69.3	96.4	119.0	162.1	179.4
Pulses	12.7	11.8	10.6	14.3	13.1
Rice	34.6	42.2	53.6	74.3	82.3
Wheat	11.0	23.8	36.3	55.1	65.9
Jawar	9.8	8.1	10.4	11.7	8.0
Maize	4.1	7.5	7.0	9.0	10.9
Bajra	3.3	8.0	5.3	6.9	7.7
Gram	6.3	5.2	4.3	5.4	5.1
Tur	2.1	1.9	2.0	2.4	1.9
Oilseed	7.0	9.6	9.4	18.6	22.0
Sugarcane	110.0	126.4	154.2	241.0	276.3
Cotton	5.6	4.8	7.0	9.8	11.1
Potato	2.7	4.8	9.7	15.2	17.8

Slowdown in Growth

Foodgrains production increased annually by 3.22 per cent during fifties mainly because of expansion in foodgrains area. Sixties recorded a low annual growth of 1.72 per cent necessitating large scale imports of foodgrains . Annual growth of 2.08 per cent was redorded during seventies. This decade was the turning point in the India's foodgrains economy and the path to self sufficiency was marked by the revolutionary changes in the seed technology that pushed up productivity levels first in whest and, later in rice in the eighties.

An annual growth of 3.5 per cent in foodgrains in eighties is the hallmark of the green revolution that enabled India to become self sufficient in foodgrains and even a marginal exporter . The decade of nineties could not maintain this pace and annual growth having fallen to 1.7 per cent is just about equal to annual population growth. This trend has to be reversed.

Rice - The production of rice has increased from 81.8 million tonnes in 1994-95 to 82.3 million tonne in 1997-98 and estimated to 82.3 million tonne in 1998-99.

Wheat - Uttar Pradesh, Punjab, Haryana and Madhya Pradesh are the major wheat growing states in India. In 1994-95, the country's total wheat production was 65.8 million tonne which has increased to 69.4 million tonnes in 1998-99.

Pulses - The country grows a large variety of pulses-the most popular are gram, moong (green gram), tur or arhar (pigeon pea), masur (lentils) and urad (black gram). Gram dominates with 40 per cent share followed by tur with about 19 per cent share. The annual production ranging from 12 to 14 million tonnes has virtually remained stagnant for over thirty five years as there is hardly any technological breakthrough in improving productivity . Consequently the per capita availability has dropped from 56 grams per day in 1968 to 33 grams per day in 1998. Dependence on imports has been increasing. In 1997-98 , 9.97 lakh tonnes of pulses valued at Rs. 1184 crore was imported , Major source of imports is Myanmar followed in some years by Canada and Australia.

Coarse Cereals - The declining trend of coarse cereals production is the direct consequence of the gradual shrinkage in its area. From a peak of 47 million hectares in 1967-68, the area declined to about 36 million hectares by 1990-91 . By 1996-97 it dropped further to 32 million hectares. Hardly 10 per cent of the area is irrigated. Being dependent entirely on rainfall, the coarse cereal output shows considerable inter year variation. In 1996-97 coarse cereal output was 34.1 million tonnes (one third of which was jowar and another one - third was maize). In 1997-98 coarse cereal output declined to a low of 31.1 million tonnes.

Commercial Crops

These crops mainly includes oilseads, cotton, sugarcane, jute, and mesta, Harticulture.

Oilsead - Amongst the nine major oilseeds, groundnut still occupies the dominant position accounting for nearly 34 per cent of total oilseeds production of 24.2 million tonnes. Rapeseed/ mustard which occupied second rank now accounts for only 26 per cent of oilseeds output. Soyabean has came to occu the second rank recently accountry for 28 per cent of production. This trend is likely to continue and groundnut may soon be overtaken by either rapeseed mustard or soyabean. Production trend shows that despite increase in production in some oilseeds notably soyabean and sunflower- India's consumption requirement of edible oils would still not be met. Imports have therefore become vital for supplementing domestic supplies. Current output of edible oils is about 68 lakh tonnes which falls short of consumption by about 15 lakh tonnes. The production of oilseeds in 1998-99 is likely to be 24.2 million tonnes.

Cotton - India is leading producer of cotton . Its production has increased from 11.9 million bales (180 kgs each) to 14.0 million bales in 1989-90 . Its production become uncertain in recent years due to the damage caused to the crop in Punjab and unexpected cyclonic stroms appears to have damaged the crop in Andhra Pradesh.

Sugarcane - The country has achieved satisfacotry perfromance in production of sugarcane. Its production has increased from 275.5 million tonne in 1994-95 to 276.3 million tonne in 1997-98 and estimated to reach on the peack of 289.7 million tonne in 1998-99.

Jute and Mesta - Jute and Mesta had for quite some time declined in importance due to falling domestic and world demand. Domestic demand was largely sustained by Government policy of mandatory jute packing of foodgrains by FCI and the packaging of cement, sugar and fertilizers. The world demand for jute arose mainly from carpet backing which , of late, had shrunk because of increased use of synthetic substitutes. World is now veering towards use of biodegradable packing and this may generate fresh hope for Indian jute.

Horticulture - The diversity of physiographic, climate and soil characteristics enables India to grow a large variety of horticultural crops - fruits, vegetables, flowers, spices, cashewnut, coconut, cocoa, arecanut, root and tuber crops, medicinal and aromatic plants, etc. India is the largest producer of fruits in the world and, second largest producer of vegetables. India enjoys the unique distinction of being single largest producer consumer and exporter of spices in the world India is also the leading producer and exporter of cashew in the world.

Production Corps

These Crops mainly includes coffee, tea and Natural rubber.

Coffee - India is the sixth largest producer of coffee in the world. Karnataka is the largest coffee producing state accounting for about 70 per cent of the total coffee output. In 1997-98 , coffee output was 2.28 lakh tonnes. In 1998-99 , output is likely to be 2.30 lakh tonnes . Nearly three fourth of coffee produced is expored . Coffee export trade was totally deregulated since 1996. Stagnation in domestic demand for coffee could possibly be because of its high price relative to tea.

Tea - India is the largest producer and consumer of tea in the world. Tea is mainly grown in Assam. West Bengal, Kerala , Karnataka and Tamil Nadu, Annual production, consumption and export of tea during the last five years is listed in table -3.

Table -3

Tea- Production, Consumption and Exports

(Million Kgs.)

Year	*Production*	*Export*	*Domestic Consumption*
1994	752.9	150.7	580
1995	753.9	167.9	595
1996	780.0	161.7	618
1997	810.6	203.0	640
1998	812.3*	188.4*	NA

* *Anticipated* @ *January- November*

Natural Rubber - India ranks fourth in the world rubber production with an annual production of about 6 lakh tonnes. The country's 97 per cent of demand for natural rubber is met by indigenous production. Only a small proportion of demand (less than 3 per cent) is met through imports. Kerala produces more than 90 per cent of the natural rubber and accounts for over 85 per cent of the area under cultivation. Most rubber plantations are small and the average size of a holding is 0.5 hectare only.

Table - 4

Natural Rubber - Production and Consumption

(Lakh Tonnes)

Year	*Consumption*	*Production*	*Yield (Kgs/Hec.)*
1991-92	3.80	3.67	1130
1992-93	4.14	3.93	1191
1993-94	4.50	4.35	1285
1994-95	4.86	4.75	1362
1995-96	5.25	5.07	1422
1996-97	5.62	5.49	1503
1997-98	5.74	5.84	1565
1998-99*	6.03	6.24	1615

*** Estimated**

Plan outlay and Actual Expenditure

In absolute terms the allocation for agriculture in plans is continuously on an increase. The amount provided in the Fifth Plan was more than 9 times that of the First Plan. However, in terms of percentage the allocation at 35% in the First Plan came down to 23% in the Second Plan and remained at around this level till the Fourth Plan . Following table will make it very clear :

Table - 5

Outlays and Actual Expenditure during the Plans on Agriculture

Plan	*I*	*II*	*III*	*Annual*	*IV*	*V*
Outlay on Agriculture	823	1,100	1,718	-	3,815	8,084
Percentage of total plan outlay	35	23	23	-	24	20
Actual expenditure	724	950	1,754	1,578	3,498	-
Percentage of expenditure on plan	37	21	21	24	24	-

In the Sixth Five Year Plan (1980-85) Rs. 12,538 crore planned to spent on agricultural and rural development.

Production Target and Achievement . A comparison of the targets and the actual achievements during the plans brings out the fact that our achievement had fallen short of targets postulated in the different plans . Only the First Plan stands out as the most successful in this regard. We had targeted to reach the production level of 129 million tonnes of foodgrains by the end of the Fourth Plan but could not reach at it even at the end of the Fifth Plan. We had planned to achieve a production of 10.5 million tonnes of oilseeds by the end of the Fourth Plan but the actual productionat the end of the Fifth Plan is merely 8.9 million tonnes.

Inputs

During the plans many changes have taken place in the use of agricultural inputs.

1. *Irrigation* . The total area irrigated in the country stood at 22.6 miilion hectares in 1950-51 . As a result of massive

investment made in successive plan periods the total irrigation facility has been more than doubled at the end of 1981-82 standing at 57.45 million hactares. The total potential created is only 50% of the ultimate feasible that means again the achievements have been than the targets.

2. *High Yielding Varieties Programmes.* It was during the midsixties that the high-yielding variety of wheat seeds were evolved . Since then a number of HYV seeds of wheat rice and other cereals have been developed and widely distributed throughout the country. In 1981-82 , 46.68% million hectares of land is covered under HYV seeds programmes whereas it was only 1.88 million hectares of land in 1966-67.

3. *Chemical Fertilliser.* After the introduction of HYV seeds, the fertilisers consumption got a boost. The consumption of fertilisers has been 6.23 million tonnes in 1981-82 whereas it was merely 0.13 million tonnes in 1950-51 and 1.1 million tonnes in 1966-67 . We are now the fourth largest consumer of nitrogen and the eighth largest consumer of phosphate in the world.

4. *Credit.* Lack of finance has been the bane of Indian agriculturists . Some progress has been made in providing credit facilities to the agriculturists. In case of short and medium term finances, it is the primary agriculture credit societies that are relevant. Their number in 1950-51 was 1.05% lakhs which increasd to 1.2 in 1976-77 and has declined to 0.94 in 1980-81 . The percentage of village covered rose to 97 and membership which was just 44 lakh in 1950-51 rose to 5.73 lakh in 1980-81 . The total short-term loans advanced by them amounted to 22.9 crores in 1950-51 which went up to 1.656 crores in 1980-81 . With regard to long term finance, it is the Land Development Banks which matter. Their number (Central and Primary) has increased from 291 in 1950-51 to 913 in 1976-77 and the amount of loans advanced by them in 1950-51 was Rs. 1.38 crores which rose to Rs. 309 crores in 1979-80.

5. *Marketing.* For it the important agency is the co-operative society. At present there are 3600 primary agricultural marketing societies. In 1978-79 they marketed produce worth Rs. 1,800 crores which was mere 179 crores in 1960-61 . Besides they are supplying inputs to their members.

Land Reforms

Although it had been recognised as the most important aspect of agriculture , has been the most neglected aspect. Major steps adopted under the programme were :

(i) Abolition of intermediaries.

(ii) Regulation of landlord -tenant relationship.

(iii) Ceiling on holding and redistribution of land.

(iv) Consolidation of scattered holdings.

(v) Development of co-operative farming.

As far as intermediaries are concerned all the zamindars, talukadars, jagirdars and enamdars have been removed of their rights and about 2 crore farmers have come into direct contact with the State.

In the field of tenancy reforms some sort of legal protection has been conferred by the State in the form of security of tenure, fixation of fair rent, etc.,

Regarding ceiling on land the State Governments have enacted ceiling laws, but in its implementation there has been lack of political will power,

In case of consolidation, except, Punjab, Haryana and U.P. the progress is very dismel . Co-operative farming has also failed to come up due to lack of necessary environment.

Evaluation of Progress

By now we have seen the progress of agriculture during the plans. We are also clear that emphasis on "growth with stability" has subsequently been strengthened and expanded to "growth with social justice". The progress of agriculture hence can be evaluated in terms of (i) growth and (ii) social justice.

Growth . For this purpose the entire periods can be divided into three periods (i) 1950-51 to 1960-61 , (ii) 1961-62 to 1966-67 , and (iii) 1967-68 to 1980-81 . The index number of agricultural production went up from 58.5 in 1950-51 (Base : Triennium ending 1969-70 =100) to 86.7 in 1960-61 . The second period has seen decrease in production creating a serious crises for whole of the economy . The production index in 1965-66 was 80.8 as against 86.7 in 1960-61. The third period is a golden period in Indian agriculture. The index number has risen to 143 in 1981-82 . All this has been possible due to adoption of the new agricultural strategy. The annual compound growth rates come to 4.1% in the First Plan, 3.1 % in the Second Plan 3.3% in the Third Plan (excluding the abnormal year 1965-66), and 2.2 % in the Fourth Plan. The adequacy of growth can be judged in several ways as under -

(a) Comparison with the Pre-planning Period. According to K. Mukherji, the annual growth rate of Indian agriculture during the first half of the 20th century came to be 0.25% . The rate was not more than this even during the 25 years immediately preceding independence. Historically, the rate of agricultural growth is higher during the plan period and thus a matter of satisfaction.

(b) Comparison with other countries at the same level of development. In judging the performance of agriculture in the countries in the period following their independence from colonial rule or domination it would be relevant to derive some idea regarding the time required to bring about a yield breakthrough from the early experience of developing countries. Comparing with the U.K. and the USA during such period . India can certainly boast of its performance in the growth of production and productivity.

(c) Comparison with other countries during the corresponding period. For this purpose the yardstick can be yield per hectare in different countries. In yield per hectare of

principal crops India is very low as compared to other countries. To illustrate yield per hectare of wheat in the UK is 3,877 kg whereas it is only 1,410 kg in India. Thus there is considerable scope to increase land productivity.

(d) Comparison with the targets and needs. In terms of targets except the First Plan growth rate of agricultural production has always fallen short of expectations. In regard to needs again the things have been unsatisfactory. India had to foot high import bills for meeting both foodgrains need and raw materials. Thus it can be asserted that our agricultural production could not fulfil the domestic requirements.

In terms of all these comparisons it is quite clear that the agriculture has certainly shown a remarkable progress, but looking at population growth there is an imbalance between the production and the needs.

Social Justice

Agriculture has failed to provide enough work for many much less for all the surplus labour . Rather the number of unemployed has further increased due to population pressure. Income levels of rural poor have recorded no increase , rather the poverty line has further expanded. Inequality in terms of land has not reduced. There are large gaps in the laws and their implementation.

Despite concerted industrialisation in the last three decades , still agriculture forms the backbone of the Indian economy. Being the largest industry in the country, It is a source of livelihood for over 70% population. Half of the national income is contributed by this sector.Virtually all the aspects of the country's life and economy bear its stamp so much so that the very existence of all the economic activities of the nation is tied up with the state and health of this sector. The importance of agriculture can be well understood by going through its role under different heads. :

1. *National Income* - The distribution of national income by industrial origin for the period 1950-51 to 1982-83 shows that the share of various agricultural commodities , animal husbandry and ancillary activity has always been more than 40% . As a matter of fact, during fifties it contributed half of the national output . In the sixties and seventies it has come down to about 44%.

Although the share of agriculture is declining after 1960-61 still it is the single most important sector contributing highest to the national income. A comparison with other countries will make it very clear. Contribution of agriculture in the UK is 3.1 % in the USA it is 3.2% ; in Canada it is 5% , and so on. The obvious conclusion is that more developed a country, the smaller is the contribution of agriculture to national output.

2. *Employment and source of livelihood.* - The size of labour force in agriculture increased from 87.72 million in 1921 to 167.33 million in 1977and is projected to grow further to 213.2 million in 1983 . This means seven out of 10 persons are engaged in agriculture to earn their livelihood. During the last 70 years of this country this proportion has almost remained stagnant. In countries like the UK, the USA , West Germany, Canada, New Zealand, etc., less than 20% of the population is dependent on agriculture. At the same time it is important to note that in these countries the proportion of people dependent upon agriculture is declining while in our country it has remained almost stationary.

3. *Food and Fodder.* According to one estimate agricultural commodities comprise almost 80% of the total consumer expenditure. In such a situation it is of crucial importance that agriculture meets almost the entire food needs of the people . Although India has made imports of foodgrains in the past, but its proportion to total food requirements has always been very small.

Agriculture also provides fodder to sustain live stock whose number runs into crores; the 1972 census puts it at 35.33 crores (cattle, buffaloes, sheep, goats , horses and ponies, etc..) and poultry at 11.5 crore. These are the sources of protective foods, including milk eggs and meat, draught power for farm operations and of commercial produces like wool and hides.

4. *Industrial Development* , - Agriculture has been source of raw materials to India's leading industries- cotton and jute textiles, sugar, tobacco, edible and non-edible oils, leather, plantation industries, all these depend on agriculture directly. There are many other industries which depend on agriculture indirectly.

Agriculture employing 7-% of the total population provides a large part of the market for industrial goods. " To the extent that modern agricultural practices are adopted the demand for inputs like seeds, fertilizers, pesticides, insecticides, implements, machinery, pumps and consumer goods goes up and sustains a larger industrial tempo, " The Japanese and Russian industrial economies could develop only because of the transfer of agricultural surplus to industrial sector.

5. *Internal Trade and Transport* - Internal trade is mostly in agricultural products. It is the trade to buy raw materials and foodgrains etc., to supply to industries and consumers respectively . It is the trade to supply industrial and consumer goods to farmers. The volume of trade definitely depends on the economic health of agriculture.

The main support for railways and roadways, which transport bulk of agricultural products from farm to mandis and factories, comes from agriculture.

6. *International Trade* - Agriculture contributes a very large part of exports and is an important segment of import of the country. In 1976-77 the agricultural products accounted for 35.4% of the total export earnings, while import of

agricultural commodities represented 32.7% of total import. If the commodities based on agriculture are also included then the export earnings will go up further. The main agricultural commodities exported are-tea, oil cakes, fruits and vegetables, spices, tobacco, cotton, coffee, rice, sugar, hides and skins, etc. Ready-made garments and jute textiles exports etc., are the commodities based on agriculture for raw materials.

The important items of import have been cereals, raw cotton, fertilizers vegetable oils and fats, dairy products, raw jute, tractors, raw wool , rubber, and agricultural machinery and implements. The foreign exchange to buy them comes from the export of agricultural commodities.

7. *Capital formation and investment.* Since agriculture contributes 44% of the national income, this sector is the primary source of savings and hence capital formation for the economy. Prior to independence there was neither inclination nor capacity to create productive assets on large scale. However, today a major part of the productive assets of the country are in the form of agricultural asset like irrigation facilities plough, storage capacity, etc. Every year addition to this stock are being made on a large scale both on government and private accounts.

8. *International ranking.* At the international level, also Indian agriculture has a fairly high ranking in certain respects. In case of groundnut India stands first in the world. ; for rice production India ranks number two; and in case of tobacco it comes to third place.

Thus it is very clear that agriculture occupies a central place in the national economy . The whole economic system gets disturbed if agriculture is affected adversely . Our experience has been that all round price rise has been caused due to shortage of foodgrains. Larger imports were due to failure on agricultural front. Failure in agriculture brings depression in business as well as state revenues. In fact not only the economy, but Indian culture, society, politics and all that constitutes life have the strong flavour and deep colopur of village life.

Indian agriculture has some *special characteristics.* A few of them are as under :

1. *Too much, dependent on uncertain rains.* In comparison with other occupations, agriculture is much larger dependent on nature. However, in India this dependence on rains, etc., is rather too much . In the absence of sufficient irrigation facilities, about 75% of the cultivation in India has to depend upon monsoon rains for water supply. But rains in India are irregular, uncertain and inadequate. In a few places and a few times it falls in torrents and heavy down pours leading to floods and run-off. At the same time in few places it is in dire scarcity. Thus, this monsoon may be said to be the pivot upon which the whole of Indian economic life swings. "If monsoon fails, there is a lockout in agriculture industry a disaster which calls forth the virtues of patience, fortitude and charitableness. " Only because of uncertain climate and agriculture's too much dependence on it we find large ups and downs in India's national income, trade, employment government budget price level and overall prosperity.

2. *Variety of crops* The large extent of its area and a great variety of physical and natural fertility of the soil, enable the country to produce the amazing variety of crops compared to countries where only a few types of crops can be grown. Due to multiplicity of crops India is able to produce tropical products like rice, coffee etc., sub-tropical crops like cotton, tea, etc., and temperate zone products like wheat, pulses, potatoes, etc.

The other peculiar feature is that about three fourths of the total cropped area is under food crops. Wheat rice and millet, maize and barley occupy about 71% of the sown area.

3. *Large variations in other aspects too.* It is not only crop pattern where we find an amazing variety , but this diversity is a unique feature of the total Indian agricultural system. Inter-regional and inter-regional varieties are there in matters such as ownership of land, mathods of irrigation , size of land holdings system of agriculture, rotation of crops, etc. Such variations are the results of the socio-economic cultural in heritage and the political system of past and present . Thus no uniform agricultural policy can be prescribed for the whole country.

4. *Semi-commercial type of farming.* - In India earlier agriculture was considered to be a way of life and people were used to produce only for their own consumption. This is known as subsistence farming. Today, the things have changed , but still the farming activities have not been fully commercialised, where the farming production is done primarily for sale in the market. This is why the farming in India is called semi-commercial . In regard to foodgrains, bulk of production in villages is still meant for consumption by farmers and their families. But in case of non-foodgrains of course, a large part is meant for marketing.

5. *Predominance of small cultivators :* According to the All India Report on Agricultural Census (1970-71) 70% of the land holdings come into the category of marginal (less than 1 hectare) and small (1 hectare to 2 hectares) land holdings. This is due to the population pressure resulting in fragmentation and sub-division and backward nature of Indian agriculture. Many of the farmers are not even owners of the land. Thus neither there is any motivation nor resources to invest for better farming.

6. *Large inequalities in ownership of land.* In India while a few agriculturists own large areas of land, a very large number of people have no or very little land. It will be clear from the fact that 4% holdings on the top have 30% of land area, the 50% holdings at bottom of the ladder have only 9% of land.

7. *Low Productivity* Productivity in agriculture can be measured through output per hectare of land or per worker. As far as total output is concerned India is on the top in the world in some of the commodities, but in average output per hectare or per labour is on the botton . Several technical, social and economic factors are responsible for it.

8. *Mass Unemployment and Underemployment* . Except a few places where irrigation facilities enable double cropping in almost the whole country people dependent upon agriculture do not get sufficient and adequate work. Not only there is unemployment during a large part of the year, but even vast of the majority employed are withdrawn will not make any adverse impact this means there is lot of disguised unemployment.

The various characteristics described above put together point out to the fact that the Indian agriculture is very weak and suffers from many shortcomings.

AGRICULTURAL PRODUCTIVITY

It can be measured from two angles- one from the point of view of productivity per acre (i.e. land productivity) and the other from the point of view of per labour employed (i.e. labour productivity). Let us study them one by one.

Land Productivity

According to the Indian Agriculture in Brief (17th Ed.) in 1979 the production of rice per hectare in India is 1667 kg. whereas it is 5,503 kg in Japan and 5,244 kg. in the USA. In case of wheat , output per hectare in India is only 1,410 kg. while in the UK. it is 4,382 kg. and 3,760 kg. in France. For sugarcane, the yield per hectare is 52,902 kg. in India and 84,976 kg in the USA. The same is the case with groundnut cotton etc., etc. However one thing should not be lost sight of that during the plans the yield per hectare is continuously on an increase . To take an example of rice between 1966 and 1975 average output of rice per per hectare has increase from 1,290 kg. to 1,880 kg. - and increase of 46% in 9 years.

Inter state variations in land productivity . We find large variations within the country. While land productivity for the whole country is worked out at Rs. 1,307 per hectare it is as low as Rs. 461 per hectare in Rajasthan and as higher as Rs. 2,716 for Kerala.

Labour Productivity

Productivity per person in agriculture is low from all standards. From occupation to occupation the earnings in agriculture per worker were estimated at Rs. 500 as against Rs. 1,500 in commerce, transport and communications. From country to country the labour productivity in India is $ 105 , as against $ 2,265 in Japan and $ 3,495 in West Germany.

Inter State Variation in Labour Productivity According to Commerce Annual , 1972 all India labour productivity has been estimated at Rs. 1,213 . It has been valued at Rs. 3,195 for Punjab and Rs. 409 for Nagaland. Thus labour productivity also shows large regional variation like that of land productivity.

CAUSES FOR LOW PRODUCTIVITY

From the discussion above , it has been well established that Indian agriculture is backward. Let us analyse the causes responsible for it under following headings :

(a) General Factors

1. *Demographic Reasons-* The most important demographic factor responsible for low yield is the increasing population . Since the growth rate i n industrial sector has been far from expectations, the increasing population has fallen back on land for its livelihood, which is already over-populated. This mounting pressure has bred a number of evils

like fragmentation and sub-division of holdings ; the supply of improved practices and inputs has always fallen short of requirements; it has created conditions of unemployment, under - employment and disguised unemployment, etc. All these evil influences collectively have been responsible for low productivity in agriculture

2. *Outdated Rural Environment* . The Indian farmers are in general illiterate, ignorant superstitious conservative and bound by age old customs and institutions such as caste system and the joing family. Superstition and belief in fate are the curses which keep the farmers fully satisfied with their primitive system of cultivation. Unless this climate is changed there is no possibility of getting agriculture out of the clutches of backwardness.

3 *Inadequate Non-farm Services.* Many non-farm services in India like credit and marketing, etc. are either non-existent or if available these are quite costly. To illustrate, till recently, farmers had to depend upon the village moneylender and had to pay very high rate of interest, high to the extent that once a farmer borrowed , he was bound to lose his land and become a landless labourer. Although other sources of finance like co-operatives and the Government did exist but were very unsubstantial and insignificant. Similarly due to lack of storage facililties, the farmers had to sell their produce at very low rates in the mandis, till now. Lack of such facilities has kept Indian agriculture backward.

(b) Institutional Factors

1. *Size of Holdings.* As already observed, the average size of holding in India is very low. The national average of the size of holding is small at 2.3 hectares, with an overshelming number of landholdings below the size of two hectares. As if this were not enough, there is the other equally big drawback of fragmentation of holdings . Many farmers

have small holdings (called 'tiny 'or 'toy') scattered over many places, often separated from each other by long distances. Due to it investment in farming cannot be a profitable proposition. Supervision and management also become difficult and no advantage can be made from the modern technology of farming.

2. *Defective Tenurial System* . Under the system of the Zamindari as well as landlordism, the tiller of the soil was not the owner. Not only he had to pay very heavy rents but the sword of eviction had also been handing over him. He did not and could not make any investment ; the system took the very basic motivation out of him. On the other land Zamindar got a lot without any work and investment . After independence some measures of land reforms have been introduced along with the abolition of Zamindari system. But in actual practice not much has changed. Due to lack of political will power and lack of administrative skill, land reforms measures have not made much headway in our country.

(c) Technological Factor

1. *Poor Technique of Production* . Poor equipment inadequacy and obsolete nature of tools has been also contributing towards backwardness. The high prices of new implements and equipment are prohibitive for small and medium farmers. Indian farmers have been using seeds of their own make, which are not very good. Use of manure and chemical fertilizer is also extremely inadequate.

2. *Poor Irrigation Facilities.* In India of the total cultivated land only 22% has irrigation arrangements and thus, still agriculture is a gamble of monsoon. Contented absence of irrigation facilities for three fourths of land have made the poor cultivator a helpless tool in the hands of his ' fate.'

3. *Research and Development* Benefits of research and development have neither reached to all the farmers nor are in a usable form. Extension is confined to individual good practices and no complete pattern of farming has been advocated.

4. *Organisation and Leadership.* There is complete lack of these two in agriculture. The philosophical outlook inclemency's of whether vagaries of monsoon, fluctuating prices, harassment by village factions and petty officials, etc. have discouraged the talented youth to come with new zest and ideas into the agricultural fold.

To sum up, we have to accept the fact that in India agriculture is backward resulting in low production. Low production leads to low marketable surplus, low bargaining power, low incomes, low investment for land improvement and ultimately leads to further deterioration . During the coming years there is no option but to strive hard to develop our agricultural productivity , which is the key to out development and national honour.

CROPPING PATTERN IN INDIA

The term crop pattern is used to study the distribution of land for different crops at a particular period of time. The Cropping pattern also refers to the choice of the crop to be cultivated. In this process, the objective is to utilise the land in the best possible way so as to get optimum benefit out of the available fertility of the soil. A change in crop pattern means change in proportionate area for different crops.

FEATURES OF CROP PATTERN IN INDIA

In India , 80 per cent of the cropped area is used for cultivation of food grains . This pattern has not changed over the years. Among food grains, there has been considerable increase in the case of wheat .. Among the commercial crops, sugercane has shown remarkable increase. In the case of food grains the increase was much more we have disscused below main feature of crop pattern in India :

1. *Amazing Variety* . India is a very large country in terms of size. It is endowed with a great variety of soils and climatic conditions. Due to aforesaid unique situation India is able to produce all types of crops- tropical, sub-tropical , temperate zone and others. Here following observations are important to note.

(i) *In the Food Crops* . Rice is the most important crop in India and it accounts for the largest are and production among the food crops. It occupies 37% of total area under food crops and 23% of the total cultivated land. Wheat comes next to rice in area as well as production. It accounts for 18% of the total area under the food crops and 11% of the total area sown in the country. Pulses come at third place. The other important food crops in terms of land area are jowar, bajra, maize , barley, millet etc.

(ii) *In the Non-Food Crops* . Sugarcane is the most important cash crop in terms of value although it holds only 1.5% of total agricultural land. Area wise cotton is very important covering about 5% area of the total crop area of the country. Highest area covered in cash is by oilseeds.

2. *Dominance of Food Crops over Non Food Crops* . Right from 1950-51 till date we find that food crops and non-food crops stand in the ratio of 3:1 . So much preponderance over food crops is due to two reasons. First, a sharp rise in their market prices on the one hand and a continuous declaration of minimum guarnateed prices on the other hand. And secondly, the High Yielding Variety seeds have opened new vistas for productivity in food crops.

3. *Dominance of Cereals Among Food Crops.* Food crops can be divided into two groups viz ; (i) Cereals like rice wheat etc. : and (ii) Non-cereals like pulses. Out of the total area under food crops, 80% is occupied by cereals cultivation. As already explained, this is due to better prices of cereals.

4. Importance to Inferior Cereals. Although wheat and rice known as superior cereals dominate in the cereals crops, still 40% of the area is occupied by inferior cereals like jowar, maize , bajra, barley, millets, etc. also known as coarse foodgrains. Such an important place is due to the fact that these crops can be produced under dry conditions.

FACTORS INFLUENCING CROP PATTERN

Crop pattern depends upon the farmers' choices and these choices are governed by number of factors as discussed under :

1. Natural and Technological Factors. Natural factors like soil, climate rainfall, etc., are very important factors in determining the crop pattern, certain type of soil and climate is very conducive for one crop and most unsuitable for the other. Black soil is good for cotton and wheat but not for coffee and rubber for which laterite is required. Where there is uncertainty of rain and no facility of irrigation the choice will be for inferior cereals. In areas where very good rains are assured the choice will be in favour of rice, jute, tobacco etc.

With the help of technological improvements these natural factors can be changed and thereby cropping pattern too. With the spread of irrigation facilities the choice has shifted in favour of crops requiring water than the dry farming ones.

2. Economic Factors. Prices, income, farm, size, risk, availability of inputs, etc. do play a major role in deciding crop pattern. The prices of all types of products, viz price of inputs, prices of agricultural products and prices of manufactured goods all have a bearing on the type of crop to be selected. Stable level of prices for a crop provides a better incentive to the producer to increase the output than what a very high level of prices does if there is no uncertainty of this level being maintained over a number of years. The farmer will go in for that crop witch provides him the largest real income . Size wise small farmers are interested in producing foodgrains for themselves whereas large farmers put commercial crops in a large area to build up cash balances. Again a small farmer cannot take much risk against rainfall and in order to asure a minimum for himself he prefers to have easy crops involving little risk. Availability of agricultural inputs like seeds, fertilizers irrigation storage, marketing transport, etc,. is also a deciding factor for a particular crop to be produced. Gestation period i.e, time required to get the crop is also important because less gestation period brings better profits to the farmers.

3. *Sociological and Historical Factors.-* Social factors such as density of population , customs traditions, philosophy towards material things and aptitude and capacity to change have an important impact on crop pattern . Prior to independence these factors were very decisive but with the spread of education and change of outlooks things are a bit different. Historically the tenure system also had a bearing on the type of crop. A tiller under the zamindari system had no say in selection of crop since it was to be decided by the zamindar according tohis own cost-profit considerations. As against this, under ryotwari system a small farmer produces all that he can and prefers foodgrains production for his self consumption.

4. *Government Policy.* Now-a-days the Government policy has been the most important factor in determining the crop pattern. Policies relating to crop priorities exports, fiscal incentives availability of credit, development of backward area minimum prices guaranteed affect the nature of crops and the area for them considerably.

PRESENT CROP PATTERN IN INDIA

During the first 50 years of this century the area under agriculture did not grow in line with the population growth. While population increased by 38% the area increased only by 18% but the growth of area under non-foodgrains was faster. In the foodgrains the largest increase was in respect of wheat. The trend of faster increase in non-food crops suffered during the Second World War with the launching of 'Grow More Food ' Campaign.

There are changes in crop pattern after independence. *Firstly*, while prior to independence the ratio of food and non-food crops was 80:20 , has been sticking at 75:25 throughout the planning period. *Secondly* , there has been sharp uptrend in some individual crops in both the groups . In food crops it is visible in wheat. In non-food crops, the largest increase has been in oilseeds. *Thirdly*, the net area sown under various crops has increased considerably which is due to multiple cropping. *Fourthly* ,while the total area is on an increase, in all the crops the area at times has gone down instead of increasing. *Finally* , in both the groups the total production has increased substantially but in regard to certain important crops the things are very dismal. Pulses, coming under the category of food crops, are the most important source of protein in the India diet. But their percentage in total food crops production has come down from 16% in the beginning of fifties to 10% in the seventies. Similarly, the situation of oilseeds in non-food crops is a matter of concern, since even scaled down targets have not been achieved.

In the Sixth Plan special attention has been paid to pulses oilseeds and cotton crops. The policy was to increase hectarage under these crops, through multiple and mixed cropping. Some area has been released from low yielding cereals crops. The national Seeds Corporation along with the State Seeds Corporations are to provide better seeds.

Suggestions

Many institutions and agricultural econonmists have given numerous suggestions for improving crop pattern. A few of them to be mentioned are :

1. The present way of haphazard allocation of area to diffeent crops by individual farmers is not in the best interests of the farmers as well as the country. Inertia and ignorance cause lot of wastage of capital, land and irrigation resources since farmers do not adhere to the crop plans drawn out for different irrigation projects. As persuasion is a slow remedy, some legislative action (like Egypt and the USA) may be thought of.

2. Some institutional arrangement be made to plan the crops for each season and all areas keeping in view the prices, yields , etc.

3. An Agriculture Mechanisation Corporation should be set up where the size of holdings is too large and where the average farmer is unable to manage with hired labour. The Corporation should provide the requisite machinery on credit.

4.Infrastructural facilities like marketing transportation and consolidation of holdings should get highest importance.

5. The research institutions should develop seeds whereby the crops can mature within 60-70 days. This way different crops can be grown on the land remaining vacant in between rabi and kharif crops.

WORLD TRADE ORGANISATION AND INDIAN AGRICULTURE

World Trade Organisation (WTO) has come into existence from January 1,1995. Mr. Renato Ruggiero is the Director-General of WTO (from May, 1995). Now World Bank IMF and WTO are the three international agencies in the field of international finance and trade. The Eighth Round of General Agreement on Tariffs and Trade, called, the Uruguay Round of GATT, was concluded on December 15, 1993 at Geneva (Switzerland). it was ratified by several countries in April, 1994 at Marrakesh (Morrocco) in Africa. The world trade would be rule based, transparent and free from uncertainties in future. Different countries would cut tariffs by about 37% on agricultural and industrial products, direct export subsidies would be reduced by 36% over 6 years, rules would govern trade in services like banking insurance, travel, etc. Multi-Fibre Agreement (MFA) would be phased out after 10 years to bring textile trade in accord with GATT rules. Patent system will have to be changed from process - patent to product patent which means that medicines under patent system cannot be manufactured by another country by changing the process as was the case, hitherto in India.

In the Uruguay Round of the GATT it was decided to establish the World Trade Organisatin (WTO) which will be vested with sufficient power the implement the various agreements reached between in the members of the GATT.

The WTO aims at improving the standard of living level of employment and output and optimal utilisation of the world resources. It will ensure preservation of environment all over the world . The thrust of its activities will be to secure better share of growth in international trade, especially, for the least developed countries.

Functions of the WTO. The WTO will perform the followingt functions :

1.Through the various councils and committees it will implement the 28 agreements contained in the final agreement contained in the final agreement of the GATT.

2.It will try to resolve trade disputes through conciliation mechanism.

3.Unresolved disputes relating to trade between the member countries will be solved by WTO's dispute settlement court.

4.WTO will keep in its data bank all vital data relating to world trade.

5.It will act as a watchdog of international trade, monitoring and examining the trade transactions of the member -countries.

6.It will implement the agreement relating to tariff and non-tariff cuts by the member-countries.

7.All the trading partners will be treated at par while settling trade disputes between them.

8.It will provide a platform to the member countries to negotiate freely on various issues relating to world trade.

In brief, WTO is a very powerful body to ensure fair distribution of world resources through uninterrupted and friendly trade environment to the member-countries.

WTO AND INDIAN AGRICULTURE

The World Trade Organisation could see light of the day under GATT agreement. Establishment of WTO is an important achievement in the field of international trade. India is a agricultural nation where agricultural commodities contribute 25% in total exports of the country. 70% of India's population is directly or indirectly dependent on agriculture for their livelihood. In national income of India, 31% is obtained from agricultural sector. Keeping in view the aforesaid facts, it is necessary to study the possible effects will fall on Indian agriculture due to GATT agreement. This bilateral agreement will influence Indian agriculture in following ways :

(1) Reduction in Subsidies - In GATT agreement, there is a provision to keep the agriculture subsidies up to 10 per cent of the total agriculture production of seeds, fertilisers, pestisides, agriculture implements, power supply and irrigation facilities. It clearly means that the countries where agriculture subsidy is more than the prescribed percentage as recommended by the GATT i.e. 10% , need to reduce the percentage of subsidies. However, this binding will not influence to Indian agriculture unfavourably.

(i) No Fear of Reduction in Subsidies - In the countries where agriculture subsidies is more than 10 per cent to agriculture need to be worried . But reduction in agriculture subsidiary is not a point of fear for India as the agriculture subsidy in India is much less than the percentage fixed by GATT i.e. 10 per cent.

(ii) More Possibilities to Increase Agriculture Subsidy- Though between 1991-92 to 1993-94 efforts have been made in India to reduce the subsidies in agriculture sector which impedimented farmer to pay more for seeds, fertilisers, pestisides, power supply , but under the current agreement there will be more possibilities for rasing the agriculture subsidy. It is because in the present time subsidies in India is equal to 5 per cent to 6 per cent of its agriculture production as against the 10 per cent approved by the GATT.

(iii) More Opportunities of Profit - India will be able to earn more profit by exporting of agriculture produce because when other countries reduce the percentage of agriculture subsidies, their cost of agriculture production will go up. In such a situation India will be able to export agriculture produce at higher price.

(iv) No Fear to Public Distribution System - There is no fear of this decision on Public Distribution System (PDS) as GATT recommended for reduction in agriculture subsidies not in consumer subsidies. Beside , it will be possible now to run the scheme in the more interest of weaker sections of the society.

(v) Minimum Support Price - The policy of Minimum Support Price in case of food grain will be continued. In this agreement there will be not any binding to keep parity in the Minimum Support Price produrement price , and market price. Hence, it will be possible for India to keep continue its policy of Minimum Support Price.

(2) Reduction in Export Subsidies - There is a provision in the agreement GATT to reduce export subsidies to be given in the form of direct grant. India need to reduce provision and qunatum of such subsidies to 36% and 24% respectively between the budgets of 1993 and 1999 .

It is expected that this provision will also not influence to Indian agriculture unfavourably as India will be able to take advantages of export subsidies under foreign exchange crisis.

(3) Reduction in Terminal Charges on Agriculture Produce - Under the provisions of GATT agreement member countries required to introduce wide-range of charges in their tax-structure. Besides between 1993 to 1999 there required to reduction of average 36% in General Terminal Charges at least 15% in the Terminal Charges of every commodity . There also provisions for some more concessions.

There are possibilities for India to take advantages of reduction in terminal charges because with the removal of tariff and other restrictions in the industrially developed countries, agriculture products of India may find more favourable competitive environment. No doubt all these efforts will provide wide market to India .

(4) Condition of Minimum Import - Though there is no need for import of food grain for fulfillment of domestic requirements in India . But condition of minimum import of food grains has been imposed. it is one of the essential part of the agreement . After implementation of the agreement, a country required to import minimum 2% of its total consumption of food grains. This minimum percentage limit will have to reach up to 3.33% till the end of 10 years from the year of its implementation.

The aforesaid compulsion of the GATT agreement will encourage competition in the domestic market of food grain. Further , it will also create obstacles in the way of becoming self-sufficiency in foodgrain production by the country. The country under compulsion will spent scarce foreign exchange reserve for import of unwanted foodgrains.

India for the time being will be free from abiding this condition because due to problem of unfavourable balance of payment, this condition will not be imposed . But the compulsion may prove costlier for India in future.

(5) Aggregate Measures of Support - The concept of Aggregate Measures of support (AMS) has been introduced, under which agriculture will get assistance/support equal to a certain percentage of the gross agricultural output.

The AMS will be restricted to only 5 per cent; however, in the case of the developing economies government service programmes such as research, pest control, training , extension and advisory services, inspection, marketing, infrastructural facilities will be keep outside the purview of the AMS . The economic aid granted to the poor farmers will also be excluded from the AMS . All these measures will benefit the Indian farmers.

It is clear from the above explanation that there is not any possibility of adverse effects on Indian agriculture since the implementation of GATT agreement. It is mainly because since the implementation of the agreement there will be not any reduction in subsidy what the farmers getting at present. Moreover there is all possibilities in enhancement of subsidy for farmers. Like wise because of balance of payment problem neither there will be any reduction in grants -in-aid available in the form of export-subsidy nor there will be binding for imports of foodgrains by India even when it is not required. Even since the implementation of Sui-Generis agreement , farmers will be free in keeping seeds and its commercial usase . Though former will not be free to sale and purchase of their seed in the open market, but they will enjoy ample opportunities in exporting their produce because reduction of custom duties and reduction of agricultural subsidy in other countries. All these measure will increase the competitive strength of farmers. Hence , at the movement there is not any danger to India because of GATT or World Trade Organisation .

No agreement could be reached in the GATT in the field of agriculture because of the adamant attitude of the USA and other European countries. In the Uruguay Round it has been decided that the domestic support to agricultural sector will be reduced and dependence on the market forces will be enhanced . Developing countries will be granted a special status. India would be able to offer a price higher than the international prices to the domestic producers. It would be possible to offer larger subsidy to irrigation , ts in Fafertilisers , power credit, etc.

POSSIBLE GAINS AND DANGER TO INDIA BY JOINING WTO

Arguments in Favour

There are following gains to India by joining WTO :

(i) Exports of textiles would increase with the dismantling of MFA after 10 years.

(ii) Total exports from India would increase as a result of liberalisation of Trade in future, thereby increasing employment and income in India,

(iii)USA would not be able to take bilateral action or unilateral action under special 301 and super 301 against a country, as WTO would intervene in the case of any trading dispute between the countries,

(iv) There won't be patents for seeds;

(v) Agricultural subsidies would not be adversely affected by joining WTO , India can give subsidy to the farmers in various forms upto 10% the value of agricultural produce. At present the level is about 5% only. Thus India would reap the benefits of globalisation under WTO.

Arguments Against

There may be following danger anticipated to India by joining WTO :

WTO may protect the interests of developed countries like USA , Japan, France, Germany, etc. only to the detriment of developing countries like India. The change in Patent Act of India may lead to a rise in the prices of drug, particularly of life saving drugs. MNCs may get benefit more by their entry in developing countries . Some fear that the farmers will have to give high prices for the imported seeds, which would be under the patent system. India may not be able to withstand the competition from developed countries in the industrial sector due to technological reasons.

After all said and done, it can be emphasised that India should continue its membership of WTO till its interests are not hurt by wrong decisions of developed nations. China wants to enter WTO and take advantage of its membership. In case India's interests are hurt in any way we can quit WTO by giving six months notice in this regard. There are many wrong notions in the minds of the people about GATT and WTO. Avoding such nations, India should take full benefit from the multilateral trading system.

4

Land Reform

In the traditional sense land reform is "the redistribution of property rights in land for the benefit of small farmers and agricultural labourers". A broad definition would mean including two types of institutional changes one related to agrarian relations and the other to the size of the unit of cultivation. Thus, land reform aims at not only redistributing ownership holdings from the viewpoint of social justice but also of reorganising operational holdings from the viewpoint of optimum utilization of land. It also aims at providing security of tenure, fixation of rents and conferment of ownership.

Need and Importance of Land Reform

(1) Promotion of Incentives— A small farmer is always unable to buy agricultural inputs in required quantity and if he happens to be farmer-in-tenancy he has no incentive to make a proper use of agricultural resources. To encourage a cultivator to work hard and to exercise a close supervision of agricultural operations, there is need to guarantee the cultivator that he will get full benefits from his labour and investment. Thus there is need for land reform.

(2) Costless Method of Raising Production— All of us will agree that in India there is scarcity of capital and whatsoever is available in the country is to be utilised in the non-agricultural sector. But production in the agricultural sector can be increased without any cost if the relationship of the

cultivator with land is improved. Such an improved relation will result in better ploughing, sowing and fertilisation of land, watering the land at right time in right quantity and better looking after all other aspects.

(3) Planned Growth— A Rational system in agricultural will help in promoting well planned development. Agricultural economy can be brought into a close integration with the planning process provided the cultivator has a direct link with the government. It will be easier for the planners to formulate and implement policies for the farm sector by eliminating the heterogeneous and large varieties of tenurial relations.

(4) Social Justice— Land reform will provide justice tolarge number of cultivators. Change in tenurial relations in favour of the tiller will mean that he is assured of his right to share in fruits of his labour and investment. Again, distribution of surplus land to marginal farmers and landless labourers will reduce inequalities of wealth. Further, consolidation of holdings is bound to increase income of the cultivators.

Objectives of Land Reform

Right from the First Plan to the Ninth Plan there have been two major objectives of land reform, viz., (1) social justice, and (2) economic efficiency. The Planning Commission has summed up these objectives thus :

"The first is to remove such impediments to increase in agricultural production as arise from the agrarian structure inherited from the past. This should help to create conditions for evolving as speedily as possible an agricultural economy with high level of efficiency."

"The second objective, which is closely related to the first is to eliminate all elements of exploitation and social justice within the agrarian system to provide security for the tiller of the social and assure equality of status and opportunity to all the sections of the rural population."

For the fulfilment of these objectives, the major steps adopted under the land reforms programme are:

1. Abolition of intermediaries.
2. Regulation of landlord-tenant relationship.
3. Redistribution of land.
4. Consolidation of scattered holdings.
5. Development of co-operative farming.

Factors Responsible for Small Holdings

Small holdings create serious imbalance in the man-land ratio, suffer from higher investment per hectare and practice inferior farm practices. Following are the factors responsible for small holdings—

1.Population Pressure— Due to heavy pressure of population, the area of farm is divided into a number of tiny fields and consequently the farm size is reduced further. The failure of agriculture and industries to develop pari passu with the increase in population has been the most responsible cause of sub-division of holdings.

2.Laws of Inheritance and Succession— According to the Hindu Code Bill and Mohammedan laws of succession all the sons and the daughters are equally entitled to a share in the ancestral property. The division is not confined merely to the total area of land but each heir claims a share in each individual field. This leads to fragmentation.

3.Disintegration of Joint Family System— With the growth of industries, towns and western culture the joint family system has suffered a great setback. This has led to sub-division.

4.The Absence of the Alternative Sources of Employment— A decline in village handicrafts and industries due to British colonial policies and a fierce competition from machine-made goods have resulted in the pressure on land. Obviously, with no other walks of life open as a choice to a farmer's son he has perforce to fall back on agriculture and insist on his share in land.

5.Rural Indebtedness and the Indigenous Moneylender— "In addition to the laws of inheritance, unequal fertility and assessment, another cause which contributed to this state of affairs is the absorption of large amounts of land into the hands of the village sowkar by means of foreclosure of mortgages or sales. The agricultural population in consequence has only a limited area to divide among themselves, so far as the occupation of the land is concerned".

6.Other Factors— Village land reform measures, land speculation, lack of literacy, a large number of local languages, inadequate transport and communication facilities, extremely poor level of income also favour concentration of people on agriculture.

Harmful Consequences of Sub-division and Fragmentation

1.Increased Cost of Production— There are two types of costs, viz., fixed and variable. Fixed cost comprises of cost of land, maintenance of pair of bullocks, the cost of a well, expenses of maintaining his (farmer's) family, etc. These costs remain the same irrespective of the size of land. The variable cost comprises of costs of fencing per hectare, fertilizers and seeds, etc. Although variable cost goes down with the reduction in size, but never in the same proportion. Thus, if the size is small or the holding is fragmented average cost of production is more.

2.Wastage of Land, Time and Energy— If the farm is too small, lot of land is wasted on account of boundary walls. In Punjab about 10% of the land is wasted due to this reason. Similarly, the farmer is not able to make optimum use of his time and energy. In case of scattered holdings lot of time and energy get waited due to movement from one holding to another. Further personal supervision also becomes difficult. Some of the farms are too small to put them under cultivation. To quote, in Punjab 6% of the land is split up in such 'tiny' or 'toy' holdings that it cannot be used for cultivation thus causing wastage of land.

3.Difficulty in the Use of New Methods— While fencing of field is necessary to protect the farms from stray cattle, the cost is very high in case of tiny fields. When the holdings are scattered a farmer has less incentive to spend money on the maintenance of proper drains to prevent water logging and on the embankments to check soil erosion. In case of fragmented holdings, even if sufficient water is available, irrigation becomes impracticable.

4.Expensive and Unnecessary Litigation— Small and fragmented holdings often result in expensive and unnecessary litigation on account of boundaries, making of pathways, moving through one another's farm, the channel along which water is to be taken as well as over its distribution, etc.

To sum up, combined results of all these are to drive the land out of cultivation and loss of time, money and energy.

Remedial Measures

These can be grouped under two heads–preventive and curative. The object of preventive measures is to prevent further deterioration of the situation and of late, to remedy the existing drawbacks. Here we can discuss them under following heads—

1.Ceiling on the Size of Holdings— Although legislative measure have been taken to put a ceiling on the size of holding, but there is hardly anything to prevent a co-sharer from sub-dividing the lands informally, various measures in the regards may be—

(a)Prohibition of partition of a holding below a certain size.

(b) Compulsory acquisition of petty and uneconomic holding and their distribution to those whose holdings would thereby be made economic.

(c) The Egyptian system whereby land is normally divided amongst heirs, but it is actually left in the hands of one to cultivate on behalf of all the members or handed to trustees to manage for all.

(d) Joint farming of the inheritance without partition.

(e) Under the policy of ceiling, the surplus land available to used to increase the size of uneconomic holdings.

(f) Some land may also be available to increase the size of uneconomic holdings through reclamation.

(g) The farmers may be withdrawn from tiny holdings by providing them alternative employment

2.*Consolidation of Holdings*— Fragmented agricultural holdings stand in the way of rationalisation of agriculture and adequate investment of capital and inputs on land.Consolidation of these fragmented holdings is thus an important measure to boost efficiency and economy in agriculture. The problem of fragmentation is to be solved through consolidation. Consolidation of holdings is the way to allot one compact block at one place in exchange of scattered plots of a cultivator. Such a pooling at one place brings economy in terms of investment, time and energy. Consolidation can be (1) voluntary, and (2) compulsory. In case of voluntary consolidation the villagers themselves take the initiative, whereas in compulsory consolidation the State Government enacts legislation whereby making it necessary.

In most of the European countries there are provisions for the prevention of fragmentation. In some Asian countries also like Japan, Iraq and Syria, there are legal provisions for the consolidation of land. In Iraq there is a special anti-fragmentation law.

Prior to independence, a number of efforts were made for voluntary consolidation but did not make any headway. Consolidation of holdings provides an opportunity for planned development of villages. Legislative provisions have been made in many states for undertaking consolidation of holding.

So far 629.73 lakh hectare of land have been consolidated. Bulk of this work has been done in Maharashtra, Uttar Pradesh, Haryana, Punjab, Bihar and Orissa.

In the programme of consolidation following difficulties have been felt-attachment to ancestral land, conservative outlook and literacy, fear of getting inferior land in exchange of superior ones, no co-operation from affluent farmers and the cost involved.

3.Co-operative Farming— Since the availability of land is inadequate, hence better alternative is to go in for co-operative farming under it, the land is pooled into a single unit, but the ownership of land remains with the individuals. The management of land is carried on jointly. Members are paid for their work and net profits are distributed among member-farmers after deducting some money for building up reserves for the co-operative society.

Line of Action on Remedial Measures

In India, land reforms have been undertaken on the following lines:

1.Abolition of Intermediaries- There were three systems, viz., the Zamindari system, the Ryotwari system and the Mahalwari system. This tenurial system resulted in low investment, no motivation and distributive injustice. Before independence 40% of the cultivated land was under intermediary tenure.

The Policy and Measures— After independence a lot of enactments were passed by State legislatures to abolish intermediaries between the tiller and the State. However, in actual practice the legislative enactment equated intermediaries with zamindars and thereby left a class of rent-receivers and absentee landlords under Ryotwari system untouched. State Government passed legislations and by 1952.

The laws enacted had two principles in Common: (a) abolition of intermediaries between the State and cultivator, and (b) the payment of compensation to land owners. The abolition of statutory landlordism has resulted in bringing 20 million cultivators into direct contract with the State and distributing 57.7 lakh hectares of land to landless agriculturists. In regard to compensation there was difference in the standard to be followed. In some of the State the net income of the owner of the land has been the basis of compensation. It was followed in A. P., Tamilnadu, Karnataka, Bengal, Delhi, Bihar, Orissa, Rajasthan, Manipur, Tripura. The compensation was high for low-income brackets and low for high income brackets. In some of the States apart from compensation some grants were also given to the zamindars with small income. In some States like Gujarat, M. P., Maharashtra, U. P. and H. P. the basis of compensation was land revenue, whereas in Kerala, the market value of land was the basis of compensation. Compensation was to be paid in cash or in bonds. A large number of the States paid in cash, but a few paid in both cash and bonds. However, the big landlords were given bonds everywhere. These bonds were to be encashed in equal instalments spread over a period varying from 20 to 40 years.

Evaluation— No doubt lakhs of cultivators came into direct contract due to abolition of Zamindari system, but the programme has been assailed on three grounds. *First,* the amount of compensation to be paid was very heavy amounting to Rs. 670 crores, whereas the revenue to be accruing to the State is only Rs. 20 crores or so. Not only this, the bulk of compensation was either frittered away in consumption or spent on buying urban property, etc. *Second,* the State has acquired only the rent receiving interests, thus the rent receiving Zamindars have been converted into landlords with superior rights in land, employing agricultural workers or share-croppers and have swelled the ranks of 'owner cultivators' without being tillers of soil. Number of studies have proved that de to these loopholes in the legislation there has been an increase in the number of feudal landlords. *Third,* the legislation provided the intermediaries to resume land for self cultivation, it resulted in large scale evictions of tenants. At last, it can be concluded that there is need to consolidate the gains and to improve upon the implementation.

2. *Tenancy Reforms*- The land reform under this category is related to those who work on land leased from others or taken on rent from others. Such cultivators can be of three type, viz.,

(i) Permanent tenants or occupancy tenants,

(ii) Temporary tenants or tenants-as-will, and

(iii) Sub-tenants.

The occupy tenants have permanent right to cultivate and this right goes from generation to generation as long as rent is paid. If they make any improvement on land it can be recovered from the owner. Thus, except the payment of land revenue to the Government by the owner there is hardly any difference between an owner and a permanent tenant on land.

But in case of rest of the two categories the position of the cultivator is very weak. They can be ejected from land at any time. Prior to independence they had to perform different types of beggar and were just like bonded labourers of the landlords. Many a time such lease deeds were oral and likely to change at the discretion of the landlord. According to the National Sample Survey (8th Round) 20% of the land is under the tenancy at will and sub-tenancy.

Measures— The principal tenancy reform measures concern three Fs to the tenant, i.e., Fixity of tenure (security of tenure)., Fair rent, and Free Transferability (right of ownership). Let us discuss them in detail.

Regulation of Rent– On the eve of independence, the rents varied from 50% to 70% of the total produce and apart from rent certain free services known as beggar was also to be rendered compulsorily thereby reducing the net income further. At the start of the First Plan it was laid down that the rent to be paid to landlord should not be more than 20% to 25%. Legislation on these lines has been enacted in all the States. However, the maximum rent differs from State to State, for example, in Kerala it is one-fourth to one-half; in Orissa and Bihar it is one-fourth of the gross produce; in Punjab it is one-third; and in Rajasthan it is one-sixth of the gross produce but in case of cash rents, at twice the land revenue assessment. The rates vary within the States also due to quality of fertility.

Security of Tenure— *Sir Arthur Young* has very rightly observed, "Give a man the secure possession of a bleak rock and he will turn it into a garden; give him a nine years' lease of a garden he converts it into a desert." Thus to involve a cultivator whole-heatedly in the operations, security of tenure is a must. The laws enacted in this regard have three objectives—

(i) evictions or ejections do not take place except in accordance with the law;

(ii) that the land resumed if at all by an owner should be for personal cultivation only;

(iii)in case of resumption, some minimum area must be left for the tenant

As regards the security of tenant-cultivator the position is as follows:

(i) Full security of tenure without any right of resumption (in U. P. and Delhi);

(ii) Right of resumption of a limited area for personal cultivation subject to the condition of area for the tenants (in Assam, Maharashtra, Gujarat, Punjab, Rajasthan and H. P.);

(iii) Provision of land resumption for self cultivation, but no such arrangement that the tenant should be left with a minimum land under all conditions (in West Bengal and J & K); and

(iv) Measures in the form of an order for staying ejectments adopted to give a temporary protection to tenants (in T. N., Karnataka, Kerala, A. P., Orissa, etc.).

Right of Ownership— The earlier two steps are the first stage in tenancy reform; the goal is to confer ownership rights to as many tenants as possible. Legislation provides for bringing tenants of non-resemble lands into direct relationship with the State in the following three ways:

(i) by declaring tenants as owners against the payment to owners by them,

(ii) through the acquisition of ownership rights by the State on payment of compensation and transferring these rights to tenants against payment in instalment to the State by the tenants, and

(iii) through the acquisition by the State of the landlord rights and bringing tenants into direct relation with the State. In this case the cultivators will have to pay rent to the State. N.P. As a result of these measures 12.40 million tenants have acquired ownership rights over 64.81 lakh hectares of land. In some of State like Maharashtra, Gujarat, Kerala, H. P. and J & K the system of tenancy has almost disappeared.All tenants are generally protected except for those like widos, member of the armed forces, minors. Unmarried women, person suffering from disability etc.

Evaluation of Tenancy Reform Measures— The Third Plan observed, "When there is a pressure on land and the social and economic position of tenants in the village is weak, it becomes difficult for them to seek the protection of law. Moreover, resort to legal processes is costly and generally beyond the means of tenants. Thus, in many ways, despite the legislation, the scales are weighted in favour of the continuance of existing terms and conditions." Thus, although considerable progress has been made in right direction, there are a number of shortcomings in the laws and their implementation:

1. The definition of the term 'tenant' generally excludes the share-croppers who form the great bulk of tenant-cultivators, thereby denying them protection.

2. While regulating rent, the rents were not reduced and in many places the rent fixed was the same prevalent at that time.

3. Fair rents have not been defined uniformly in the State laws. For any demand for fair rents on the part of share-croppers and tenants-at-will leads to ejectment.

4. There are many exemptions and escape clauses which have been misused against the interest of cultivators. To illustrate, there are provisions of land resumption for self cultivation by owners, but the definition of the term personal cultivation is so loosely described that lot of land has been resumed by land owners.

5. Voluntary surrenders are a big fraud. Since surrenders were made under duress and correction of the landlords.

6. The object of conferring occupancy rights on a large body of tenants did not materialise because of high rates of compensation.

7. The administrative difficulties, fear of landlords to officials, non-maintenance of correct and uptodate land records have been great lacunae in tenancy reforms.

3. *Ceiling on Land Holding*- One of the basic objective of land reform is to bring about a more equivable distribution of land. The main instrument for realising this objective is the imposition of ceiling on land. Since the supply of land is limited and claimants are extremely numerous. Hence no single individual can be allowed to possess unlimited amount of land. The ceiling on land holding is intended to meet he longer hunger of the landless, to reduce large inequalities in land ownership and to enlarge self-employment in owned land. There are two aspects of land ceiling

(i) fixation of ceiling above which nobody can hold land and this will be applicable to future holders also, and

(ii) acquisition of surplus land from those who have extra land and to distribute this surplus among small farmers and landless labourers so as to increase the size of their holdings within the maximum limit of land ceiling.

The provisions under the ceiling laws may be analysed as under:

(i) unit of application,

(ii) upper limit for land,

(iii) exemptions allowed, and

(iv) availability of surplus land and its distribution.

(i) Unit of Application— Under the old Acts (Prior to 1972) the basis of ceiling fixation was an individual instead of a family which helped the cultivator-families to possess large areas of land. To illustrate, a family of 5 members in A. P. could

have 1,620 acres. Since 1972, the basis has been shifted from an individual to a family. The family is defined as consisting of husband, wife and children. For families with more than 5 children, there is provision for holding land in excess of the ceiling for every additional member, subject to the condition that in no case the total land with a family exceed twice the ceiling limit for a family.

(ii) Maximum Limit or Level of Ceiling— The national guideline on land ceiling were evolved in 1972 after a conference of Chief Ministers of States. The level of ceiling applicable to family as applicable to a family as recommended in these guidelines varies from 10 to 18 acres for the best category of land capable of producing two crops a year to 54 acres of dry land.

(iii) Exemptions— In the new policy, exemptions have been rationalised and considerably reduced thus a large surplus of land can be expected.

(iv) Availability of Surplus Land and Its Distribution—

Evaluation— In India, ceiling on land holding has aroused a great deal of controversy. There are lobbies on both the sides, one in favour and the other in opposition. Those who support the policy opine that to bring social equity and even distribution of economic power, it is a must. There is evidence that while a majority in rural area lives in poverty, a few are very rich. The green revolution has further winded rural disparities. Secondly, small peasant farming is more suitable in India's labour surplus economy. Through ceiling, while increasing the number of small peasants, it will result in more employment and production. Though ceiling the surplus land may be distributed to the co-operatives of the landless agricultural labourers.

On the other hand there are a few who are basically concerned with development and do not pay even lip service to the cause of egalitarian aspect. Their main arguments against ceiling are :

(i) In India, already the size of holding is uneconomic and it will further aggravate the situation.

(ii) Small cultivators do not have adequate resources to make any investment in land.

(iii) Economic of large scale cannot be obtained.

(iv) Small farmers will have less propensity to save.

(v) Since small farmers firs of all produce food crops for them, there will be adverse impact on supply of raw materials to industries.

(vi) Ceiling might displace a large number of agricultural workers.

(vii) Since even after ceiling everybody in villages cannot be distributed land, so why do it?

(viii) Unless there is ceiling on incomes in other sectors, e.g., industries, trade and services, it is unfair to prescribe a ceiling on agricultural income alone.

(ix) And, the ceiling is likely to affect adversely the leadership in rural areas. But all these arguments have little validity in the context of social justice as well as development and some of them are ill founded also.

As regard to implementation we have already seen that the progress has been very slow and tardy. The total area so far declared surplus under the programme of Distribution of ceiling of surplus land is 30.34 lakh hectare out of which 26.64 lakh hectare have been taken under possession . A total ares of 21.06 lakh hectare has been distributed to 51.47 lakh beneficiaries of whom 36 per cent belongs to scheduled caste and 14 per cent belongs to scheduled tribes. The reason responsible for the unsatisfactory progress are summarise below:-

(i) The new policy was announced on 26 September, 1970 but came into effect from 24 January, 1971, thus the big landlords had all the time for sale of land and fictitious transfers to avoid the sale. Delay occurred further due to legal cases.

(ii) The law itself was not clear and many loopholes were left to give advantages to landlords' lobby.

(iii) Poor records and inefficient administration.

(iv) Unfavourable political climate, and

(v) Litigation (although they are covered by the Ninth Schedule of the Constitution which bars judicial scrutiny).

4. *Agricultural Reorganisation* - One of the reasons of low productivity in India has been small size of land holding which is due to sub-division and fragmentation. In this regard we have already studied the nature, reasons responsible and progress made insolving the problem in the last chapter.

5. *Co-operative Farming* - Since the availability of land is inadequate , hence better alternative is to go in for co-operative farming under it, the land is pooled into a single unit, but the ownership of land remains with the individuals. The management of land is carried on jointly. Members are paid for their work and net profits are distributed among member-farmers after deducting some money for building up reserves for the co-operative society.

6. *Land Record* - It is the pre-condition for effective implementation of land reform measure to correct and keep up to date record of land reform. It is necessary particularly for providing security to tenure to tenents and share-cropper and also for smooth flow of credit and agricultural inputs to the land holders . So far, financial assistance to the tune of Rs,. 96,91 crores has been provides to the states / union territories towards the central share for this purpose.

7. *Land Acquisition* - Land Acquisition Act 1894 provide for compulsory acquisition of land needed for public purposes and for companies. The Act was extensively amended in 1984 with a view to serve the interests of the community in

harmoney with the rights of individual. The provision of amended Act. provides for a three years time limit for completion of the acquitition proceedings and makes generous provisions in respect of payment of compensation to land holders.

An Over-all Appraisal of Land Reforms

"By and large land reforms in India enacted so far and those contemplated in the near future... are in the right direction; and yet due to lack of implementation the actual results are far from satisfactory." A number of studies conducted by the individuals like Dr. Mukherjee, Dantwala, Ladenjinsky, Gunnar Myrdal, Baljit Singh, etc., etc., and by the committees and commissions like Mahalnobis Committee, Nanda Committee, the Planning Commission, the U. N. O., the F. A. O., the Congress Agrarian Committee, etc., etc., have all in one voice expressed their sorrow and anger over the slow and defective progress of land reform measures in India. According to the Task Force of the Planning Commission the main reasons for the poor performance are:

(i) Lack of political will.

(ii) Absence of pressure from below.

(iii) The lukewarm and apathetic attitude of bureaucracy.

(iv) Legal hurdles.

(v) Absence of correct up-to-date land records.

(vi) Lack of financial support.

(vii) Land reforms treated as an administrative issue rather than political issue.

(viii) Components of land reforms were treated as disjointed programmes.

Suggestions for Improvement— As long as the policy of land to the tiller is not faithfully followed, the Indian agriculture cannot be modernised. The National Commission or Agriculture has made following suggestions to improve the position.

(1) Agriculture should be treated as a family occupation of the peasant-cultivator and not as a source of subsidiary unearned income. Thus *the landlord-tenant nexus be broken up.*

(2) The State Government should institute *enquiries into benami transfers* and those found guilty (of such transfers to avoid ceiling law) must be punished.

(3) The process of acquisition and redistribution of surplus clear that they will not be allowed to sell or mortgage such land

(4) Not only the administrative machinery needs an overhaul but the legal machinery should also go in for simplification and speed.

****

5

Agriculture Finance

Emphasising the importance of Credit in the field of agriculture *Kindle Berger* observed that growing population needed more production, which in turn needed more capital (credit) because it was not possible to expand area of land. So more production could be possible only by the use of better seed, number etc. In India, farmer's need for capital is all the more acute as he is poor. Each agricultural operation requires that the peasant should get credit at a proper time and at reasonable rate of interest. To understand the role of different rural credit agencies, it is essential to understand the nature of agricultural credit in terms of borrowers, purposes, time period, suppliers and risk. This can be understood from the following chart:-1

Nature of Farm-Business— This basis tells about the different aspects of rural business activities.

Economic Status— The All India Rural Credit Survey (1951-52) for the first time made an attempt to classify the borrowers on the basis of the size of their land holdings.

Utility— It has been divided into parts. The Production Credit or the Producer's credit is the credit taken for the purpose carrying on productive activities with a vies to augmenting the income. It may be needed to create some fixed assets like a well in the land and/or for meeting current needs

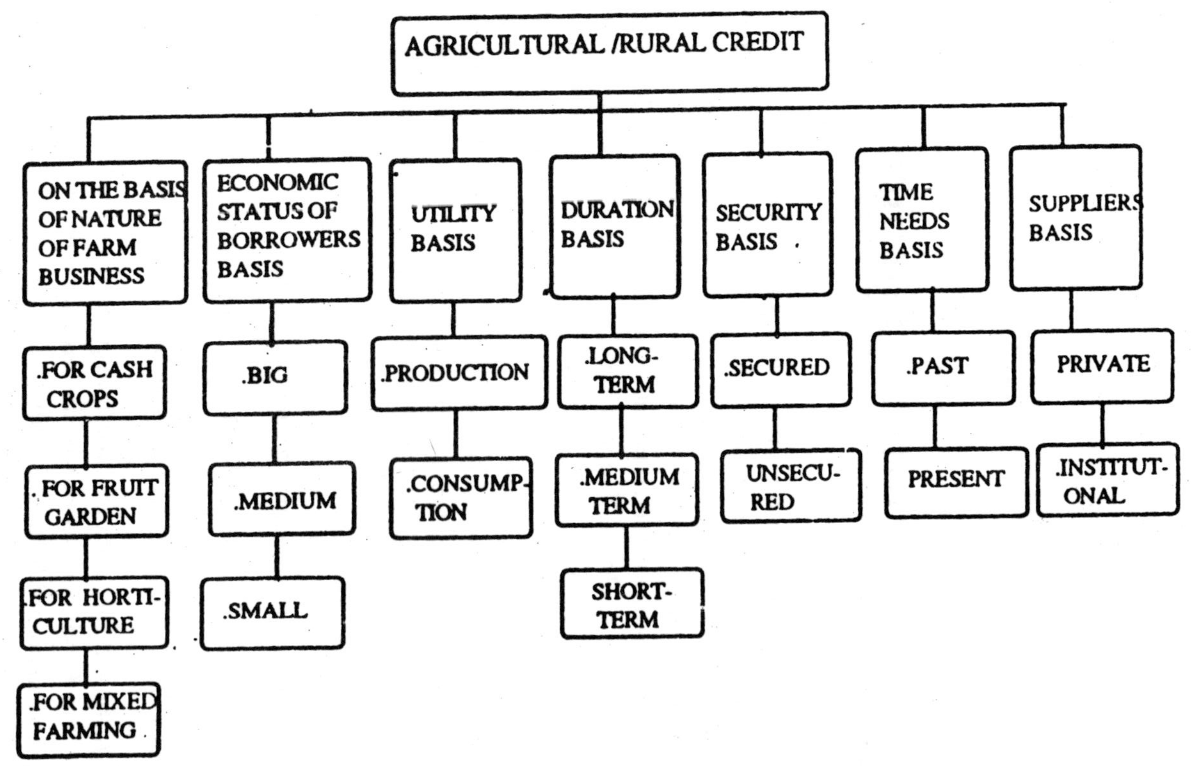
AGRICULTURAL /RURAL CREDIT
ON THE BASIS OF NATURE OF FARM BUSINESS
.FOR CASH CROPS
. FOR FRUIT GARDEN
.FOR HORTI-CULTURE
.FOR MIXED FARMING
ECONOMIC STATUS OF BORROWERS BASIS
.BIG
.MEDIUM
.SMALL
UTILITY BASIS
.PRODUCTION
.CONSUMP-TION
DURATION BASIS
.LONG-TERM
.MEDIUM TERM
SHORT-TERM
SECURITY BASIS
.SECURED
UNSECU-RED
TIME NEEDS BASIS
.PAST
PRESENT
SUPPLIERS BASIS
PRIVATE
.INSTITUT-ONAL

like buying seeds or other inputs. Producer's credit is often divided into settlement credit (needed for new settlement, rehabilitation and construction of farm house etc.), development credit (needed for levelling of fields, construction of drainage or digging a well), and equipment credit (needed to buy a tractor, pump-set or to repair machines and to meet their running expenses). Such a classification helps the lending agency to make a proper evaluation of loan proposals and to make a decision in regard to quantity of assistance, duration, interest rate, security and mode of payment.

Consumption need is taken to satisfy needs of consumption goods or services of a former's family. Its repayment is expected to be made out of future anticipated income. There was a time when institutional suppliers used to refuse credit for consumption, but now the attitude has got a sea change.

Duration— Although there is no hard and fast rule regarding duration of loans to distinguish long; medium and short period loans. However, by convention and experience the time period for these three as has been broadly accepted is...loans for a period of 3 months to about 18 months are termed as short-term loans. Such loans are normally required for current production needs or for consumption needs or for carrying on marketing operations. Medium-term loans are given for a period ranging from 2 to 5 years and are used for buying bullocks or milch cattle, small agro-machinery, digging a well etc. Loans taken for over 5 years come under the category of long-term loans. Such loans are given for purchase of new land or to bring some permanent improvement on the land, or purchase of some costly agro-machinery.

Security— Loans covered by some security are termed as secured loans. If the loans are secured by mortgage of immovable property then they are known as mortgage credit. Loans secured by pledge or hypothecation of movable property are termed as collateral credit. And, if the loans are secured by promissory note or by guarantee of a third party, then they come under the category of personal credit. Normally the lending agencies are keen to have adequate and satisfactory security against loans to fully cover the risk involved in granting of loans to agriculturists.

Time Needs— Credit may be needed to meet out past needs and present needs. Past needs mean to pay off the past debt. Such a loan or credit is important in view of the reason that if the poor farmer does not repay the past debt he may have to part with his land or may be required to sell his produce to the creditor at a lower price under durers and thus lose in the bargain.

Supplier of Credit— The credit agency may be a private agency *viz.* money-lender, indigenous banker, wholesale trader, retail trader, relative or some friend. Private credit maintains a great deal of secrecy and has been exploitative by nature.

Institutional suppliers comprise of co-operative credit societies, commercial banks, regional rural banks and alike. These agencies operate within a framework of rules and regulation and their accounts are open to public scrutiny and audit.

Rural credit institutions or the rural money market (most commonly used term) from where the farmers get their credit needs fulfilled may be divided into two parts *viz.*, Organised and unorganised. These two can be further classified.

Composition of Rural Credit

As clearly shown in the chart that Indian farmer meets his credit needs by borrowing from several sources. Sources of short-term and medium-term credit are: Money-lenders, Traders, Co-operative Credit Societies, Banks and Government. Long-term credit is obtained from Land Development Banks, Money-lenders and Government. Table 5 shows important sources of agricultural credit in India.

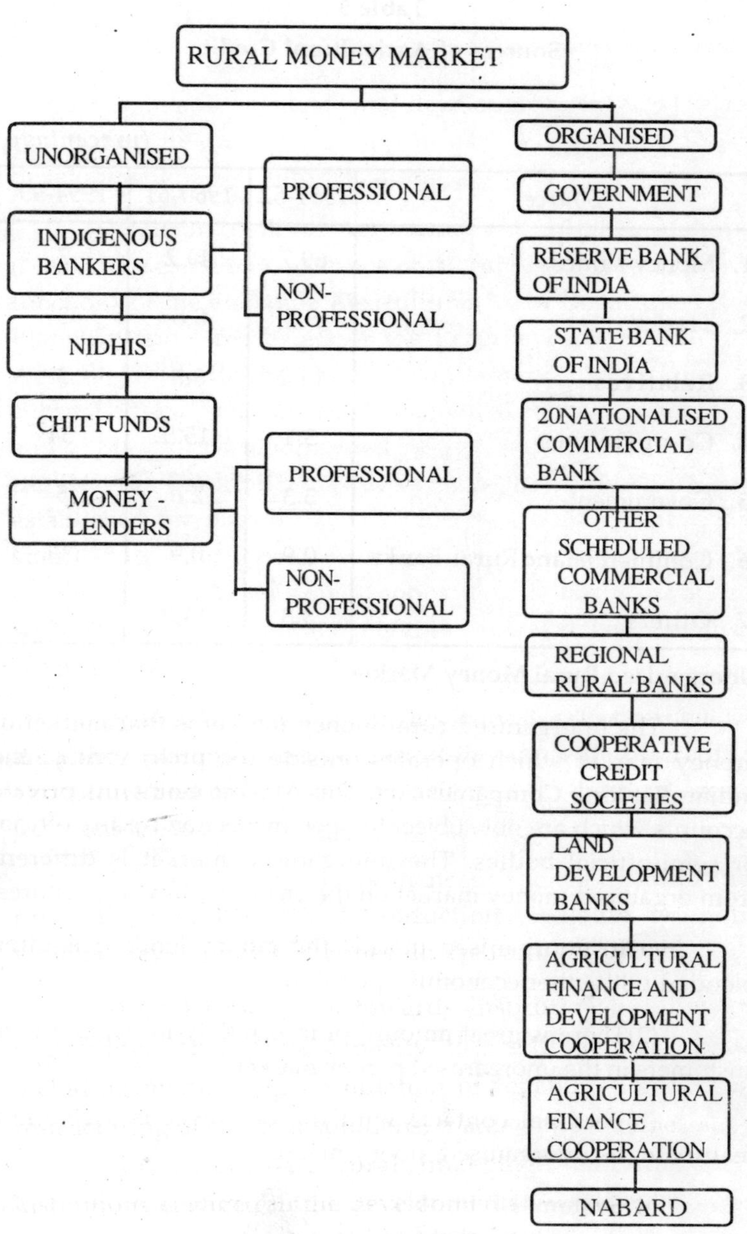

RURAL MONEY MARKET
UNORGANISED
INDIGENOUS BANKERS
PROFESSIONAL
NON-PROFESSIONAL
NIDHIS
CHIT FUNDS
MONEY - LENDERS
PROFESSIONAL
NON-PROFESSIONAL
ORGANISED
GOVERNMENT
RESERVE BANK OF INDIA
STATE BANK OF INDIA
20NATIONALISED COMMERCIAL BANK
OTHER SCHEDULED COMMERCIAL BANKS
REGIONAL RURAL BANKS
COOPERATIVE CREDIT SOCIETIES
LAND DEVELOPMENT BANKS
AGRICULTURAL FINANCE AND DEVELOPMENT COOPERATION
AGRICULTURAL FINANCE COOPERATION
NABARD

Table 5

Sources of Agricultural Credit

(percentage)

Source	*1951-52*	*1960-61*	*1994-95*
1. Money lender	69.7	49.2	7
2. Trader	5.5	8.8	5
3. Relatives	14.2	8.8	3
4. Co-operatives	3.1	15.5	34
5. Government	3.3	2.6	5
6. CommercialandRural Banks	0.9	0.9	35
7. Others	3.3	14.2	11

Unorganised Rural Money Market

The unorganised rural money market is that market of money market which operates outside the provisions of the Indian Banking Companies Act. This Market maintains private accounts which are not subject to open inspection by any official or semi-official bodies. The unorganised market is different from organised money market on the basis of following features:

(1)In unorganised market the money lending is often blended with other economic operations.

(2)There is great amount of informality in dealing with customers in the unorganised money market.

(3)Personal contacts with the borrower is a common feature in the unorganised money market.

(4)System of book-keeping is quite simple in the unorganised money market.

(5)Fairly great amount of flexibility in matters of loan operations is maintained in the rural unorganised money market.

(6)In the unorganised money market secrecy of operations is the rule of game.

Let us discuss different agencies operating in such market.

Money-lenders— These are of two types, *viz.*, professional and non professional. Professional money-lenders are those whose only occupation or profession is money-lending, whereas non-professional money lenders carry on money-lending as a side business. To find a professional money-lenders in rural areas is difficult. Non-professional money lenders comprise of village traders, landlords, well-to-do agriculturists, friends, relations, relations, retired officials, widowers etc. etc., who apart from doing their regular activities also lend money to farmers.

Over the years the importance of money-lenders is declining. While in 1951-52 the money-lenders provided 70% of the total rural credit needs, the share went down to 49% in 1961-62 and remained only 7% in 1994-95. However, there are many reasons for the preponderance of money-lenders in rural areas . They were popular in rural areas because :

(a)The money-lender freely supplies credit for productive and non-productive purposes and also for short-term and long-term requirements of the farmers.

(b)The money-lender is easily accessible and maintains a close and personal contact with the borrower often having relations with family extendity over generations.

(c)His business methods are quite simple and elastic.

(d)The money-lender has local knowledge and experience, therefore, can lend against land as well as against promissory notes. he knows how to protect himself against default.

Objectionable Practices— There are number of malpractices associated with village money-lenders. The most usual types of objections have been : Usurious rates of interest, demand for advance interest, demanding a present for doing business and general manipulation of accounts to the disadvantage of the debtors. Unless their activities are controlled and alternative sources of credit provided to the farmers, it would be difficult to improve the conditions of the peasants. For the planned development of the agriculture, it is all the more important. The All India Rural Credit Survey has rightly concluded, "Private credit, generally unsuitable, is wholly unsuitable in the context of planning for larger production".

In the recent past number of steps have been taken by the Government and the Reserve Bank of India to reduce the importance of money-lenders through enactment of law and development of alternative institutional agencies framework.

Indigenous Bankers— The Indian Central Banking Enquiry Committee has defined an indigenous bankers as any individual or a private firm receiving deposits and dealing in hundis or lending money. Normally people et confused between the two terms-money-lenders and indigenous bankers. But this is not true. The distinctions between the two are as under:

(a)The money-lenders only lend money and that too with their own resources (sometimes borrowed from their relations or other money-lenders also). Whereas, the indigenous bankers accept deposits and deal in hundis. thus they perform a total banking function.

(b)While indigenous bankers mostly finance trade and commerce, money-lenders provide finance often to meet consumption needs and other expenses arising out of social and religious functions.

(c)Indigenous bankers are more careful than money-lenders regarding objectives and purposes for which money is lent.

(d)The amounts advanced by indigenous bankers are more substantial than those lent by money-lenders.

(e)While financial transactions of indigenous bankers are mostly based on short-term credit instruments (*i.e.*, hundis), the dealings of money-lenders are mostly in cash and at the most in only one type of paper, namely promissory note.

(f)Indigenous bankers keep accounts more systematically, receive repayments more regularly and charge lower interest rate than money-lenders.

(g)While money-lenders have their business at one place and do not have relations with other money-lenders; indigenous bankers have their branches at other places and also have fairly close relations with one another.

(h)Indigenous bankers have good and close relations with organised sector of banking and often borrow from State Bank of India and other commercial banks to augment their resources, the money-lender never does so.

Nidhis— Nidhis are mutual loan associations. Nidhis came into existence in the mid nineteenth century, mainly in south India, essentially as 'Loan societies'. But in course of time, these Nidhis have developed into a sort of semi-banking institutions enjoying a great amount of credibility and respectability in the rural areas where normal banking facilities are not available.

Chit Funds— Chit Funds have been defined as loose voluntary associations for mobilising rural savings and to give loans to members. Normally, an entrepreneur starts a Chit Fund and is known as a 'promoter'. A number of persons who join the Chit Fund as members agree to make periodical contributions to the promoters who appropriates for himself as his remuneration the collection of the first instalment of members.

There are hundreds of Chit Funds in southern India. While some of them are well managed, many of them resemble gambling or lotteries appealing to gambling instinct of people in the area. Because of the these reasons only the Chit Funds (along with Nidihis) have attracted lot of public and government attention. Recently, the Central Government has enacted legislation to regulate the working of Chit Funds of all types throughout India.

Conclusion

The agencies operating in unorganised market are progressively losing their importance. While they contributed about 94% of the total rural credit in 1951-52, their share came down to 26% in 1994-95. Among these agencies the role of money-lenders is dominant. Despite the increasing role of institutional financing, they will still be needed to help the rural credit requirements.

ORGANISED RURAL MONEY MARKET

Organised rural money market comprises of institutional credit made available by co-operatives, commercial banks, regional rural banks, and the Government. Institutional finance is better than private credit described as under:

(a)Its basic purpose is to help the farmer to raise his productivity and maximise income and hence never exploitative.

(b)Not only rate of interest is lower, but for different groups of farmers at different rates for different purposes.

(c)Institutions also make a clear distinction between short-term and long-term credit requirements and give loans accordingly.

(d)Institutional credit is fully integrated with other needs of agriculturists.

Government— The Government has also been a source of rural credit both for short and long term periods. The Government provides both direct and indirect help. Indirect credit is provided through the co-operative societies. In this manner, the government is playing a complimentary role to the RBI in the development of co-operative credit.

Direct assistance to farmers is given in the form of taccavi loans. These loans are generally given in times of emergency or distress, such as famine, flood, etc. The rate of interest is low and the mode of repayment is also very convenient. But these loans are not very significant looking at them in view of the total credit needs. In 1951-52, the share of Government finance in the total credit to cultivators by different organised and unorganised agencies was merely 3.3% which further came down to 2.6% in 1961-62. In 1980-81 out of total institutional finance for agriculture of Rs. 3448 crores, the Governments' contribution was a meager Rs. 144 crores, just 4.3%. During 1990-91 , the state governments had advanced nearly Rs. 350 crores as short term loan to agriculture.

There are number of problems associated with these loans because of which the progress has been so declining:

(a)Inadequacy of amount, inequality of distribution and inappropriateness of security;

(b)Inconvenience of timing, incidental delays and impositions of various kinds on borrowers;

(c)Inefficiency of supervision and incompleteness of co-ordination;

(d)Illegal ratification by the village patwari and the BDO to get loans sanctioned.

Hence, the taccavi loans did not become as popular as they should have been.

Reserve Bank of India— Among the central banks of different countries in the world, the role of Reserve Bank of India, right from its inception, both in absolute and comparative terms is most significant. In the beginning the RBI did not do much for agriculture, inspite of the fact that a separate department *viz.*, the Agricultural Credit Department, existed. In 1950-51 the RBI provided only about Rs. 3 crores to the financing of agriculture. It was after 1954, when in presuance of the recommendations of the All-India Rural Credit Survey Committee, the RBI enlarged its contribution to this sector.

Since its establishment in 1935, the Reserve Bank of India has been playing a significant role in the analysis and solution to the problems related to agricultural finance. In this regard the role of the bank has passed through sheveral phases.

The role of the RBI in the sphere of agricultural credit was just advisory during the period between 1935-47.

The Reserve Bank of India called upon to play a more significant and active role in the reorganisation of co-operative credit facilities and disbursement of a large volume of credit through co-operative . This phase covered the period between 1947-1954. During this phase in August 1951, the RBI constituted a committee of Directors to conduct an All India Rural Credit Survey. The Committee submitted its report in December 1954 and marks the begining of the third phase in the evalution of the Bank's role.

During the period between 1955-1982, since the beginning of 1955, the Reserve Bank of India assumed the role of finance, promoter, co-ordinator and the regulator in the sphere of agricultural credit . As a leading financer the RBI provided agricultural finance not directly to the farmers but indirectly through co-operative and State governments. The aforesaid role of the Bank becomes evident from the certain facts. [1]

In its promotional role in the sphere of agricultural credit the Bank worked in close co-ordination with central and state Governments, the planning commission , the National Federation of the State Co-operative Banks.

(1)*State Bank and Agricultural Credit*— State Bank of India was established in 1955 with a view to implementing Integrated Rural Credit Scheme as recommended by Rural Credit Survey Committee. This bank helps the farmer in many ways.

(1) Order to develop banking habit among the farmers, it has opened branches in small towns and mandis.

(2)It has introduced Village Adoption Scheme to provide more credit to agriculture.

(3)It gives loans at low rate of interest to Co-operative Societies.

---

1. (a) It provided short term finance to state cooperative banks at 2% below the Bank Rate.

(b) It provides medium term loans to state cooperative banks at 1-1.5% below the Banks Rate.

(c) It established two funds-

(i) National Agricultural Credit (Long term operation)fund and

(ii) National Agricultural (consolidation) fund. Out of the former, the Bank provided long term loans to state government to enable them to contribute to the share capital cooperative credit institutions, whereas out of the second fund, it granted medium term loans to state cooperative banks to enable them to convert short term agricultural loans to medium term loans.

(d) Various credit agencies were governed by the RBI norms.

(4)It gives loans to the farmers to install tubewells or to buy tractors etc.

The bank is actively engaged in financing to agriculture since its inception. Agricultural financing activities of the Bank gathered momentum in recent few years. The Bank is actively

engaged in granting direct and indirect advance to agriculture. Besides granting advances Bank has shown ample interest other activities related to agricultural finance such as opening of Agricultural Development Branches and adoption of villages.

As a result of Bankès concern towards agricultural finance , its total of direct and indirect advances showed a rise of Rs. 329 crore in 1980 to Rs. 8,794 crores in 1997-98 . The Bank has sponsored 30 RRBs spread over 75 districts in 13 States. A network of 2,383 branches of these RRBs accounts for 16% of all RRB branches in the country . During the year (as at end-September 1997), the deposits and advances of the RRBs sponsored by the Bank stood at Rs. 2,666.45 crore and Rs. 1,183.22 crore respectively.

(2)*Commercial Banks*— Before nationalisation of 14 commercial banks in 1969, Commercial Banks contributed barely 0.9 percent of the total agricultural credit. After nationalization of the 14 banks in 1969 and 6 banks in 1980, the share of commercial banks in total agricultural credit increased to 13 percent. After nationalization, commercial banks have opened branches in rural areas in large numbers. In 1969, of the total loans given by the commercial banks, share of agricultural loans was 5.5 percent. It went upto 16 percent in 1995. These banks mainly advance short-term loans.

(3)*Regional Rural Banks*— On the occasion of the birth anniversary of Mahatma Gandhi on 2 October 1975, a new agency called Regional Rural Bank was inaugurated to provide rural credit. These banks have been established as a supplement to commercial banks. The special function of these banks is to provide loans and other facilities mainly to small and marginal farmers, agricultural labourers, artisans and small entrepreneurs.

Regional Rural Banks (RRBs) had been established to take the banking services to the doorsteps of rural masses especially in remote rural areas with no access to banking services. These banks were to provide institutional credit to the weaker sections of the society at concessional rate of interest, who had perforce been depending on private money-lenders. The banks were also intended to mobilise rural savings and channelise for supporting productive adtivities in the rural savings and channelise for supporting productive activities in the rural areas. As at end-March 1997, there were 196 RRBs covering 436 districts with a network of 14,450 branches. The loans and advances stood at Rs. 7,852.7 crore as at end-September 1996. As much as Rs. 15,423 crore were mobilised as deposits by RRBs as at end-September 1996. Consequent upon the permission permission of the Resrve Bank to determine their own lending rate with effect from 26 August 1996, most of the RRBs have been charging interest rate on loans varying between 13.5-19.5 per cent per annum. The minimum and maximum rates of interest charged were 12.0 per cent and 22.0 per cent, respectively.

CO-OPERATIVE CREDIT INSTITUTIONS

Co-operation is in no way new to India. It has been known and practised in this country since time immemorial. The growth of modern movement of co-operatives is 95 years old, beginning with the enactment of Co-operative Credit Societies Act, on 25th March, 1904. However, the movement of Co-operation in general and credit agencies in particular got impetus with the start of planning phase in India. The First Plan very rightly recognised co-operatives as an "instrument of planned economic action in democracy". The co-operative agency was recognised as better suited than the state for ensuring proper utilisation of credit for productive purposes.

Co-operative finance is the cheapest and has proved best for the Indian former. Under this type of banking organisation , people voluntory co-operate with each other with a view to promote their economic interest. The Co-operative credit movement has a three-tier organisation as illustrated bel;ow.

(a) Primary Credit Societies (at village level)

(b) Central Co-operative Banks (at district level)

(c) State Co-operative Bank (at state level) .

The Structure of Co-operative Credit

The co-operative credit agencies can be divided into two parts on the basic of duration or length of period of credit. We have already discussed that the credit, on the basis of duration can be short-term, medium-term and long-term. However, here we will have only two groups, (i) short-term and medium term and (ii) long- term.

Short-term and Medium-term Co-operative Credit

It is a three tier system. At the village level there are Primary Co-operative Credit Societies, which are generally affiliated to District Central Co-operative Banks (One each in every district). The District Central Co-operative Banks in turn are affiliated to the State Co-operative Banks (one each in every State), also known as Apex Co-operative Bank. Thus, this segment of rural credit forms a pyramid and strength of each part depends on the strength of each of the three parts.

Agro-Credit Co-operative Structure

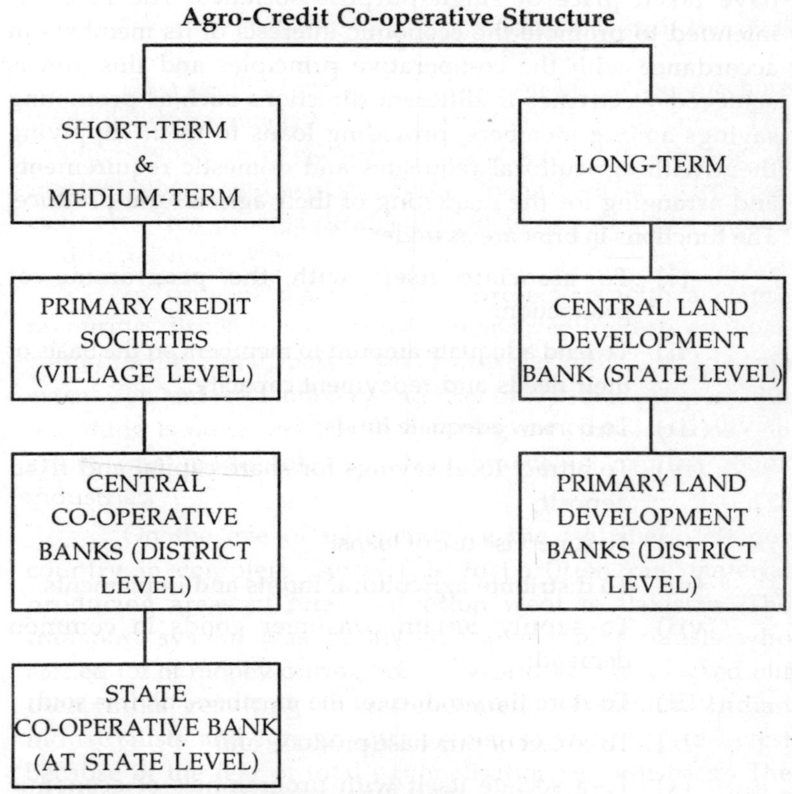

1. Primary Agricultural Credit Society

"The agricultural primary credit society is the foundation stone on which the whole co-operative edifice is built". These have been also called as kernel of the co-operative institutions. The organisation of these societies dates back to 1904 when the first Co-operative Societies Act was planed. The Primary Agricultural Credit Societies provide short and medium term loans to formers.

Functions— The main functions of a PACS is to provide short and medium-term credit; supply agricultural and other production requirements and undertake marketing of agricultural produce. Now-a-days multi-purpose societies have taken place of single-purpose societies. The PACS is intended to promote the economic interests of its members in accordance with the co-operative principles and this aim is achieved y activities in different directions such as promoting savings among members, providing loans to them supplying them with agricultural requisites and domestic requirements and arranging for the marketing of their agricultural produce. The functions in brief are as under:

(i) To associate itself with the programme of production;

(ii) To lend adequate amount to members on the basis of their needs and repayment capacity;

(iii) To borrow adequate funds;

(iv) To attract local savings for share capital and fixed deposit;

(v) To supervise use of loans;

(vi) To distribute agricultural inputs and implements;

(vii) To supply certain consumer goods in common demand;

(viii) To store the produce of the members, till it is sold;

(ix) To collect or purchase produce; and

(x) To associate itself with programmes of economic and social welfare for the village.

In 1951-52, Primary Agricultural Credit Societies, advanced loan worth of Rs. 23 crore which has increased to Rs. 6,461 crores in 1993-94 . The total number of primary credit societies operating in the country stood at 88,000 in 1992-93.

2. Central Co-operative Banks

These are federations of primary credit societies in a specified area, normally a district, that is why these banks are called District Central Co-operative Banks. The DCC Banks are of two types, one, membership confined to PACSs only, hence known as 'Banking Union'. And two, membership granted to both PACSs and individuals possessing some financial status or influence or some special business capacity or experience in the field of co-operative banking. Such individuals are of great asset to DCCBs in inspiring confidence in the public for these banks.

Functions— The main functions are:

(i) To meet credit requirements of member PACSs.

(ii) To undertake ordinary commercial banking business.

(iii) To act as balancing centres for PACSs by making available funds of surplus societies of deficit societies and also from DCC Bank's own funds.

(iv) To undertake non-credit (distribution) activities.

(v) To maintain close and continuous contacts with the PACSs and to provide leadership to them.

(vi) To supervise and inspect the PACSs.

(vii) To provide a safe place for investment of the resources of primary societies.

3. State Co-operative Banks

Also known as Apex Bank, forms the apex of the co-operative credit structure in each State. It serves as a link between the RBI on the one hand the DCC Banks and the PACSs on the other.

Functions: Their main functions are as under:

(i) They act as bankers' bank to the DCC Banks in the district.

(ii) They co-ordinate their own policies with those of the co-operative movement and the government.

(iii) They form a connecting link between the Co-operative Credit societies and the Commercial money market and the RBI.

(iv) They formulate and execute uniform credit policies for the Co-operative movement as a whole.

(v) They promote the cause of co-operation in general they grant subsidies to DCC Banks for development of co-operatives.

(vi) They act as clearing house for money flows.

(vii) They supervise, control and guide the activities of the DCC Banks through regular inspection working as their friend, philosopher and guide.

4. Land Development Banks

Land development banks are advancing long term cooperative credit to the farmers against the mortgage of their lands for its permanent improvement , purchasing agricultural implements and for repaying old debts. The amount of loan sanctioned by the Primary. Land Development Banks has increased from Rs. 3 crore in 1950-51 to Rs. 2039 crores in 1993-94 . Presently there are 19 central Land Development Banks and 440 Primary Land Development Banks working in the country . But benefits from these land development banks could not reach to small farmers and only big landlords have been taking advantages out of them.

National Bank for Agriculture and Rural Development

In March 1979, Reserve Bank of India appointed Shivaraman Committee with a view to studying problems relating to agriculture credit. On its recommendations National Bank for Agriculture and Rural Development was set up on 12 July 1982. This bank has been set up an as Apex bank of the country with regard to agricultural credit. It is popularly known as NABARD. It plays a significant role in agricultural as well as rural development. The main function of the bank is to refinance state governments, State Co-operative banks, Land Development Banks, Regional Rural Banks and other financial institutions that give loans for agriculture, small ad cottage industries, handicrafts and rural development. In 1994 the bank sanctioned loans amounting to Rs. 4,334 crore for the development of agriculture.

National Bank for Agriculture and Rural Development (NABARD) came into existence on 12 July 1982. It took over the functions of the erstwhile Agriculture Credit Department Rural Planning and Credit Cell of the Reserve Bank of India and Agriculture Refinance and Development Corporation. Its subscribed and paid up capital stands at Rs. 500 crore at the end of March 1996, contributed by the central Government and the Reserve Bank of India at various phases. NABARD was established for providing credit for promotion of agriculture, small-scale industries cottage and village industries, handicrafts and other allied economic activities in rural areas with a view to promoting integrated rural development and securing prosperity of rural areas.

NABARD as the apex institution, is concerned with all policy planning and operation in the field of credit for agriculture and other economic activities in the rural areas. It functions are to :

(i) serve as an apex refinancing agency for institutions providing investment and production credit for promoting various development activities in the rural areas;

(ii) take measures towards institution building for improving absorptive capacity to credit delivery system including monitoring, formulation of rehabilitation schemes, restructuring of credit institutions, training of personnel, etc,

(iii) co-ordinate rural financing activities of all institutions engaged in the developmental work at field -level and maintain liaison with Central State Governments, Reserve Bank of India and other national institutions concerned with policy formulation and also;

(iv) undertake monitoring and evaluation of projects refinanced by it.

NABARD provides refinance to the state land development banks, state co-operative banks, scheduled commercial banks and regional rural banks, while the ultimate beneficiaries of investment credit can be individuals, partnership concerns, companies, state owned corporations etc. During 1996-97, NABARD sanctioned short-term credit limits aggregating Rs. 789-9 crore (as of September 1996) , comprising an amount of Rs. 552.2 crore for seasonal agricultural operations (SAO) and an amount of Rs. 146.68 crore for other seasonal agricultural operations (OSAO) in respect of 103 RRBs . Separate credit limits were sanctioned for OPP (Rs. 62.39 crore) and for DTP (Rs. 28.63 crore) to 48 RRBs each. The outstanding refinance under SAO and other short-term limits for RRBs stood at Rs. 833.11 crore as on end-September 1996.

INSTITUTIONAL FINANCE FOR AGRICULTURAL CREDIT - A REVIEW

Institutional funding of the farm sector is mainly by commercial banks , regional rural banks and co-operative banks. Agricultural credit provided by various agencies rose from Rs. 16,494 crore in 1993-94 to Rs. 30,976 crore in 1997-98 . In 1998-99 it is likely to rise to Rs. 38.054 crore. Disbursement of Agricultural credit for the period 1993-94 to 1997-98 is listed in Table 1 .

Share of commercial banks in total institutional credit to agriculture is almost 48 per cent followed by cooperative banks with a share of 46 per cent. Regional Rural Banks account for just about 6 per cent of total credit disbursement. It is important to highlight the continued importance of short-term credit which accounts for two third of the total institutional lending to agriculture as depicted in Table -2.

Table-1

Disbursement of Agricultural Credit

Institutions	*1993-94*	*1994-95*	*1995-96*	*1996-97*	*1997-98**
Co-operative Banks	10,117	9,406	10,479	11,944	14,339
Regional Rural Banks	977	1,083	1,381	1,684	2,175
Commercial Banks	5,400	8,255	10,172	12,783	14,808
Total	16,494	18,744	22,032	26,411	30976
Growth Rate (%)	9	14	18	20	17

* *Estimated*

Source : The Economic Survey 1998-99 P. 125.

The problem of overdues in agricultural credit continues to be an area of concern. However there has been some improvement in the recovery in 1997-98. Table -3

Table -2

Flow of Institutional Credit to Agriculture

(Rs. crore)

Year	*Short Term*		*Medium and Long Term*	
	Amount	*Percent*	*Amount*	*Percent*
1993-94	11,271	68.4	5,223	31.6
1994-95	7.938	42.3	10,806	57.7
1995-96	14,525	65.9	7,507	34.1
1996-97	16,998	64.4	9,413	35.6
1997-98*	19,875	64.2	11,101	35.8
1997-99$	23,577	62.0	14,477	38.0

* *Estimated* $ *Target*

Survey : The Economy Survey 1998-99 P. 126

Table-3

Recovery of Agricultural Advances

(Per cent)

Institutions	*1993-94*	*1994-95*	*1995-96*	*1996-97*	*1997-98*
Commercial Banks	56	58	60	62	63
Co-operative Banks					
SCARDBs *	57	62	61	61	60
PCARDBs**	59	67	61	61	56
State Co-operative Banks	89	90	90	86	81
District Central Co-operative Banks	64	73	69	69	66
Regional Rural Banks @	46	51	55	57	NA

@ RRBs recovery percentage pertains to the period ended June 1993 to June 1997.

* SCARDBs - State Co-operative Agriculture and Rural Development Banks.

** PCARDBS- Primary Co-operative Agriculture and Rural Development Banks.

Source : *The Economy Survey 1998-99 P. 126.*

Measure Taken for Recovery

The measures taken by the Government in resent year to improve credit flow to agricultural may be describe as follows :

Procedural simplification for credit delivery (following R.V. Gupta Committtee Report) through rationalisation of internal returns of banks.

Delegation of more powers to branch mangers.

Introduction of composite cash credit limit to farmers, introduction of new loan products with saving components, cash disbursement of loans, dispensation of no due certificate and discretion to banks on matters relating to margin security requirements for agricultural loans above Rs. 10,000.

Introduction of at least one specialised agricultural bank in each state to cater to the needs of high-tech agriculture.

Introduction of cash credit facility.

Issue of Kisan Credit Cards to farmers to draw cash for their production needs on the basis of the model scheme prepared by NABARD.

Hassle-free settlement of disputed cases of over dues.

Augmenting Rural Infrastructure Development Fund (RIDF) with a corpus of Rs. 10,000 crore with NABARD to finance rural infrsastructure development projects by States.

Investment in Agriculture

Public investment measured in terms of gross capital formation in agriculture which had been rising till 1970s , decelarated during the 1980s . Public investment in real terms at 1980-81 prices was Rs. 1796 crore in 1980-81 but declined to Rs.1154 crore in 1990-91 . After modest increase in 1994-95 to Rs. 1316 crore, public investment declined to Rs. 1132 crore in 1996-97 as depicted in Table -4 .

Table - 4

Gross Capital Formation in Agriculture

(Rs. crore)

Year	*Total*	*Public*	*Private*	*Per cent share*	
				Public	*Private*
		(At 1980-81)Prices			
1960-61	1668	589	1079	35.3	64.7
1970-71	2758	789	1969	28.6	71.4
1980-81	4636	1796	2840	38.7	61.3
1990-91	4594	1154	3440	25.1	74.9
1991-92	4729	1002	3727	21.1	78.8
1992-93	5372	1061	4311	19.7	80.3
1993-94	5031	1153	3878	22.9	77.1
1994-95	6256	1316	4940	21.0	79.0
1995-96	6961	1268	5693	18.2	81.8
1996-97	6999	1132	5867	16.2	83.8
		(At 1993-94) Prices			
1993-94	15845	4468	11377	28.2	71.8
1994-95	18214	4970	13244	27.3	72.7
1995-96	19944	4776	15168	23.9	76.1
1996-97	19902	4347	15555	21.8	78.2
1997-98	20995	4416	16579	21.0	79.0

Source : CSO , The base year has been changed to 1993-94 from this year.

Decelarating trends in public investment is a matter of concern. However , private investment in agricultureal has grown substantially in the nineties . Even after shifting of the base year to 1993-94 , the general trend of decline in public investment is clearly visible.

****

6

India's Industrial Policy

The 'Industrial Policy' is a policy covers all those procedures, principles, policies, rules and regulations used for control the industrial undertaking of a country and shape the pattern of industrialisation.Industrial Policy is a comprehensive concept which covers all those principles, rules and regulation which control and direct the pattern of industrial development of a country . It is the industrial policy by which industrial development and expansion of a country is guided and fostered. Through this policy Government of a country expresses its national priority and the ways and means to achieve those priorities. Industrial policy also indicate the respective rule of private, public, Joint and co-operative sector in the industrial development of the economy.

Industrial Policy refers to the principles or philosophy of industrial development of framework visualised by the Society and covers all those procedures, rules and regulations which control the industrial undertakings in a country and determine its industrial structure. It also incorporates the relevant aspects of fiscal and monetary policy, labour policy and Government's attitude towards the foreign assistance and iserception of the public and private sectors as well.

India's Sixth Five Year Plan (1980-85) document observed "Industrial policy cannot be static and will have to respond to changes in the economic scene. The framework of rules and regulations relevant to the nascent stage of development is not necessarily appropriate to the complex industrial structure which has since been builtup. Without sacrificing the basic principles of a planned economy, sufficient flexibility would need to be built up into a system to impart a sense of dynamism to take advantage of a considerable technological and managerial capabilities that have been developed over the years.

OBJECTIVES OF INDUSTRIAL POLICY

Industrialisation is one of the importans conditions to accelerate economic growth . But industrialisation is not a spontaneous process. It is the process which requires encouragement by the Government by adoption of appropriate promotion policies Nature of industrialisation and the Government's promotional attitude toward industrial development deffects in the industrial policy announcement of the nation. Some of the important objective of industrial policy stated below :

1. *Best Utilisation of National Resources* - Industrial policy assists in discovery, integration and full exploitation of natural resources. It is the prime responsibility of the industrial policy to see that country's natural resources are fully and properly utilised. Proper utilisation of natural resources proves helpful in increase in National Income.

2. *Increase in Industrial Production* - The success of industrial policy determined as how the policy succeeds in changing the rate of growth of industrial production without any undesirable effects. Industrial policy boosts to industrial development which ultimately augment to industrial production.

3. *Innovations and Modernisation* - A good industrial policy tends to promotes innovations and modernisation. It facilitate to use modern and latest techniques in the industrial sector. All these steps privious down the cost of production.

4. *Balanced Industrial Development* - Industrial policy open avenuesw for balanced development of industries and agriculture . It also assists in balanced development of rest of the sectors economy.

5. *Balanced Regional Development* - In order to prevent lopsided development industrial policy encourage balance regional development. To promote balanced regional development under industrial policy backward regions are equipped with paper infrastructure alongwith concessional facilities.

6. *Selecting Appropriate Industrial Strategy* - One of the important objective of industrial policy is to select appropriate industrial strategy for rapid industrial development. While selecting appropriate industrial strategy varieties of issue requard to be resolved e.g. , selection of large size or small size industries, urban or rural industries, heavy or light industries consumer or capital goods industries export promotion or import substitution industries etc. It also includes determination of the role private and public sector particularly in the mixed economy.

7. *Selection from choices.* - Government's policy presents a set of choice. A large number of choices have to be made in case decision making problem arises. These choices may be related to selection of a particular project, technique of production, specific industrial location, specific market location etc.

8. *Determining Intervention by State* - The industrial policy plays key role in determining extent of State intervention in the economy. What will be areas reserved for operation of public sector, which industries will operated by private sector and where will be the state enjoy complete monopoly are determined under the provisions of industrial policy. The industrial policy also clarify as to which industries may be taken by the state and under what conditions if required.

9. *Achievement of Self-reliance*- In order to achieve viable economic system efforts are made under industrial policy for self-reliance. While doing so efforts should be made in the direction of strengthening international economic relation, export promotion and bringing down the burder of external desirs.

10. *Provides Infrastructure for Growth* - Avaliability of proper infrastructure in a prime condition for industrial growth . An industrial policy provides basis infrastructure to accelerate economic development by faster industrialisation.

11. *Providing Gainful Employment* - An Industrial Policy also aims to increase employment opportunities , income and standard of living. By providing gainful or productive employment to all compitent Job-seekers the policy foster the pace of industrial development.

12. *Cordial Industrial Relation* - Cordial industrial relations are key to the success of industrial development . Industrial policy bring together capital and labour by avoiding conflicts. A comprehensive and appropriate industrial policy takes come all those aspecet which may foster cordial relations between employer and employees.

INDUSTRIAL POLICY OF INDIA

Before the advent of the Britishers India was rich in natural resources and her people were prosperous . Handicrafts and products of handlooms were popular throughout the world. Because of her prosperity, India was called 'Golden Sparrow'. India as traders along with Portuguese and French people. Brithisers formed East India company to trade with India. In fact they took advantage of the weaknesses of the Indian kings and ultimately became the rulers of the country. Industrial revolution had brought about sweeping changes in the British economy during the 17th century. The Britishers exploited the situation and made India an exporter of raw materials and importer of finished products from Britain.

As a result of industrial revolution in Europe, machine made goods became cheap and started pouring into India. The products which were cheaper . India was made an importer of finished goods and exporter of raw materials such as iron ore, coal, etc. This process ultimately led to the decay of India's traditional industries.

In spite of discriminating protection with a clause favouring British goods, some Indians ventured to establish cotton textile, sugar, paper, woolen textiles mills, and to some extent iron and steel industry and they made some progress. But one thing is quite obvious that during the British period no effort was made for the development of capital goods industries.

On the eve of independence the Britishers left our country in complete chose. Due to partition raw material producing areas of jute and cotton went to Pakistan. The transport system was paralysed.Many industrialists who earned lot of money during Second World War had locked out their mills resulting in retrenchment of labour. Indian industrialists and foreign entrepreneursa were shy to invest because of the fear of total nationalisation of industries . The Industrial relations were very disturbing . In this atmosphers, general need was felt that the government should frame a far reaching policy for better industrial relations and progress.

In 1948 the then Minister for Industries Dr. Shyam Prashad Mukherjee convened a tripartite conference of Indian labour, industrialists and the government and evolved a government policy for the growth of industries . This policy is known as the First Industrial Policy Resolution . Following were the essential features of the Industrial Policy Resolution (I.P.R,),1948 .

Industrial Policy 1948

The Industrial Policy Resolution (I.P.R.) 1948 contemplated the establishment of mixed economy where a sphere was reserved for the private sector and another was left for public sector to be owned and controlled by the government . The industries were divided into four categories wherein the cottage ad small scale industries were assigned a significant role to play in the national economy. The Industrial Policy Resolution also favoured the need for securing participation of foreign capital to speed up the pace of industrialisation. The Industrial Policy Resolution evolved a scheme of maintaining healthy industrial relations. The Industrial Policy Resolution also required the evolution of a tax system for encouraging more savings and investment.

The main features of Industrial Policy Resolution (I.P.R.) 1948 were:

(i)*Demarcation of Industries* - The industrial Policy Resolution (I.P.R.) divided industries into four groups:

(a) The Central Government will have exclusive monopoly in the industries manufacturing arms and ammunition, production of atomic energy and the railway transport.

(b) The State, will undertake the industries consisting of coal, iron and steel, aircraft, ship building etc.

(c) The Central government would plan and regulate industries of basic importance. It comprised industries of automobiles, heavy machine tools, heavy chemicals and fertilizers etc.

(d) The reminder of the industrial field was left open for private enterprise.

(ii) *Cottage and Small-Scale Industries*— These industries were assigned an important role in the national economy because they provide good scope for employment in rural and urban areas. They help in decentralisation and equal distribution of income and wealth.

(iii)*Industrial Relations*— It was felt that healthy industrial relations between the employers and employees maintain industrial peace and help the growth of industries. Tripartite machinery was evolved to solve industrial disputes. The Indian Labour Organisation was created. The Industrial

Policy Resolution (I.P.R.) also emphasised the need for fair wages, housing, bonus, etc.

(iv)*Foreign Capital*— The industrial Policy Resolution (I.P.R.) 1948 recognised the need of foreign capital for speeding up the pace of industrialisation. However it was laid down that the major interest in ownership and effective control should always be in the hands of the Indians.

(v)*Tax System*— A tax system encouraging savings for investment should be evolved.

Industrial Policy Resolution (I.P.R.) of 1956

The Industrial Policy of 1948 lasted till 1956. Between 1948 and 1956 three major developments of far reaching consequence took place. *One* was the enactment of our constitution, which guaranteed certain fundamental rights and also laid down certain directive principles for the state of follow. *Secondly* the country decided to become Democratic Socialistic Republic. *Thirdly* the government adopted the method of planning for economic progress of the country. The First Five Year Plan was successfully completed in 1956. The new circumstances necessitated a revision of the then existing industrial policy.

The 1956 Resolution laid down the following objectives for the industrial policy :

(i) to accelerate the rate of growth and to speed up industrialization;

(ii) to develop heavy industries and machine making industries;

(iii) to expand public sector,

(iv) to reduce disparities in income and wealth;

(v) to build up a large and growing co-operative sector, and

(vi)to prevent private monopolies and the concentration of wealth and income in the hands of a small number of individuals.

Salient Features of the Industrial Policy of 1956

Division of the industrial Sector : As against four categories in the 1948 Resolution, the 1956 Resolution divided industries into the following three categories:

(1) *Monopoly of the state*— In the first category, those industries were included whose future development would be the exclusive responsibility of the State. Seventeen Industries were included in this category and were listed in Schedule A (appended to the Resolution). These industries can be grouped into the following five classes:

(i) defence industries,

(ii) heavy industries,

(iii) minerals,

(iv) transport and communications, and

(v) power.

(2) *Mixed sector of public and private enterprise*— In this sector 12 industries listed in Schedule B (appended to the Resolution) were included. In these industries, State would increasingly establish new units and increase its participation but would not deny the private sector opportunities to set up new units or expand existing units.

(3) *Industries left for private sector*— All industries not listed in schedules 'A' or 'B' were included in the third category. These industries were left open to the private sector. Their development was to depend on the initiative and enterprise of the private sector, though even here the State could start any industry in which it was interested. However, the main role of the State in this category was to provide facilities to the private sector to develop itself.

(4) *Mutual dependence of public and private sectors*— The public and private sectors were not be exclusive and totally independent of one another. The government could establish units in any of the industries (included in any category) on the one hand and could also allow the private sector to operate in any field reserved for the public sector. The only four industries

in which private sector was not allowed to function were arms and ammunition, atomic energy, railway and air transport.

(5) *Assistance and control of private sector*— According to the 1956 Resolution, the government could assist expansion and development of private sector through participation in its risk capital and share capital and by providing other types of services, fiscal incentives, etc.

(6) *Importance of small-scale and cottage industries*— The 1956 Resolution recognised the importance of small-scale and cottage industries just as the 1948 Resolution had done. Such industries could create large scale employment opportunities, ensure a more equitable distribution of income and wealth, and help in effective mobilization of human and physical capital. Assistance to this sector was to be provided either through direct means or through indirect means.

(7) *Reduction of regional inequalities*— The 1956 Resolution called for reduction in regional imbalances and inequalities. For this purpose it was advocated that transport facilities, power and other facilities should be provided in the backward regions. Stress on balanced development of agriculture and industry in each region was also laid.

(8) *Technical and managerial personnel*— Shortage of technical and managerial personnel to carry out the programmes of industrial development in economy has been accepted and emphasized by the government right from the beginning of the planning era. Accordingly, the 1956 Resolution advocated the establishment of proper technical and managerial cadres through the organisation of apprenticeship schemes of training on a large scale, establishment of technical institutions, organisation of management course in universities, etc.

(9) *Industrial peace*— For industrial progress to take place in a congenial atmosphere, it is necessary that relations between the mill owners and the workers should be cordial and amicable. However in the capitalist system of production industrial relations are generally exploitative 'cordiality' is,

therefore, the first casualty. Accordingly, the 1956 Resolution reiterated that in a 'socialist society' the rights of the workers should be protected.

As compared to the 1948 Resolution, the 1956 Resolution considerably enlarged the area of the State was enlarged from 6 to 17 industries (Schedule A). In addition, another category including 12 industries (schedule B) was defined where the State could participation an increasing scale, however, the 1956 Resolution dropped the 'threat' of nationalization that the 1948 Resolution contained and the division of industries in different categories was more flexible in the former as compared to the latter. The fact is that the basic objective of both the Resolutions was the same-strengthening the mixed economy structure of the country.

Nehru was particularly enthusiastic about the role of such a policy in the volution of a 'socialist' society. Accordingly it was natural for him to emphasize the role of the public sector through the 1956 Resolution.

Critical Appraisal of the Industrial Policy of 1956

Although the 1956 industrial policy was more explicit and clear and carried a greater amount of flexibility as compared with the 1948 policy, it was not welcomed by all and sundry. Despite its emphasis on the creation of infrastructure for development, increased financial and other assistance, etc., it did not evoke a favourable response from the private sector. The private industrialists accepted the importance of public sector and the logical of the mixed economy, but were apprehensive about the 'relatively greater role' of the public sector only to the limit where it could help the private sector and not beyond.

A serious analysis of the criticism of 1956 Industrial Policy as put forward by private capitalists, exposes the weakness of this criticism. It is clear that this criticism was based on the individual selfish interests of the capitalists and did not take into account the needs of the time. It is impossible to think of industrial development in under-developed countries without a strong and vibrant public sector. In pre-independent India, the participation of the state in industrial development was minimal. However, it is only natural that such development in the post-independence period should have seen the progress of both the sectors public as well as private - together. In fact, the expansion of the public sector created an environment for the private sector to expand the area of its activities.

However, the implementation part of the Industrial Policy Resolution, 1956 was wrought with deficits. Because of the loopholes and exceptions in the legislation, the basic concept of socialism and the underlying goals were glossed over. Licences were issued to private sector units in areas exclusively reserved for the State sector or where future expansion was intended to be in the public sector. These include coal, oil, fertilisers, chemicals, engineering etc. As noted by Rangnekar, "proposal for setting up State owned steel mills were held back for years (in the earlier phase) in preference to the expansion of the private units. Schemes for setting up public sector units in new fields were watered down under pressure for private sector participation, association or continuance". For several years after its adoption, the Resolution was not even fully implemented, planning and industrial administration tended to be too slow reflecting the reluctance of the implementing authorities to carry out the Resolution in true spirit and ideals.

INDUSTRIAL POLICY -1980

On July 23,1980 , the new Industrial Policy Statement was announced by the Government . It reiterated the basic Industrial Policy Resolution of 1956.The following are some of the important policy decisions.

1. *Revamping of Public Sector Undertakings* - The public sector undertakings were set up with the objective that it would serve as a 'people's sectors'. Of late, , the people have lost their faith in the public sector undertakings. Unless efforts are taken to restore this faith, the public sector would be quoted only as "Nobody's Sector'.

For the purpose of improving the performance of public sector undertakings, a " unit by unit examination" of the undertakings is necessary. Such an exercise should be organised on a timebound basis, depending upon the nature and size of the undertaking.

2.*Inter-dependence of Small and Large Scale Industries*- Efforts would be taken to set up few nucleaus plants in districts which have been identified as industrially backward. These nucleus plants would pave the way for the generation and growth of as many ancillaries as and small and cottage industries, as possible. As a result the large as well as small scale industries will grow simultaneously and would ultimately lead to the formation of economic federalism.

3.*Re-definition of Small Scale Industries* - The investment limit which was earlier fixed at Rs. 10 lakhs for a small scale unit has now been raised to Rs. 20 lakhs. Similarly, the investment fixed at Rs. 15 lakhs for the ancillary units has now been raised to Rs. 25 lakhs. In addition , flow of finance, in a systematic way, into small units will be ensured.

4.*Legitmisation of Additional Production Capacities*- As a result of replacement or modernisation , the excess capacities created by the undertakings over and above the licensed capacity will be legitimised.

5.*Automatic Expansion* - In order to have full utilisation of installed capacity a measure of automatic expansion will be permitted to a large number of industries with a limit of 5% per annum, i.e. 25% over a period of five years.

6.*Export- Oriented Units* - Requests for setting up of 100% export units will be sympathetically and favourably considered.

7.*Research and Development* - Industrial will be persuaded to constantly update the technology and pass on the benefits to small and medium scale units.

8.*Induction of Advanced Technology for Economies of Scale* - If the industries are capable of producing more at international competitive levels, then in such cases, the Government would encourage induction of advanced technology and also permit creation of additional capacity.

9.*Packaging* - Small scale industries will be encourated to produce modern packing materials.

10.*Co-ordinated Industry - Energy Policy* - A co-ordinated policy for industry and energy will be evolved for the purpose of maintaining simultaneous growth in both the industries.

11. *Streamlining of Licencing Procedures* - The existing licensing procedures will be simplified and streamlined.

12.*Identification of Symptoms of Sickness* - Efforts will be taken to introduce effective checks to identify symptoms of sickness at an early stage.

13.*Maintaining of cordial Industrial Relations* - Cordial employer employee relations will be maintained by reviving labour conferences.

14.*Industrial Pricing* - For the purpose of evolving a price policy , necessary efforts will be taken in consultation with industry.

New Industrial Policy: 1991

In the root of the industrial policy, 1991 was the liberalisation policy of the Government. The government had adopted the liberalisation policy in 1991 to remove the existing economic crisis. The objectives of this liberalisation policy were: increase industrial production, to improve disequalibrium in balance of payments, to get rid of the sick units of public or private sectors and to control inflation by increasing production and regulating money supply. To enforce the devices of liberalisation the Government of India announced a new industrial policy in 1991.

The new Industrial Policy aims at:

(1) To maintain the gains from industries already made.

(2) To improve deficiencies or imbalances which emerged in the economy from previous policies.

(3) To maintain international competitiveness, that is, the formation of internal competitive market.

(4) Continuity in the increase in production.

(5) More opportunities of employment

(6) Efficiency operation of the public sector enterprises.

(7) More freedom to the private sector.

The objectives are similar to those specified in earlier Industrial policy resolutions, of course, but the difference lies in the strategy to achieve these objectives. The strategy now shifts from controls to liberalisation and from nationalisation to privatisation.

Features or Strategy of New Industrial Policy

With a view to bring revolutionary charges in the industrial scene of the country, Central Government announced the New Industrial Policy on July 24,1991. Following are unique feature of the policy.

(1) *Contraction of Public Sector*— The public sector has been given indirect role in industrial development. According to the new Industrial Policy the number of industries reserved for the public sector has been reduced from 17 to 6, the remaining industries have been opened for the private sector. The six industries reserved for the public sector are as follows:–

(1) Defence (2) Atomic Energy (3) Coal and lignite (4) Mineral Oil (5) Control of consumption and production of atomic energy (6) Railway Transport.

(2) *Privatisation of Public Sector*— The public enterprises incurring losses will either be closed or handed over to the private sector. About 20% shares of the public sector undertakings will be sold to the mutual funds and the employees. Much autonomy will be given to public sector management so that they can operate on commercial lines.

(3) *Industrial Licensing*— The government reformulated its industry policy. The industrial licensing has been abolished, except for 15 industries like petroleum, sugar, motor car, paper, medicines etc. These 15 industries will be given opportunities to make them competitive and modern in national and international spheres.

(4) *Abolition of Registration*— All existing registration schemes are sought to be abolished. In respect of new projects for manufacture of articles not covered by compulsory licensing or their substantial expansion the only requirement would be that the industrial undertaking shall file a memorandum in the prescribed form to the secretariat for industrial approvals (SIA) in the Minister of Industry.

(5) *Foreign Capital*— The new policy welcomes foreign investment with its attendant advantage of technology transfer, marketing expertise introduction of modern managerial techniques in the country and export promotion. Capital investment limit has been raised from 40 percent to 51 percent in equity. In this policy direct investment has been accepted for high priority industries. In 34 high priority industries foreign equity up to 51 percent will be permitted without any bottleneck and red-tapism.

(6) *Foreign Technology*— There is great need for promoting an industrial environment where acquisition of technological capacity receives priority with a view to injecting the desired level of dynamism in Indian industry, it has been decided to provide automatic approval for technology agreement related to high priority industries within specified parameters. For identified high priority industries, automatic permission has been given to the agreement of foreign technology use. It means these industries the use of foreign technology has been accepted with foreign investment.

(7) *Facilities to Labourers*— In order to rehabilitate retrenched employees and workers, the policy provides for social security mechanism. With a view to providing social security to the workers, *National Renewal Fund* is proposed to be set up. This fund will provide relief to the workers affected by technological changes.

(8) *Concessions from MRTP Act*— The new policy has given concession to companies under MRTP Act. This has been amended remove the limits of assets in respect of MRTP companies and dominant undertakings. In this way more freedom will be given to the big industries. There will be no restriction on big companies and industrial houses with regard to expansion or existing, or setting up of new industries, taking over of or merging into companies. But active control and check will be kept on these industries to safeguard the interest of the consumers.

(9)*Small Scale Industries*— The them of the Industrial Policy emphasises on continuity with change. While freedom has been given to major industries to grow, reservation of items for small scale will continue so as to promote industrial and agro industrial employment basis.

Critical Appraisal of the Policy

The Industrial Policy initiatives undertaken by Government since July 1991 have been designed to build on the past industrial achievements and to accelerate the process of making Indian industry internationally competitive. It recognises the strength and maturity of the industry and attempts to provide the competitive stimulus for higher growth.

Arguments in favour

1.*Deregulation of Industries* .- This policy has given freedom to industries from government and statutory controls. The policy deregulates the industrial economy in a substantial manner. It will reduce delays in project implementation.

2.*Industrial Competition*-The simplified and liberalised industrial at policy has encouraged for healthy competition among domestic industrial units. It will be achieved through increased uses of technology .Increased competition will lead to enhanced pressure on enterprise to reduce their cost and to improve quality.

3.*Correcting Distortions* - The new policy measures aim at correcting the distortions and weaknesses that had crept the regulatory and protective Indian economy. The policy aims at minimising of corruption and red-tapism by removing of unnecessary licensing and controlling, methods. Many of the evils relating to licensing could be minimised. The simplified and liberalised industrial at policy has encouraged for healthy competition among domestic industrial units. It will achieved through increased uses of technology. In short, new industrial policy is a very liberal policy. It aims at providing freedom to large-scale industries with greater areas of operation in an environment of competition rather than 'controls'.

4.*Sustain Growth in Productivity* -The liberalised industrial policy will maintain sustained growth in productivity and gainful employment. It will encourage growth of entrepreneurship and upgrade technology in order to compete in the world market.

5.*Reform Public Sector* -The disinvestment of a part of the equities of some selected public sector undertaking will help to raise non-inflationary finance for development. The policy of disinvestment will also bring in greater public accountability and improve the efficiency of these enterprises.The policy will also be helpful in improving the functioning rehabilitation of sick units. This policy has initiated the process of privatisation of public sector. In this regard beginning has been made in Air India,ONGCetc.

6.*Liberalisation of Foreign Investment-* The policy has encouraged the inflow of foreign capital in Indian industries through investment agreement with foreign firms. The policy of liberalisation of foreign investment will help facilitate the inflow of direct foreign investment. In this form non-debt creating inflows will reduce reliance on fixed-interest debt and also bring in new technology, marketing expertise and modern managerial practices.

7.*Attration For Non-Resident Indians -* There have been serveral liberalisation measure announced by the Government in this policy for investment by non-resident Indians. Non-resident Indians will be able to make more capital investment in India so as also to set-up industrial units in India.

8.*Encourageement to Tiny and Small Industries.-* The policy relating to tiny and small industries will impact more vitality and encourage the growth of employment and exports.

9.*Availability of Adequate Foreign Exchange -* Indis is facing acute crisis of foreign exchange . Since in this policy encouragement has been given to development of foreign trade. more foreign exchange could be possible for the country to earned.

10.*Multi -dimensional Effects.-* The liberalised foreign investment policy as well as exemption of corporate sector from licensing and quotas will bear favourable effect on the industrial and commercial function and also will also help in bringing revolutionary changes in cultural and social fields.

11.*Increase in Production -* The policy has been streanlined with a view to increase in production by according specific attention to the working and economic freedom of the country. Under this policy every industry will also enjoy freedom to diversify their activities and will able to increase in production capacity within the prescribed limits.

12. *Safeguarding worker's interest's* - This policy also committed in providing added improtance to the workers for safeguarding their interests in the industrial set-up.

13.*Withdrawal of monopoly restriction* - In this policy provisions have been made for withdrawal of restrictions from monopoly companies. According , all types of companies will now get equal opportunity for development.

14.*Other Favourable Aspects* - There will be fall in price of commodities due to liberalisation in licencing procedure and full use industrial capacity. Researched and developmental activities will also be encouraged which will open avenues for development of new industries.

Points Against the Policy

1.The abolish of licence will encourage rush of entrepreneurship in certain industries. The policy related to free entry and free exit might result into fierce competition in some industries, especially in some consumer goods industries.

2.If a substantial part of Indian market will be under the control of foreign collaborating companies. Indian government will not be in a position to exercise control over them.

3.The raising of financial limit of small-scale industrial units to Rs. 60 lakh would encourage richer section of the society to enter this field or large industrial house would enter this field in the name of their relatives or friends etc.

4.Participation of foreign equity capital in any Indian establishment (except some strategically important industries) may also create a humbler of problems. Foreign companies in the craving of maximum profit would enter into only those industries which cater to consumer needs of elite classes. This tendency would divert country's resources into production of goods for richer section of the Indian community. The dire requirements of our country is to develop heavy and basic industries by injecting huge investment and modern technology.

****

7

Industrial Development

On the eve of planning era the Indian industrial structure had a narrow base and a lop-sided size pattern, while, the composition of manufacturing output reflected the preponderance of consumer goods industries vis-a-vis capital goods industries. The drive to broadbase and diversify this structure, a drive linked to the search for self-reliance, has been the keynote of the industrial strategy of our plans.

With a pronounced emphasis of government policy on diversification of industrial sector through a focus on investment in intermediate, capital and basic goods industries their share in the total value added by the factory sector increased over the years. More rapid growth of the non-consumer sectors of industries than of consumer goods is an important feature of India's industrialisation strategy.

Development Strategy

Strategy implies essentially a deliberate choice - a choice of the point and the manner of attack on the problem at hand. The First Plan, really speaking, was no plan but was a list of a few projects which were already in operation or were about to be taken in hand. Though development of agriculture and transportation and communications were given a high priority there was no strategy as such. Prof. Mahalanobis, the real architect of the Second Plan; enunciated a definite strategy based on the experience of the Soviet Union which skipped the earlier stages and started their plans directly with the development of heavy industries. This strategy emphasized investment in heavy industries to achieve rapid industrialisation, which in turn, was a *sine qua non* for rapid economic development, Second Five Year Plan Framework put it in clear terms, "In the long run, the rate of industrialisation and the growth of the national economy would depend upon the increasing production of coal, electricity. Iron and heavy industries generally–which would increase the capacity for capital formation. One important aim is to make India independent, as quickly as possible, of foreign imports of producer goods so that the accumulation of capital would not be hampered by difficulties in securing supplies of essential producer goods from other countries. The heavy industry must, therefore, be expanded with all possible speed". The thrust of the strategy adopted for the Second Plan, and with minor modifications for the subsequent Plans; is on rapid industrialisation through heavy investment in heavy, basic and machine-building industries.

The main thrust of the investment strategy has been to achieve self-sustained growth by diverting increasing proportion of investment into the establishment of basic and capital goods industries.

Export Promotion— After the foreign exchange crisis of 1956-57, the planners realised that the creation of export surplus and export promotion should go side by side with rapid industrialisation. The Third Plan noted the weakness in the earlier period when it observed in clear terms "One of the main drawbacks in the past has been that the programme for exports has not been regarded as an integral part of the country's development effort". Export promotion has always been an important aspect of the successive five-year plans. The Fifth Plan even went for a near zero rate of foreign aid. Along with export promotion, import-subsituation has been emphasized all along.

Supply of consumer goods— It was duty recognised that the growth of heavy industries would be limited by the growth of consumer goods in the household sector. For, the Second Plan framework categorically stated: "The greater the marketable surplus of consumer goods in the household or hand industries, the greater will be the possibilities of investments in heavy industries without any fear of inflation'. In the Mahalanobis model, there was active encouragement for cottage industries producing consumer goods. In spite of the favourable factors for increasing the supply of consumer goods in the cottage and small-scale industries (*i.e.* low input-output ratio and the shorter gestation period) Mahalanobis did anticipate shortages in supply of consumer goods and the consequent high prices and costs obstructing the planning process. As such, he provided for fiscal controls.

Role of public sector— As investment in the heavy industries was very high and as the gestation period was also long while the profitability would below, the planner felt that heavy industries should be, by and large, in the public sector. Further, the control of the public sector would enable the government to exercise the control over the commanding heights in the economy. In the interest of evolving a socialist economy, the public sector would help in the redistribution of income and the prevention of concentration of wealth and monopoly power which are inherent in the private sector.

Balanced growth— The Second Plan, though it assigned top priority to the capital goods sector stated: "The Central objective of public policy and national endeavour in India has been the promotion of rapid and balanced economic development". It also observed, 'Continuous growth of national income and employment requires simultaneous development all over the economy".

Industrial Growth Under the Plans

Industrial and the First Five Year Plan (1951-56)— The First Plan was a transitional plan meant to rehabilitate the Indian economy hit hard by the war and the Partition. No big effort was contemplated to industrialise the economy. Rather it put emphasis on the creation of the necessary economic overheads like power and transport for industrialisation in the subsequent plans. Accordingly, industrial and mineral development was primarily left to the private sector, the State's share being 6 per cent in the total outlay of the Plan. The total expenditure on industrial development by the State was Rs. 117 crores as against Rs. 370 crores by the private sectors.

Industrial production increased by 38 per cent during the Plan period. Progress in various industries was not uniform. Production of consumer goods increased by 34 per cent, of capital goods by 70 per cent and of industrial raw materials by 34 per cent. The increase in cotton textiles and iron and steel output was 28 per cent and 22 per cent respectively. The production of paper-board, bicycles and sewing machines matched the Plan targets.

The First Plan saw the establishment of the Sindri Fertilizer Factor, Chittranjan Locomotive Factory, Indian Telephone Industries, the Integral Coach Factory, the Cable Factory and the Penicillin Factory, Newsprint Factory. In the case of steel, aluminum, fertilizers, etc., the targets set under the Plan were not reached. Despite a modest Plan investment, the overall industrial production registered a comfortable increase and created a wide industrial base.

Industries and the Second Five Year Plan (1956-61)— The Second Five Year Plan programme for industrialisation was based on the IPR of 1956 which envisaged a big expansion of the public sector in the sphere of minerals and basic and heavy industries development. Accordingly, top priority was accorded to the development of heavy machine building, heavy electricals, steel, machine tools, and non-ferrous metals. Employment potential of heavy industries being limited over the short-run, attention was focused on the development of cottage and small-scale industries. The actual investment in the public sector on organised industry was Rs. 870 crores. Private sector investment was Rs. 675 crores during the Plan periods -more than envisaged in the Plan. investment in village and small industries was Rs. 265 crore. Taken together, total investment in industries was Rs. 1,810 crores, *i.e.,* 27 per cent of the total investment during the Second Plan.

The index of industrial production rose from 72.7 at the end of the First Plan (base 1960) to 100 in 1960. There was significant advance in certain spheres, the production of iron ore and aluminum rose by 150 per cent, of steel ingots by 100 per cent and of machine tools by 50 per cent.

During the Second Plan one of the major steps towards building a solid capital base was the establishment of three steel plants in the public sector with an initial capacity of 10 lakh tonnes at Rourkela, Bhilai and Durgapur. In the private sector, the production capacity of TISCO, IISCO and MISW was raised by 7 lakh tonnes, 5 lakh tonnes and 75000 tonnes respectively. The other programmes of industrial development included the manufacture of electrical equipment, expansion of Hindusthan Machine Tools, expansion of Sindri Fertiliser Factory and the establishment of a fertilizer plant at Nangal, further expansion of Hindusthan Ship-yard and Chittaranjan Locomotive Factory. Quite a number of new industrial items, *e.g.,* industrial boilers, milling machines, tractors, motor cycles, scooters etc., were also produced in large quantity. Rapid progress was made in the production of consumer durables like fans, radios, electric goods, etc.

The Second Plan witnessed a major diversification of the industrial spectrum, as also, the rise of a class of small entrepreneurs. It strengthened further the programmes of development in respect of oil exploration and coal and made a beginning in the field of atomic energy. however, the Plan failed to achieve physical targets of steel, fertilizers, newsprint, dyestuffs, soda ash, cement, chemicals, pig iron and cotton textiles. This was due to the foreign exchange crisis which emerged in 1957, as also, the non-availability of machinery, equipment and technical know-how from foreign countries in time.

Despite shortfalls in various sectors, the Second Plan heralded a veritable industrial revolution by laying the solid foundation of a strong industrial base.

Industrial progress in the Third Plan (1961-65)— The Third Plan was the first step towards the long-term industries development effort of the economy over the next 15 years. The major objective towards this end was "to expand basic industries like steel, chemicals, fuel and power and establish machine building capacity, so that the requirements of further industrialisation can be met within a period of ten years or so mainly from the country's own resources". The industrial sector was regarded as a crucial sector for securing rapid economic advance. With the base created in the first two Plans, the Third Plan called for the maximum rate of investment *(i)* to strengthen industry, power and transport sector and *(ii)* to hasten the process of industrial and technological change. The role of cottage and small industries was conceived as one of providing larger employment opportunities and of increasing the supply of consumer goods. The key role in industrial development programme was assigned for the public sector. An overall target of 70 per cent increase in industrial production was envisaged in the Plan. In keeping with these objectives, Rs. 1723.6 crores were spent on organised industry and minerals in the public sector and Rs. 1050 crores in private sector, while Rs. 236 crores and Rs. 275 crores were spent by public and private sectors respectively on the development of village and small industries.

Industrial progress during the Third Plan was uneven. During the first four years, industrial production increased by 8 to 9.6 per cent and by 4.3 per cent in the last year, giving an annual average of 7.9 per cent against the estimated 11 per cent. This shortfall was due to : *(a)* shortage in the infrastructural field of transport and power; *(b)* scarcity of imported raw materials, spares and components; *(c)* the impact of war with China; *(d)* dislocation caused by Indo-Pak conflict and the resultant disruption in the flow of external assistance; *(e)* the unprecedented droughts causing the shortage of raw materials; and *(f)* inflationary pressures within, the economy. As a consequence, shortfalls in various items ranged between 30 and 60 per cent or more, and physical targets were not achieved in the majority of industries. Compared with the general index of industrial production, output in industries like basic metals, fertilisers, heavy chemicals, machinery and generation of power grew at a relatively faster rate, whereas, consumers' goods industries which formed a substantial portion of the total output-more specifically cotton textiles–increased at a very slow rate.

Table 1
Index of Industrial production
(Base 1960)

Item	*1961*	*1966*
Food Manufacturing	101.6	129.3
Textiles	103.8	109.3
Chemicals & Chemical Product	115.9	177.4
Basic Metals	118.7	166.5
Electric Machinery	114.5	233.5
Machinery (other than item 5)	126.9	307.4
Transport Equipment	120.5	163.4
General Index	110.0	15.19

Table 1 indicates that thought the general index of industrial production increased from 110.6 to 151.9, yet, with the exception of textiles and food manufactures, the increase in the index of new items was much higher. Notable progress was recorded in the spheres of import-substitution, diversification and setting up of new industries. Despite the shortfalls, the Third Plan period attainments reflected the first stage of a decade or more of intensive development paving the way for self-reliant and self-propelling economy.

Industries and the Annual Plans (1966-67 to 1968-69)— To meet the twin requirements of defence and development, it was considered imperative to reframe the Fourth plan which was to be launched in April, 1966. To avoid delay the Annual Plan for 1966-67 was prepared. The process continued for three years. The emphasis was placed on the fuller utilisation of the existing capacity and to fill in the gaps created by the Third Plan. For this, the emphasis was on higher public and private investment. Accordingly, the expenditure on industry and minerals was of the order of Rs. 1575 crores and private investment Rs. 580 crores. Public and private expenditure on village and small industries was Rs. 144 crores and Rs. 250 crores respectively.

There was sharp deceleration in industrial production during 1966,1967 and 1968 due to an increase in unutilised capacity in a number of industries. Industrial output fell by 0.2 per cent in 1967 and by 0.5 per cent in 1968. This was due to drought in 1966-67 and the consequent short supply of agricultural raw materials and the slackness of demand for a number of capital goods and consumer goods industries. Some of the contributory causes of industrial recession were : *(i)* gheraoes; strikes and lockouts, *(ii)* inadequate foreign exchange allotments for importing equipment and industrial raw materials, and *(iii)* disturbed political situation after the fourth general elections.

Industries and the Fourth Plan (1969-74)— The Fourth Plan set before itself two principal objectives, *viz.*, 'growth with stability' and 'progressive achievement of self-reliance'. The Plan observed, "the total overall rate of industrial development has necessarily to be related to the development in the rest of the economy which can be sustained within given limits of technological capacity and of resources, physical and financial; and its pattern must be shaped in relation to the specific situation obtaining in the country". The fourth plan, therefore, laid down the following objectives of industrial development :

(i) completing investments in relation to which commitments had already been made;

(ii) increasing existing capacities to levels required for present or future developments, in particular for export promotion or import substitution;

(iii) taking advantages of internal development or availabilities to build new industries or new bases for industries; and

(iv) increasing industrial production at an average annual rate of 8 to 10 per cent. The policy of investment was directed in such a manner as to lead to industrialisation on a large scale and to encourage the emergence of new entrepreneurship and greater decentralisation in the ownership and control of industries.

A total investment of Rs. 5300 crores was envisaged (23.4 per cent of total plan investment). Out of this Rs. 3,050 crores were to be invested in the public sector and the balance of Rs. 2,250 crores in the private sector. however, the actual outlay on organised industry was of the order of Rs. 2,700 crores in the public sector. Thus the actual investment was short of the targets set in the Fourth Plan. Nearly three-fourths of the total investment was in the core sector, *viz.*, iron and steel, non-ferrous metals, fertilizers, petroleum and petro-chemicals, coal and iron ore.

The achieved rate of growth of industrial production was only 3.9 per cent per annum as against the targetted growth rate of 8 per cent. There was shortfalls in the production of almost all the industrial products as evident from Table 2

Table 2

Fourth Plan — Targets and Achievements

Industry	Unit	Base (1968-69)	Target (1973-74)	Achievement (1973-74)
Steel Ingots	million Tonnes	6.5	10.8	5.8
Finished Steel	-do-	4.7	8.1	4.5
Cement	-do-	12.2	18.0	14.7
Iron Ore	-do-	28.1	5.14	35.7
Coal	-do-	71.4	93.5	81.9
Sugar	-do-	3.5	4.7	3.9
Aluminum	000 tonnes	125.3	220.0	147.9
Cotton Cloth	m. meters	4297.0	5100.0	4083.0

Source: Fourth Five Year Plan, and *Economic Survey*, 1975-76.

There were two types of factors that held back industrial progress during the Fourth Plan period. firstly, those inhibiting utilisation of capacity; and secondly, those inhibiting the creation of new capacity. The first category of factors holding back industrial production were :

(i) insufficient demand for such industries as coal, machine tools, textile and other categories of industrial machinery;

(ii) shortage and irregular supplies of raw materials, components and spares;

(iii) shortage of erratic supplies of power in northern India;

(iv) operational problems in the case of fertiliser, heavy engineering and steel;

(v) transport bottlenecks;

(vi) disturbed industrial relations and management problems in the sick mills, steel and other industries;

(vii) faulty industrial licensing policy that led to the creation of excess capacity in a number of industries and inadequate capacity in some others.

The second category of factors (inhibiting the creation of new capacity) were:

(i) delay in the construction phase of the public sector projects;

(ii) delay in administrative sanctions;

(iii) lack of integrated planning and deficiencies in design etc.;

(iv) delays in getting domestic and foreign plant and equipment.

These factors were responsible for the deceleration in the growth rate of industrial production from 7.4 per cent in 1969-70 to 3.0 per cent in 1970-71, 3.3 per cent in 1971-72, 5.3 per cent in 1970-71, 3.3 per cent in 1971-73, 5.3 per cent in 1973-73 and 0.5 per cent in 1973-74.

Fifth Five Year Plan— Industrial development programmes in the Fifth Plan proposed to lay emphasis on the following:

(i) Rapid growth of core sector industries by giving high priority to steel, non-ferrous metals, fertilizers, mineral oils, coal and machine building.

(ii) Development of industries which promise a rapid diversification and growth of exports.

(iii) Enlarging the production in industries supplying mass consumption goods, *viz.*, cloth, edible oils and vanaspati, sugar, drugs, etc.

(iv) Restraint on the production of inessential goods, except for exports.

(v) Development of small industries by reserving 124 items exclusively for them and by initiating an intensive programme for the development of ancillary industries as feeder industries to large-scale units.

In *The Fifth Plan* the outlay was Rs. 9,582 crores for the development of industries and minerals. This was 24.3 per cent of the total Plan outlay. The growth rate of output f the manufacturing sector was estimated at 6.9 per cent annum.

The industrial development programmes during the Fifth Plan had been formulated keeping in view the twin objectives of self-reliance and growth with social justice. The strategy laid down in the Plan was as follows:

(a) Emphasis had been laid on the rapid growth of the core sector industries such as steel, non-ferrous metals, fertilisers, coal, mineral oils, and machine buildings. The development of these industries was vital for the long-run sustained growth. They also helped to save foreign exchange.

(b) There was to be greater effort to create surplus capacity in manufactured goods for exports, and towards their rapid diversification.

(c) Greater attention was to be paid towards the substantial expansion of production of essential commodities of mass consumption like cloth, edible oils, vanaspati, sugar, drugs and consumer durable goods like bicycles, fans, etc. The production programmes were supported by appropriate distribution arrangements.

(d) There was to be restraint on the production of non-essential goods except for exports. But scarce resources were to be diverted to the production of such goods.

Besides, "the other socio-economic objectives of diffusion of ownership, maximisation of employment, dispersed growth of industries and upgradation of scientific and technological capabilities were sought to be achieved through encouragement of village and small-scale industries, development of industrial backward areas and application of science and technology.

These objectives of industrial growth were sought to be achieved by means of :

(i) the maximisation of output from existing capacity;

(ii) speedy completion of projects already taken up for implementation;

(iii) technological improvements and expansion of existing units where substantial additional production could be achieved expeditiously;

(iv) the creation of new capacity in accordance with the priorities in the Plan; and

(v) the initiation of advance action on long-gestation projects".

During the Fifth Plan, the growth rate of industrial production was 6.2 per cent as against the target of 6.9 per cent. "Major factors responsible for a general setback in industrial production during 1977-78 were power shortage, industrial unrest and demand constraints affecting certain industries.... The year 1977-78 was among the worst attected in regard to industrial unrest as over two million mandays were lost every month. These factors affected capacity utilisation in a large number of industries'.

The Sixth Plan spent 16 per cent of the total outlay on the development of industry and minerals. The Plan envisaged an annual growth rate of 8 per cent in industrial production. To achieve it, a significant improvement in the functioning of the infrastructure particularly coal, power and railways was emphasised. The Plan gave high priority to the creation of adequate capacity in basic industries such as steel, non-ferrous metals, capital goods, fertilisers and petro-chemicals. The public sector had been assigned a major role in the expansion of these industries. Besides, the private, joint and co-operative sectors were expected to contribute significantly in the production of fertilisers, cement, paper, textiles, chemicals, pesticides, drugs and pharmaceuticals.

In keeping with the Industrial Policy Resolution of July 1984, emphasis was laid on the induction of advanced technology, introduction of processes which would aim at optimum utilisation of energy as also for the establishment of appropriate capacities to achieve economies of scale. Special efforts were made to establish export-oriented units. To protect employment and to provide more employment opportunities, encouragement was given to the growth of cottage, village and small industries. Consistent with the emphasis on technological self-reliance, adequate stress was laid on keeping the technology in use uptodate. For this purpose, the import of technology was liberalised.

The Sixth Plan achieved a growth rate of 6.4 per cent per annum in industrial production and the Seventh Plan 8.5 per cent per annum.

Seventh Plan (1985-90)- The objectives of the industrial development programmes and policies during the seventh plan has been -

(i) to ensure adequate supply of wage goods and consumer articles of mass consumption at reasonable prices and of acceptable quality;

(ii) to maximise the utilisation of the existing facilities through restructuring improved productivity and upgradation of technology;

(iii) to concentrate on development of industries with high growth potential and relevant to our needs; and

(iv) to usher in "sunrise" industries with high growth potential and relevant to our needs; and

(v) to evolve an integrated policy towards self reliance in strategic field and opening up of avenues for employment of skilled and trained man power.

The plan aimed at an overall annual average rate of over 8 per cent in the industry sector, certain selected , segment of it having been projected to grow at much higher rates.

The growth rate in the industrial sector would be supported by (a) improving performance and efficiency of the core sector namely, power, railways, steel and coal, and (b) enlarging purchasing power through overall economic growth and the specific poverty alleviation and employment generation programmes.

The overall outlay envisaged in the Seventh Plan for industrial and mineral programmes in the public sector is Rs. 19,708 crores, out of which Rs. 17,268 crores are in the central sector, and the balance of Rs. 2,440 crores is in the Plans of states and Union territories. The actual expenditure is estimated at Rs. 23,175 crores in the Central Sector and Rs. 3,120 crores by States and Union Territories.

Strategy of the Seventh Plan - As a part of its strategy to achieve the target, the plan emphasises on :

(i) *Restructuring of industry* - To recognise the importance and growth of non-traditional industries. The investment pattern and policy frame work should facilitate such structural changes. The main objective of the restructuring process would be to usher in a pattern of industrial development which would take India into the ranks of leading industrial countries of the world;

(ii) *Efficient* use of capital to generate surplus for further investments;

(iii) *Improving infrastructure facilities* - The resource allocation strategy for the public sector has been built on this premise. A coordinated approach to the functioning of the different sub-sector of infrastructure is expected to lead to efficient use of the existing capacities, and yield higher productivity;

(iv) *Modernisation* and up-gradation of technology;

(v) *Increasing the productivity* - Specific productivity targets for major industries like steel, fertilizers, non-ferrous metals, petrochemicals, paper and cement planned to set for the plan;

(vi) *Export as an integratl part of production in the domestic economy* - A special effort is proposed to be made in selected industries in which the country has comparative advantage and has already reached a degree of industrial maturity. This is with a view to maximise foreign exchange earnings.

Performance - *During the 7th five year plan , the overall performance of industrial sector has been quite satisfactory attaining an average growth of 8.5 per cent per annum as against the target of 8.7 per cent.* Year wise achievements were 8.7 per cent in 1985-86, 9.1 per cent in 1986-87 , 7.3 per cent in 1987-88 , 8.8 per cent in 1988-89, and 8.4 per cent in 1989-90 . Considering the several handicaps like severe droughts in 1987-88 and the consequent decline in demand for consumer goods as well as inadequate availability of foreign exchange for import of key inputs, growth rate during the seventh plan has been a matter of satisfaction expecially when compared to the growth in the earlier plan periods. The liberalisation of industrial policy and procedures initiated in the 6th plan continued in the 7th plan. It has succeeded in creating proper environment for sustained industrial growth by providing the industry the degree of flexibility essential for smooth adjustment of changing demand and supply.

As regards broad sectoral performance during the 7th plan, the growth in mining and quarrying sector has been 5.7 per cent, in electricity generation, it has been 9.4 per cent and in manufacturing, it has been 10.5 per cenbt. The respective targets of the plan in these sectors were 13 per cent, 12 per cent and 8 per cent.

Eighth Plan (1992-97) - The average annual growth rate of the industrial sector including mining, manufacturing and electricity generation during the 7th plan period was 8.5 per cent, which was much higher than the achieved growth rate during the sixth plan. The projected growth rate druing the VIIIth plan period in industry and minerals is stated to be 8.2 per cent. The outlay on industry and minerals happens to be Rs. 46921.75 crores, which is 10.81 per cent of the total public sector outlay.

The private sector of industries during the plan period is expected to play an increasing role in industrial activities. The public sector will concentrate increasingly on basic and core sectors. The emphasis would be more on competitiveness of industries and efficiency of operations.

The qualitative performance in the capital goods industries is emphasised. This is in view of the fact that the sector decides the efficiency of operators of the various user sectors.

In the area of machine tools, transport equipment and accessories and instrumentation, with upgradation of facilities, it is attempted to achieve good growth in production as well as exports.

Attention is drawn towards capacity utilisation and lowering the cost of production in ship building industry. The growth of ship repairing industry, in particular is emphasised . Similar emphasis is on the growth of electronics sector and fertilizer industry.

Similarly a package of reforms causing restructuring, (involving modernization rationalisation of capacity, product-mix changes and making public enterprises efficient and competitive), increase in autonomy , and changes in management practices in public sector enterprises is envisaged during the plan period.

Performance - The 8th plan started against the back drop of impressive industrial growth during the Eighties. The average annual growth rate of the industrial sector including mining, manufacturing and electricity generation during the 7th plan period was 8.5% which though marginally lower than the targetted 8.7 % was much higher than 5.9 per cent achieved during the 6th plan. The significant growth in industrial production during the 7th plan provided a base for a higher targetted growth for industrial sector in the 8th plan. The 8th plan envisaged a growth of 8 per cent in mining, 7.3 per cent in manufacturing and 7.8 per cent for electricity. This targetted rate of growth for industrial production could not be achieved during the first two years of the 8th plan, only 2.3 per cent rate of growth was achieved in the first year of the 8th plan (1992-93). In the second year (1993-94), the growth rate achieved was only 4,1% . Though during the period 1994-95 , and 1995-96 , the rate of growth improved to approximately 8 per cent, in 1996-97 , it further declined to 3.5%.

The slow growth in industrial production can be attributed to the *demand constrants* faced by industry *poor performance of domestic capital goods sector,* liberal imports due to reduction in custom duty which adversely affected capacity utilisation in domestic sector industries like copper , lead, zinc, etc; and increased cost due to increase in administrative prices of some infrastructural items like coal and petroleum.

Current Industrial Production

As part of the quick estimates of Index of Industrial production , the overall growth of industrial production during April-June 1996 was 8.5 per cent over the corresponding period of 1995. As per the use-based classification of industries, the overall industrial growth has been broad based. After being relatively sluggish in the last two years, Intermediate Goods recorded a growth of 11.9 per cent in April-June 1996. Within the manufacturing sector, all the 17 broad categories had recoreded positive growth rates during April-September 1995. Performance of the major 172 industries with a weight of 88 per cent of IIP indicate a growth of 9.98 per cent in April -June 1996 , indicating that industrial growth has so far remained buoyant.

The performance of six infrastructure industries comprising of electricity, coal, saleable steel, petroleum refinery products, crude petroleum and cement is given in Table-3 ,

Table -3

S.No	*Industry*	*Growth Rate*				
		Weight	*1992-93*	*1993-94*	*1994-95*	*1995-96*
1.	Electricity	11.4290	4.9	7.5	8.5	8.2
2.	Coal	6.6082	3.8	3.4	3.0	6.4
3.	Saleable Steel	5.2090	7.0	4.6	11.1	8.5
4.	Crude Petroleum	2.4073	-11.2	0.3	19.3	7.2
5.	Refinery Products	1.5192	4.0	1.5	4.1	3.6
6.	Cement	1.5983	0.3	7.1	7.6	11.2
	Overall	28.7712	3.0	5.3	8.4	7.8

The office of the Economic Adviser, an attached office of the Department of Industrial Policy and Promotion in the Ministry of Industry also collects advance information on the production performance of 24 selected industries which have a weight of around 50 per cent in the IIP. According to the information available , these industries have recorded a growth of 5.6 per cent during April-August 1996.

The process of adjustment , however, seems to have had a much shorter time span compared to international experience. Overall industrial growth, though moderate, has remained positive. From April 1994 industrial recovery has become more apparent and spread to the sectors which were depressed earlier.

Investment Scenario

The thrust of the new industrial policy has been to enable entrepreneurs to take investment decisions based on their own commercial perception with a greatly reduced regulatory role of the Government Licensing stands abolished for most of the industries , and the entrepreneurs are only required to file an investment intention. The response of the entrepreneurs to the policy initiative has been very encouraging. The industrial investment intentions from the year 1991 to August 1996 is given in Table-4

Review of Industrial Development

Industrial development in India has been playing a crucial role toward structural diversification, modernisation and self-reliance. The progress of industrialisation over the last thirty-five years has been a striking feature of Indian economic development. The process of industrialisation was launched as a conscious and deliberate policy in the early fifties. In pursuance of this policy, large investments have been made in building up capacity over a wide spectrum of industries. Industrial production has gone up by about five times during this period. Apart from quantitative increases in output, the industrial structure has been widely diversified covering broadly the entire range of consumer, intermediate and capital goods. In most of the manufactured products, the country has achieved a large-measure of self-sufficiency, providing the capability to sustain the future growth of vital sectors of

INVESTMENT SCENARIO

Year	Industrial Entrepreneur Memoranda (IEMs)			Letters of Intent (LOIs)		
	Number Filed	Proposed Investment (Rs. Crore)	Proposed Employment ('000)	Number Issued	Proposed Investment (Rs. Crore)	Proposed Employment ('000)
1991	3084	76.310	769	195	2,071	34
1992	4860	1,15,872	923	620	13,994	97
1993	4456	63,976	703	528	12,845	100
1994	4664	88,771	829	546	17,937	130
1995	6503	1,25,509	1,114	355	14,265	91
1996 (Up to August)	3392	54,754	512	369	25,525	129
Total	26,958	5,25,192	4,850	2,613	86,637	582

the economy primarily through domestic effort. This is reflected in the commodity composition of our international trade in which the share of imports of manufactured products has steadily declined. On the other hand, industrial products, particularly engineering goods, have become a growing component of our exports. The rapid stride in industrialisation has been accompanied by a corresponding growth in technological industries and agro-based industries.

INDUSTRIAL DEVELOPMENT & TRENDS TOWARDS LIBERALISATION

In Indian economy, liberalisation took place on two fronts as mentioned below:

(I) *Domestic Liberalisation*— Domestic liberalisation in Indian economy began in the mid seventies. However, a formal liberalisation of economic policy in India was started in 1973 when a number of industries were open for participation by large business houses and companies comes under the purview of MRTP and FERA Act. The real beginning of domestic liberalisation have taken from 1975 with the modification of the licensing procedure. The government exempted several medium entrepreneurs from obtaining of industrial licences. On the way of further liberalisation, the licensing policy was further liberalised between 1975 and 1979. The Government exempted from licensing for investment up to s. 3 crore in 1978 and to Rs. 5 crore in 1983.

The process of liberalisation gathered momentum in 1980 with the announcement of industrial policy. The provision of the policy focussed attention for encouraging competition in the domestic market with technological upgradation and modernisation. The policy laid the emphasis for an increasingly competitive export base and for encouraging foreign investment in the areas using high technology.

The liberalisation process which till then primarily concerned with removing of the supply constraints. Since 1985-86 entered in a new phase with the introduction of liberalisation measures on the demand front alike, especially on the demand of consumer durables. A number of policy measures have been implemented in order to :

(i) limiting the role of licensing;

(ii) expanding the scope for contribution to growth by large houses,

(iii) encourage modernisation,

(iv) raising the investment limits for the growth of Small Scale Sectors,

(v) providing fiscal incentives for Small Scale Sectors.

Some important liberalisation measures as a part of liberalised Economic Policy of government of India includes the following:

(1) *Delicensing*— Since June 1988, a number of industries have been de-licensed the number of industries subject to statutory licensing reduced to only 18.

(2) *Exemption Limit*— The exemption limit for industrial licensing has been raised from Rs. 5 crores to Rs. 25 crores since June 1988 for those units that are set-up in non-backward areas and Rs. 75 crores for those units that are set-up in backward areas.

(3) *Liberalised the MRTP Act*— The government has liberalised the operation of the MRTP Act in phase manner. As a result, large business houses have been given the opportunity to enter a number of industrial fields which were formerly closed for them.

(4) *Encouragement to Small Scale Industries*— Investment limits for small scale sector have been raised. The liberalised policy also providing fiscal incentive for their growth.

(5) *Export Promotion*— The policy exempted from licensing requirements to 100 per cent export oriented units. Since February 1990 even the units which undertake to export 60 per cent of their total production have been exempted from these requirements.

(6) *Import of Technology*— The liberalised economic policy making it easier to import foreign technology for purpose of modernisation and upgrading of quality.

The process of liberalisation was further accelerated with the announcement of the new industrial policy in July 1991. Some important factors of the new liberalisation policy are detailed below:

(i) The policy abolished licences for all industries, except for 18 industries related to strategic significance, security, social reasons, hazardous chemical and overriding environmental reasons and items of elitist consumption.

The number of items, in which industrial licensing remains, reduced to 15. These industries account for only 15 per cent value added in manufacturing sector.

(ii) The policy provides for automatic approval for foreign technology agreements. Automatic approval of foreign investment up to 51 per cent and foreign technology agreement permitted for 35 priority industries which account for about 50 per cent value added in the manufacturing sector.

(iii) The policy provides for raising limits of foreign investment equity from 40 per cent to 51 per cent, except in cases of a few industries of strategic importance.

(iv) The policy provides a new broad banding facility to existing units to enable them to produce any article without additional investment.

(v) The policy provides for abolition of all existing registration schemes.

(vi) The policy provides that entrepreneurs will hence forth be required to file an information memorandum on new projects and substantial expansion.

(vii) More and more private initiative encouraged in the development of infrastructure like power, roadways, tele-communication, shipping and ports, airports and civil aviation etc.

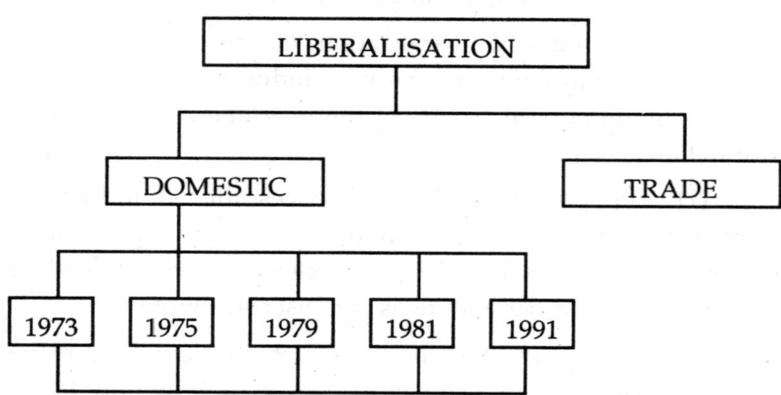

(II) *Trade Liberalisation*— Trade liberalisation generally means reducing restrictions on trade or making trade free than before. In a technical sense, trade liberalisation may be defined as any policy change which makes a country's system more natural. A completely natural system would mean a free trade system and moves towards neutrality means *trade liberalisation*. However, there is not a single nation on the glob which has completely free trade as there is always some scope for a movement towards neutrality.

India's trade policy has shown trend towards liberalisation characterised by gradual liberalisation of (i) complicated licensing system and (ii) high tariff import regime.

****

8

Development of Large Scale Industries

In a country like our, keeping in view the rising pressure of population on economy, the need for development of cottage and small scale industries need not to be explained. But at the same time it is equally true that no country can develop merely by developing its small scale and cottage industrial sector. In the process of economic development, the development of large scale industries possesses prominent place. While mentioning the importance of large scale industries, *T. Thomas observed* "To hold that only small is beautiful is to be oblivious of the fact that everything that is alive has to grow. Today's small-scale industry is going to be medium-scale industry of the next decade and, hopefully, the large-scale industry of the following decade.We must find ways of enabling complementary growth of large and small–not conflict and compartmentalisation. Very important factors such as consumer interest, market linkages, the efficient use of resources, and the need for innovation necessitate the continuous growth of large-scale industry."

In this chapter, importance, factor responsible for localisation, present position, development and problem with regards to few large scale industries has been explained.

Meaning

Meaning of Large Scale Industries : Large scale industries are the industries having capital investment in plant and machinery of more than Rs. 70 lakh

LARGE SCALE INDUSTRIES IN INDIAN ECONOMY

Importance

Large scale industries play an important role in the development of a country these industries are considered to be inevitable in certain field. Importance of these industries in Indian economy can be explained as follows :

1. *Big push to Development* : Large scale industries have a key role in the development stately of under developed countries . These industries produce the goods without which no country can do. These industries help these countries in jumping over their economic obstacles.

2. *For Strengthening the Eonomic Base* : Large scale industries are essential to set up certain basic and capital goods industries for example transport, communication and power etc. These industries cannot be set up in small units.

3. *For Raising Level of Productivity* : Large scale industries help in raising the level of productivity . These industrise also in the level of productivity in the country is beneficial from many points of view. It is beneficial for agriculture and small scale industries also.

4. *For Mass Production and Cost Reduction* : Large scale industries enable goods to be produced on a mass scale and at reduced cost. Thus, these industries put the goods within the react of many.

5.*Contribution in Exports.:* Large scale industries are making great contribution in exports of the country. These industries produce goods at mass level, which in turn enable the country to export the surplus goods.

6. *Helpful in the Development of Small Scale and Cottage Industries* : Large scale industries are helpful in the development of small scale and cottage industries also. A large number of small scale and cottage industries are established to supply the material required by large scale industries . Besides the equipment's and machines required by the small industries are produced by the large ones.

7. *Helpful in the Development of Agriculture* : Development of large scale industries is essential for the development of agriculture also because all the agriculture machinery is produced by these industries.

8. *Improvement in the Standard of Living* : Large scale industries provide goods and commodities to the people of country of latest quality and technology . These industries are helpful in the improvement of standard of living of the people.

9. *Contribution in Gross National Product* : Large scale industries are making great contribution in Gross National Product of the country. At present , total production of large scale industries is about 85,000 crores of rupees.

10. *Development of Large Scale Industries is the development of Economy* : Development of large scale industries means the development of an economy itself. It enables the country to stand in the line of industrial countries of the world. It brings , prosperity to the country . It increases national income national production and per capita income.

Large Scale Industries-

Capital Goods And Consumer Goods

Large scale industries of India can broadly be divided in to two parts : Capital goods Industries and Consumer Goods industries. Capital goods industries are the industries which produce goods and equipment's that are used by other industries for producing consumer goods. Examples of capital goods industries are - Iron and Steel Industry. Cement industry,

Coal industry. Consumer goods industries are the industries which produce for ultimate consumption . Examples, of such industries are - Cotton Textiles industry, Jute industry, Sugar industry and paper industry etc.

STEPS TAKEN BY GOVERNMENT FOR THE PROMOTION OF LARGE SCALE INDUSTRIES

The role of public sector enterprises in Indian economy was quite negligible before independence but revolutionary changes have taken place in this field during these 48 years after independence. Government of India has taken many steps to promote these industries. Some important steps are as follows :

1. *Expansion of Public Sctor* : Government has expanded public sector rapidly during planning period. In 1951 , there were only 5 industries in public sector having investment of Rs. 29 crores only while this number has gone up to 222 having investment of Rs. 97.535 crores as on 31st March ,1996.

2. *Development of Basic Industries* : Government has laid due emphasis upon the development of basic industries like iron and steel, heavy engineering, chemical industries etc.

3. *Infrastructural Development* : Due attention has been paid to the development of infrastructure facilities in the country. Means of transportation, communication, warehousing, power and energy etc. have been developed to help in the development of industries in the country.

4. *Expansion of Technological and Managerial Skill* : Government is making best efforts for the expansion of technological and managerial skill in the country. Many engineering colleges management institutes , technical institutes and industrial training institutes are making their contribution in this direction.

5. *Increase in Foreign Collaborations* : An important achievement of Government during planning period is the rapid increase in industries established with foreign collaborations, In 1957 there were only 57 such industries which art the end of 1996 has gone up to 78918 .

6. *Regional Balance of Industries* : Government has taken steps to establish the industries in the manner that it many achieve balanced industrial growth. New industries have been established only at such places where there was no industrial development far.

7. *Establishment of Important Substitution Industries* : Government has emphasised upon the establishment of import substitution industries. These industries have contributed a lot in saving the valuable foreign currency.

8. *Development of Industrial Co-operatives* : Industries co-operation has been duly emphasised by government during planning period.

9. *Establishment of Specific Fnancial Institutions* : Many specific financial institutional have been established during planning period to provide finance to the industries.

COTTON TEXTILE INDUSTRY

Importance

Cotton textile industry is the premier national industry of India; premier in the sense that of all her industries, it employs the largest number of worker, about 10 lakhs and if we include the number of people engaged in the cultivation and distribution of cotton as well as those who deal in cloth, 1.5 crore persons depend upon this industry. From the point of capital invested in it, it occupied till recently the top position- with an investment of more than Rs. 122,crores but now it has come to be exceeded by iron and steel industry. It is the third largest foreign exchange earner .

Growth

Pre-Planning Period— The first cotton textile was set up in 1918 industry on the world map of production is evident from the fact that as against the output of 10,000 million yards in the USA, India is now producing nearly 5,000 million yards.

The first cotton textile was set up in 1818 in Calcutta. But the real beginning of the industry was made in 1854 with the establishment of the first textile in Bombay. Later it spread to the interior, though Bombay is still the most important single centre of the industry. It received a great stimulus during the Swadeshi Movement in the beginning of the century. World War I gave it an excellent opportunity of which it took good advantage. Its condition, however, became precarious after the war specially on account of severe Japanese competition. Protection was granted in 1927 and the industry began to make rapid progress.

Before World War II greatly benefited the cotton mill industry. It was a period of extraordinary productivity. Foreign competition, especially fromJapan, ceased. But the industry had to face many difficulties. Its machinery had been overworked during the war and had, therefore, undergone excessive wear and tear. The return of competitive civilian market revealed its weakness. The boom times and sellers market had created a feeling of complacency. That is why technological improve meant were neglected. Partition of the country was another serious blow -it made the supply position of raw cotton very difficult.

In 1947, protection was withdrawn, but still the industry continued to grow. Production in 1950-51 on the eve of planning had reached 584 kg. of yarn and 4,215 million meters of cloth.

Post-Planning Period— The textile sector plays a vital role in the overall economy of the country. Textile export accounts for over 30 per cent of the total exports from the country. The burgeoning growth in exports from the textile sector in recent years has been one of the most striking features of India's economic development. The textile sector occupies a very prominent place in terms of employment generation. The development of the cotton textile industry and its present position is explained in the following explanation.

First Plan— The cotton textile industry showed a remarkable expansion under the First Plan. Production of cloth rose continuously from 340 crore meters in 1950-51 to 466.5 crore meters in 1955-56. It was on all-time record and greatly in excess of the first.

Second Plan— The condition of the industry deteriorated during the Second Plan owing to foreign competition (from Japan, China and Pakistan). The industry was also suffered because of high cost of production and diminished demand due to low purchasing power of the people resulting from high prices of foodgrains.

The per capital availability of cloth was 16 yards in 1955-56 and the target in the Second Plan for 1960-61 was placed at 18.4 yards. In order to fulfil the aforesaid requirement, 7500 million yards cloth required for home consumption. Unfortunately, due problem faced by the industry as mentioned above, the availability of cloth for domestic consumption in 1960-61 was of the order of 6.750 million yards.

Third Plan— The Third Plan envisaged the total requirement of cloth for domestic consumption in 1955-56 at 8,450 million yards. But due to difficulties arising out of shortage and high prices of raw cotton, power cut, heavy taxation and obsolete machinery, these expectation could not be fully materialise during the plan period.

Fourth Plan– The target for the production of cloth was fixed at 9350 million meters. But certain disturbing trends were witnessed in the working of the cotton textile industry in our country with the result that production target could not be achieved by the end of the plan period. The cloth production in the country by the end of Fourth Plan was 7,946 million meters.

The failure to achieve the Fourth Plan's target for cotton production and the extensive power shortage of a large magnitude were two most important canses responsible for shortfall in production of both cotton earn and cloth during 1973.

Fifth Plan— During this plan, the overall production of cotton was proposed to be stepped upto 10,000 million by 1978-79. In accordance with the target, a significant share of the additional production during the Fifth Plan was allocated to the decentralised sector. The actual production till the end of the plan (1977-78) was of the order of 8141 million meters.

Sixth Plan— The programme for the development of cotton textile industry during the Sixth Five Year Plan was essentially guided by the textile policy announced in March 1981. The policy, *inter alia,* emphasised the multi-fiber approach for harmonious growth of all sector of the industry and accorded top priority to the faster growth of handloom sector" The target of production was placed at 13,300 million meters to be achieved by 1984-85 against the actual achievement of 10,362 million meters in 1979-80.

Seventh Plan— The Seventh Plan expects to achieve a production target of 14,500 million meters of cloth by 1989-90. This was anticipated to ensure a per capita consumption 15.14 meters by 1989-90 from the level of 13.7 meters. The target of spun yarn was fixed at 1.542 million kg. The capacity of looms in the textile sector was projected to be 2.13 lakh and he export target has been placed at 1,300 million metres of cloth and 50 million kg. span yearn.

Eighth Five Year Plan (1992-97) - During this plan target of production of 350 crore metre for mills sector and 2,120 crore metre for decentralised sector was fixed. In 1996-97 actual production of mills sector was around 251 crore metre and for decentralised sector of 2136 crore metre.

Present Position— The textile industry continuous to be the largest in industry in India. It accounts for 20 per cent of total industrial production provides employment to 20 million people and contributes nearly 38 per cent of the total value of exports. As depicted in the table that production of cotton textile recorded an increasing trend over the years, except for a marginal setback in 1980-81 and 1988-89.Total production of cotton textile was 422 crore meters in 1950-51, increased to 2,013 crore meters in 1996-97.

In line with the general policy of liberalization, several measures have been undertaken to eliminate/reduce control and bring about greater transparency in the textile sector. The export of cotton textile has also been increasing at a fast rate during the last few years.

Table-1

Development of Cotton Textile Industry

Year	*Production by Mills Sector*	*Handloom & Powerloom (Crore Metre)*	*Total Production (Crore Metre)*	*Yarn Production in kg.*
1950-51	340	82	422	53
1960-61	465	209	674	80
1970-71	406	355	761	93
1980-81	343	494	837	107
1990-91	186	1,357	1,543	151
1995-96	196	1,607	1,803	179
1996-97	191	1,822	2,013	181

Main Problems

The main problems facing the industry are discussed below :

(1) *Obsolete Plant and Machinery*— The first problem is that of replacement of old plant and machinery. This has reduced the productivity of the industry and thus increased the lost of production. The industry lacks adequate reserves to finance such replacement. A recent estimate puts the immediate requirements of the industry for rehabilitation and modernisation at Rs. 200 crores in a phased programme of Rs. 50-60 crores a year for the next five year. The industry is caught in a vicious circle. Unless the textiles are modernised they cannot make profit and unless they make profit they cannot modernise. At present there is neither profit nor modernisation.

(2) *Lack of Modernisation*— Closely connected with the firs problem is that of rationalisation and modernisation. The present machinery is not only old and worn out, but also obsolete in design and out-dated. Thus, it requires to be replaced by modern equipment such s installation of automatic looms. But the difficulty is that of unemployment being caused thereby and, therefore, that of serious opposition to it by organised labour.

(3) *Export Promotion*— Another problem is connected with export promotion. A large section of the home market has been reserved for the handloom industry and it is expected to promote textile exports to the target of 1,000 million yards a year. But the record of cotton textile exports has not been satisfactory. Recently, three major factors undermined its competitive strength, viz., devaluation of June 1966, withdrawal of export incentives as a follow-up measure and rise in wage as well as the cost of cotton and textile machinery. Unless the quality of our textiles is improved and they are offered at reasonable prices, it would be difficult to compete with our rivals.

(4)*Erratic Power Supply*— Another problem is regarding the supply of power. It is inadequate and irregular. The shortage of coal has adversely affected the progress of the industry in the western section.

(5)*Statutory Controls*— Statutory controls have been imposed in respect of production, prices and quality. The various types of restrictions which the Government have put on the expansion of the cotton textiles industry are not only irksome to the industry, but a factor in keeping down production.

(6)*Burden of Heavy Taxation*— Taxation is another worry of the industry. The increase in excise duty on yarn and cloth resulted in an additional burden of nearly Rs. 90 crores in 1968-69 as compared to 1955-56. A burden of another Rs. 45 crores has been imposed by a number of ceases lived by the Central, State and Local Governments.

(7) *Uneconomic Units*— The existence of inefficient and uneconomic units constitutes yet another problem. Many of them are working at a loss and some are working at marginal or slightly above marginal efficiency.

(8)*Regional Imbalances*— There is a certain amount of imbalance in the distribution of the textile industry between north and south India. To remove this imbalance, the Union Government decided in 961 to allow five south Indian firms to set up textile units with a total capacity of 50,000 spindles for the manufacture of cotton yearn.

(9)*Non-availability and Poor Quality of Raw Materials*— The raw material (cotton) presents another problem. The quality is poor and the price is high. The yield per acre being low, the farmer has to be paid more to make it worth his while to grow and supply cotton. The yield per acre in India is only about a third of the world average and less than half of that of our neighbours, Pakistan and China, Besides, present shortage of raw cotton has resulted in step rise in its price.

(10) *Low Labour Productivity*— Although wages have gone up, labour productivity continuous to be low and compares very unfavorably with labour productivity in other countries. For instance in the United States, 1.9 persons are employed for running 1,000 spindles, in India 10 persons are employed in this job. In India, a worker looks after two to four ordinary looms, whereas his counterpart in Japan manages 48 automatic looms and in the United States 60 automatic looms and even in Uganda, which has only recently started this industry, a worker manages 24 automatic looms. Unless the output per worker improves, the Indian industry cannot obviously withstand competition in foreign markets. The continuous upward revision of wages has considerably reduced profits and landed the industry into a financial mess. The wage policy should be 'production oriented' and not 'need-based'.

JUTE INDUSTRY

In the ancient period, jute industry was organised as a cottage industry. The first modern jute mill was established in Bengal in the year 1935 . In 1938-39, only 15 per cent of total looms of the world were held in India. During the second world war, the demand for Indian jute goods increased substantially. Consequently the production of jute industry and the prices of jute goods also increased. The partition of the country in 1947 proved detrimental for Indian jute industry. Nearly seventy right per cent of the area of jute production went to Bangla Desh ((then East Pakistan) whereas most of the mills manufacturing jute goods remained in India. Right from the beginning till today the industry has been dominated by the British in respect of capital and enterprise. This industry has been organised on a large scale and there is big concentration in it. As late as 1959 , four Managing Agents controlled thirty two jute mills. Most of the jute mills are to be found in West Bengal. More than sixty per cent of the jute production takes place in this state. This heavy concentration of jute mills in Bengal is mainly due to factors such as the availability of raw jute in this state, the easy supply of finance from the British Managing Agents and the existence of loading and unloading facilities at Calcutta port.

There are 73 jute mills in India at present , employing 2.5 lakh workers. About 40 lakh farmers are engaged in the cultivation of raw jute in India.

Table-2 gives the data related to production of jute goods in India for selected years:

Table-2

Production of Jute Goods

Year	*In Lakh Tonnes*
1950-51	8.4
1970-71	10.6
1993-94	14.5
1996-97 (Target)	16.0

Thus the production of jute goods was 14.5 tonnes in 1993-94 while it was 13.1 lakh tonnes in 1992-93 . It is interesting to note that the output of jute goods had reached the level of 14 lakh tonnes in 1965-66 which could not be sustained in subsequent years due to problems of raw material and demand facing the industry.

The exports of jute goods in 1993-94 were of Rs. 389 crore which were more than the previous year.

Problem of Jute Industry

The main problems of the industry are related to production raw materials, exports and prices of the jute products. They are discussed below :

(1) *Lack of Raw Materials:* After the partition our country has been facing acute shortage of raw jute. Under the five year plans the Government always fixes a high target of raw jute production but it fails to achieve it. The shortage of raw jute has proved to be detrimental for Indian jute industry, twelve per cent of the looms of this industry are already idle and if the problem of the shortage of raw materials is not solved soon, many more mills may have to be closed down. The shortage of raw jute has impaired the productive efficiency in the industry anhd reduced the competitive power of the country in the world.

(2) *Foreign Competition* : In world jute market , Bangladesh has become the greatest competitor and rival of India. Good quality raw jute is produced in that country although the number of mills there is less than in India. Since jute mills have developed in Bangladesh from the very beginning , modern machines have been installed there. This has naturally given an impetus to the jute industry there. While the cost of jute goods in Bangladesh is less than in India, India has to import large quantity of raw material for her mills.

(3) *Lack of Spinning Capacity* : In India we have to face the shortage of spinning machines and consequently the capacity of spinning is very low.

(4) *Problem of Modernisation* : A large number of Indian jute mills were established during the first world war and since then these machines have not been replaced. Most of the equipment and machines have become outdated. As a result of this, the cost of production is comparatively high.

(5) *Problem of Exports* : The exports of just manufactures were Rs. 389 crore in 1993-94 which form a very small part of our total exports.

In the light of the above mentioned problems of the industry which are urgent , we can say that in order that the jute industry should continue to remain competitive and viable in the modern conditions and enlarge its contribution to national and foreign exchange earnings, it is necessary that following steps should be taken to revive the industry.

(1) *Modernisation*-The old machines of the industry must be changed. The industry should be completely modernised.

(2) *Improved Cltivation* -Intensive cultivatin with a view to improving the yield of raw jute per hectare is the main solution to the problem of production.The facilities, like the availability of seeds and irrigation, are needed to increase the production of raw jute in India.

(3)*Regulated Market*- The Jute Commission has recommended the establishment of regulated markets and buildings up of buffer stocks of raw jute in India.

(4) *Diversification* -Jute products should be diversified; and for this new uses of jute should be found. This will require investment in research and development of new products.

(5) *Financialy Strengthen*- In order to improve and strengthen the financial position of jute mills, exports of jute goods should be increased. The government should give sufficient financial assistance to the jute mills. Modernisation and diversification of jute mills should be encouraged by all means.

It is heartening to note that the Government has announced the following measures in recent years to improve the working of the jute industry. (i) Diversification of industry to increase the product range; (ii) Passing of Jute Packaging Materials (Compulsory use in Packing Commodities) Act, 1987 to protect the interests of this sector; (iii) Creation of Modernisation and Development. Funds to revamp the industry , and (iv) a joint programme of UNDP and the Government for the overall development of the industry including raw jute , modernisation , diversification and export promotion aspects.

CEMENT INDUSTRY

Cement , an important infrastructure core industry, is one of the most advanced industries. Cement like steel is a primary material for economic development of the country. Cement industry is a basic industry and its development is of crucial importance to national growth . Healthy and orderly growth of such a key industry is a pre-requisite for rapid and balanced development of the national economy. The 1980s witnessed India emerging as a major cement producing country in the world . India ranks fifth in the total world production of cement after china, USSR , USA and Japan.

Product Mix and Scale of Operations

A large variety of cement is produced in the country viz. Ordinary Portland Cement (OPC), Portland Pozzolonic Cement (PPC) , Portland Blast Furnace Slag Cement (PBFSC) , High Strength ordinary Portland Cement (HSOPC) , Low Heat/Rapid Hardening Cement, (LH/RHC) , Oil Well Cement (OWC) , White Cement (WC) and Sulphate Resistant Cement (SRC) . Special cements like WC and OWC are used in manufacture of light coloured mosaic tiles or cement based paints and for cementing oil wells after they are drilled and cased up, respectively. SRC also is a special cement which finds application in structures exposed to saline and polluted waters such as ports dams etc.

Growth

The cement industry in India is growing year after year both in terms of installed capacity and production. . In India the cement industry has gone through various phases in the course of its development. The industry which was one fully controlled by the government , experienced partial control during the eighties and today it is completely decontrolled. The policies of partial and complete control have however, affected various aspects of the cement industry including production, price , exports, imports, etc., Table-3 gives the quinquential status of the cement industry in terms of capacity production and capacity, utilisation. .

Table-3

Cement Production In India

(Million Tonnes)

Year	*Capacity*	*Production*	*Capacity Utilisation (Percentage)*
1950-51	3.28	2.95	90
1955-56	5.02	4.60	92
1960-61	9.30	7.97	86
1965-66	12.00	10.82	90
1970-71	17.59	14.35	82
1975-76	21.14	17.29	82
1980-81	26.59	18.56	70
1984-85	40-69	29.56	77
1990-91	59.12	45.76	84
1991-92	61.34	50.61	88
1992-93	64.84	50.72	85
1993-94	77.24	57.96	80
1994-95	79.00	62.35	86
1996-97	90.00	76.20	85
1997-98	93.00	81.00	87

Production Performance

Cement an important infrastructure core industry , is one of the most advanced industries in the country. Till about a decade ago, the country was deficient in cement and it had to resort to import in order to fill up the gap in supply. Production of cement has increased from around 2.95 million tonnes in 1950-51 to over 81.50 million tonnes in 1997.98. Industry recorded a growth of 11.2 per cent in 1995-96.

After the complete de-control of price and distribution on 1 March 1989 and introduction of other policy reforms, the cement industry has made rapid strides both in capacity /production and in production and process technology. At present there are 107 large plants with an installed capacity of about 79 million tonnes. In addition , there are about 250-300 mini cement plants with an estimated capacity of seven million tonnes. The total operate installed capacity is estimated to be around 86 million tonnes.

India is producing different varieties of cement like Ordinary Portlant Cement (OPC), Portland Pozzolana Cement (PPC) , Portland Blaster Furnace Slag Cement (PBFS) , Oil Well Cement , while Cement etc. These different varieties of cement are produced stricity under BIS specifications and the quality is comparable to the best of the world.

Installed Capicity & Utilisation

The installed Capacity of cement industry has increased from 3.28 million tonnes in 1950-51 to 93.00 million tonnes in 1997-98. The Table -3 shows that installed capacity had higher growth rates in alternate years with few exception when the rate of growth was depressed. At present there are 107 large plants with an installed capacity of about 81 million tonnes. In addition , there are about 250-300 mini cment plants with an estimated capacity of seven million tonnes.

The rate of capacity utilisation in cement industry is quite high and even exceptionally high during few years.

DEVELOPMENT OF CEMENT INDUSTRY DURING FIVE YEAR PLANS

On the eve of independence there were only 18 plants engaged in production of cement producing 14.4 lakh tonne cement in the country. By the end of 1950-51 , 4 more cement plants were established resulted which total number of cement plants reached to 22 and production to 27 lakh tonne.

First Plan (1951-56) -During this plan 5 new cement plants were established and 13 were permitted for expansion. Hence the total number of Cement plants reached to 27 whereas total available production capacity was more than 50 lakh and actual production to 46.7 lakh tonnes by the end of 1955-56.

Second Plan (1956-61) - Keeping into consideration the ever increasing demand of cement 6 new cement plant were established and several existing plants permitted for expansion of production capacity . With the result of all these efforts production of cement by the end of 1960-61 reached to. 79.7 lakh tonne and number of units to 33.

Third Plan (1961-66) - During this plan 5 new cement plants were established and permission were granted for the expansion of few old plants. By the end of this plan number cement plants reached to 38 and production to 108.2 lakh tonne. In this plan cement worth of around Rs. 1 crores were also exported.

Three Annual Plans (1966-69) - During this period no new cement plant was established but emphasis was given to expansion and development of existing units. The level of cement production by the end of 1968-69 had reached to 122 lakh tonne.

Fourth Five Year Plan (1969-74) - In this plan extensive programme for the development of cement industry was undertaken. With the result of these expansion programme the production capacity of cement in the country targeted to enhanced by 215 lakh tonne and actual production was anticipated to 180 lakh tonne. By the end of this plan 13 new cement plants came in to operation. Till the end of plan number of cement plant increased to 51 and production of Cement reached to 146.7 lakh tonne.

Fifth Five Year Plan(1974-78) -Keeping in to consideration the rising future demand of cement , in the original plan 6 new cement plant proposed to establish and planned to raise the production capacity upto 245 lakh ton and ne. But till the end of 1977-78 number of cement plants reached to 55 production to 193 lakh tonne.

Two Annual Plans (1978-80) -Efforts for rasing production of cement continued during these plans. The cement production capacity till the end of 1979-80 was reached to 234 lakh tonne and actual production was 176.8 lakh tonne.

Sixth Plan (1980-85) - The Government adopted liberal attitude for the development of cement industry in Sixth Plan. In 1982 announcement was made for partial de-control and concessional attitude was adopted with regards to price and distribution of cement. It was targeted to establish 8 new cement plants having production capacity 10 lakh tonne. With the result of these efforts the production of cement reached to 425 lakh tonne and actual production reached to 300 lakh tonne by the end of this plan. At the end of this plan total number of cement plants reached to 66.

Seventh Plan (1992-97) - In this plan it was targeted to make the country self-sufficient with regards to production of cement . With a view to achieve this objective a target to enhance the production capacity up to 600 lakh tonne and actual production up to 490 lakh tonne was fixed . Bharat Cement Corporation established 3 new cement plant of 10 lakh tonne, production capacity at Tandur, Nayagavon and yeratungla. Besides several Mini Cement Plants were also established.

Cement-Industry During Five Year Plans - A Review

During 48 years of planned economic development, cement industry in India has grown rapidly. Whereas production of cement was 27 lakh tonne and number of plants were 22 in 1950-51 , has increased to 762 lakh tonne by 187 plants in Eighth Plan. A review of progross of Cement Industry during various five year plan illustrated in Table-4

Table-4
Development of Cement Industry During Plans - A Review (1950-98)

At the End of Plan	*No. of Cement Plants*	*Production of Cement*	*New Large Size Cement Plant (In each Plan)*
At the commencement of First Plan (1950-51)	22	27.0	-
First Plan (1955-56)	27	46.7	5
Second Plan (1960-61	33	79.7	6
Third Plan (1965-66	38	108.2	5
Three Annual Plans (1968-69)	38	122.0	-
Fourth Plan (1969-74)	51	146.7	13
Fifth Plan (1977-78)	55	193.0	4
Sixth Plan (1984-85)	65	300.0	8
Seventh Plan (1985-90)	155	458.0	90
Eighth Plan (1996-97)	187	762.2	25

Regional Imbalances

Table 5 indicates that the performance of the Cement units have had a regional distortion with the units in Sourthern and Western India doing reasonably well. The Industry has 73 per cent of its total production capacity in these regions and during 1992-93 , 77.4 per cent of the production was in western and sourthern region. The three states Madhya Pradesh (12.5 million tonnes) , Andhra Pradesh (8.52 million tonnes) and Rajasthan (5.41) million tonnes) together accounted for 52 per cent of the production. In Tamil Nadu the growth rate was 9 per cent , while the Northern states like Uttar Pradesh , Bihar, Rajasthan had negative growth rates. The same is true for both demand and consumption.

The Eastern region showed a demand depression of three percent, while the sourthern states whose public spending on welfare and developmental activities have grown , especially in states like Tamil Nadu and Kerala where demand increased by as much as twelve percent.

Table-5

Regionwise capacity and production

(large plants)

(million tonnes)

Region	*1990-91*		*1991-92*		*1992-93*	
	Inst. Cap	*Prod.*	*Inst. Cap.*	*Prod.*	*Inst. Cap.*	*Prod.*
North	11.19	7.99	11.39	8.47	12.63	8.75
East	4.99	2.83	4.76	2.97	4.87	2.70
West	21.97	18.83	23.68	20.00	25.62	20.36
South	20.97	16.11	21.48	18.67	21.70	18.91
Total	59.12	45.76	61.31	50.61	64.84	50.72

Export - Apart from meeting the entire domestic demand for cement, the industry is also exporting a large quantity. The export of clinker and cement has increased from 0.36 million tonnes in 1990-91 . The export in 1994-95 was to the tune of 3.38 million tonnes. At present there are about 30 mega plants of one million tonnes capacity and above operating with state -of-the-art technology and pollution control equipment.

Table-6

Export of Cement

Year	*Quantity (Lakh tonnes)*
1980-81	0.20
1984-85	0.28
1990-91	0.36
1992-93	1.18
1993-94	2.85
1994-95	3.38

At global level prospects for the cement export are very much favourable. However,. in past the export of cement remains negligible. The poor performance can be attributed to variety of factors *e.g.* cost competitiveness, exhorbitantly high fright rates, low unit cost and bulk nature of producer etc. These constraints have to be overcome if a fillip is to be given to export business in a bigway.

Mini Cement Plants

In the context of acute shortage of cement in late 70's , it was felt that mini cement plants can prove an effective instrument for satisfying demand in hilly and remote areas, exploitation of small and scattered deposit and for dispersal of cement production and reducing the burden on railway transportation. Mini cement plants played a very active role in supplementing the cement industry's efforts at increasing aggregate capacity and production . Mini cement plants came into operation sometime after 1982 to take advantage of the cement prevailing at that time. Their number increased from 26 in 1984-85 to 98 in 1986-87 and their capacity increased from 0.94 m.t. to 2.70 m.t. At present there are about 250 to 300 mini cement plants with an estimated capacity of seven million tonnes. The advantage of mini cement plants over larger cement plants are many. These include:

(i) *Less Time*-The time required to commission a mini plant is half of that required for a larger one.

(ii) *Low Capital* -It requires lower capital and minimum infrastructural facilities , and

(iii) *Low Instalation Cost* -The installation cost per tonne as also fuel cost are much lower.

Problem

Important problem facing cement industry in India analysed below :

1. *Location Imbalances* - One of the important problem of cement industry relates to locational imbalances. There is surplus capacity and production in the sourth and west of the country with deficit in the North and North -East thus putting further pressure on the already overstraned transport system and pushing-up the retail prices of cement.

Efforts are needed to reduce this imbalance to the extent possible in the coming years.

2. *Fast Escalation in Costs-* In fact, Fast escalation in investment cost is a major cause for concern for all concerned. The investment cost of a million tonne cement plant has gone up quite high in recent years. The operating cost and manufactureing expenses have also been rising significantly, notwithstanding the economies of scale and induction of modern technologies.

3. *Rise in input costs.* At a time when the cement prices have been on the lower side, the industry has been hit by a rise in the input costs. This rise has been mainly due to a rise in coal prices, increased power tariff , freight costs and increase in central excise duty.

4. *Erratic Power Supply* - The cement industry is a bulk consumer of electric power. The average power consumption for productionof one tonne of cement is 123 kwh. But the industry has been facing power cuts, voltage fluctuations and trippings year after year. To combat this, many cement companies have set up their own capitative power plants.

5. *Short Supply of Coal*- Coal is a basic necessity for cement but coal receipts have always fallen short of requirements and thereby affect cement production adversely. Moreover, the quality of coal received is not upto the mark.

6. *Inadequacy of Transport*- With cement being produced mainly in the regions where coal or limestone is easily available and the consumption centres are far away cement industry heavily depends on railways not only to transport of cement from plants to consumption centres but also to move coal from coalfields to cement plants. Hence, cost of transportation is an important factor, which influences the profitability of the industry.

Many of the units have been facing inadequate wagon facility as percentage of wagons received compared to wagons indented have been decreasing year after years.

7. *Technological Obsolescence* _ A major problem facing the industry is the technological obsolescence of the process used by a large number of units. The wet process, which is the oldest one, by its very nature requires higher thermal energy as compared to the dry process, Since the licensing policy favours only the setting up of dry process units for its obvious advantages . Nevertheless 30% of the capacity of large units in the industry is in the outdated wep process kilns. Apart from conversion of the inefficient wet process to dry process , many of the dry process units installed before 1982 also have problems of obsolescence.

8. *Other Problems* - The fixed costs constituting overheads, interest and depreciation are much higher for new cement plants. The cost of transportation of cement, average price of coal, wages, packaging charges, excise duty power tariff all have gone up forcing the price of cement to go up. Imposition of surface transport charges, overloading charges, grade changing classification by railways & collieries further added to the fuel bills.

Utilising a part of the funds provided by the World Bank to the cement industry and the grant from DANIDA, Denmark, a Human Resource Development projects is being implemented for providing demand driven training to the operatores, line managers and supervisors to enhance their skills for handling latest equipments. Four Regional Training Centres (RTCs) have been set up at ACC, Jamul (MP) , Dalmia Cement , Dalmiapuram (Tamil Nadu), J.K. Cement Nimbahera (Rajasthan) and Gujarat Ambuja, AmbujaNagar (Gujarat). A large number of personnel of the cement industry and part-time trainers have already been trained in these RTCs.

FERTILISER INDUSTRY

Four decades of planning and development of fertilizer industry have brought India to the front-line of fertilizer producing countries and India today is the third largest producer of nitrogenous fertilizers in the world, There are at present, 61 fertilizer units manufacturing a wide range of nitrogenous and complex fertilizers including 36 units producing urea and nine units producing ammonium sulphate as a by-product. Besides there are about 81 units producing single superphosphate.

The production capacity of nitrogen has increased from amodest 85,000 tonnes in 1951-52 to lakh tonnes as on 31 March 1997 and that of phosphatic fertilizers from 63,000 tonnes to 29.05 lakh tonnes of during the same period. Against the nominal production of 16,000 tonnes of nitrogen and 11,000 tonnes of in 1951-52 , the country produced . Despite massive increase in the indigenous capacity and production of fertilizers over the years substantial imports either in the form of finished fertilizers or its raw materials and intermediates, are required every year to meet the country's growing demand.

The consumption indigenous production and imports of fertilizers during 1991-92 to 1996-97 are given in Table-7

Table -7

(Tonnes)

Year	*Consumption*	*Production*	*Imports*
1991-92	127.28	98.63	27.69
1992-93	121.55	97.36	29.08
1993-94	123.66	90.47	31.67
1994-95	135.63	104.38	29.65
1995-96	138.77	113.35	39.55
1996-97[1]	149.31	111.55	20.33

1. *Provisional*

Two gas based urea plants at Aonla, district Bareilly (Uttar pradesh) and Vijaipur, districdt Guna (Madhya Pradesh) each with a capacity of 7.26 lakh tonnes of urea (3.34 lakh tonnes of nitrogen) per annum started commercial production in November 1996 and March 1997 respectively.

At present only urea which is the main nitrogenous fertilizer constituting about 60 per cent of the total fertilizer consumption in the country, is under statutory price control . Following a 10 per cent increase in the controlled issue price with effect from 21 February 1997, the farmgate price of urea has been fixed at Rs. 3,660 per tonne, excluding local levies. Notwithstanding this increase the Indian farmgate price of urea is amongst the lowest in the region and is heavily subsidized in order to provide this vital input to the farmers at an affordable price.

During 1996-97 the total subsidy borne by the Government on controlled fertilizers was of the order of Rs. 6,093 crore (Rs. 4,743 crore for indigenous and Rs. 1,350 crore for imported fertilizers). As per the budget estimates for 1997-98 the subsidy outgo is likely to be of the order of Rs. 7,190 crore (Rs. 5,240 crore for indigenous fertilizers and Rs. 1,950 fro imported fertilizers). Apart from the subsidy on controlled fertilizers under a scheme being implemented by the

Department of Agriculture and Cooperation the Government has been giving a special concession on decontrolled fertilizers in order to promote balanced use of plant nutrients. The quantum of special concession on indigenous DAP was increaseed with effect from 6 July 1996 from Rs. 1,000 per tonne to Rs. 3,000 per tonne and on imported MOP from Rs. 1,000 per tonne to Rs. 1,500 per tonne. There was a proportionate increase in the special concession on complex fertilizers , while the concession on indigenous SSP was raised from Rs. 340 per tonne to Rs. 500 per tonne. A concession of Rs. 1,500 per tonne on imported DAP was also introduced. In tandem with the 10 per cent increase in urea price effected on 21 February 1997 it was also decided to increase with effect from 1 April 1997 the concession on indigenous DAP from Rs. 3,000 to Rs., 3,750 per tonne and on imported DAP from Rs. 1,500 to Rs. 2,000 per tonne and on SSP from Rs. 500 to Rs. 600 per tonne. There has also been a proportionate increase in the concession on indigenous complex fertilizers. These measures are calculated to induce the farmers to optimise the use of the three major plant nutrients.

In order to enable the domestic industry to reduce the cost of production and remain competitive vis-a-vis the imported products, the special concession on phosphatic fertilizers is weighteed inf avour of the indigenous products. The customs duty on import of phosphoric acid the main intermediate used in the manufacture of DAP , was abolished inSeptember, 1992. Import substitution incentives are also being given on the use of indigenous rock phosphate and iron pyrites. As a long term measure to reduce the capital cost of fertilizer plants, the customs duty on capital goods imported for setting up new fertilizer plants as well as renovation and modernization of existing plants was abolished in September, 1992. Besides , Government has also introduced a scheme for interest rate concession upto a maximum of three per cent on longterm loans for establishing new fertilizer projects and revamping existing plants.

Public Sector Undertaking

The public sector has been playing a dominant role in the fertilizer industry. The first state owned fertilizer unit was set up in 1951 at Sindri in Bihar which was followed by another plant at Nangal in Pubjab. With the coming up of another fertilizer plant at Trombay, Government decided to bring all the public sector fertilizer units under the management of a single undertaking and the fertilizer corporation of India limited (FCI) was accordingly incorporated in January 1961 . The National Fertilizer Limited was established on 23rd August 1974 . Thereafter the Fertilizer Corporation of India and the National Fertilizers Limited were re-organised into four companies on the basis of feed stock and geographical considerations from 1 April 1978. At present, the basis of feed stock and geographical considerations from 1st April 1978 . At present, there are nine public sector undertakings under the administrative control of Department of Fertilizers. FCI has now four units, one each at *Sindri* (Bihar), *Gorakhpur* (Uttar Pradesh) , *Talcher* (Orissa) and *Ramagundam* (Andhra Pradesh) , with a total installed capacity of 5.87 lakh tonnes of nitrogen. The National Fertilizers Limited (NFL) has at present, five operating units viz the calcium ammonium nitrate plant at Nangal and the urea plants at Nangal , Bhatinda, Panipat and Vijaipur. With the commissioning of the Vijaipur expansion plant, the total installed capacity of NFL has gone up to 13.70 lakh tonnes of nitrogen making NFL the largest producer of nitrogenous fertilizers in the country.

Rashtriya Chemicals and Fertilizers Limited (RCF) is operating five fertilizer plants at Trombay set up during the period from October 1965 to July 1982 and a large gas-based fertilizer plant at Thal which started commercial production in 1985. The installed capacity of the RCF plants is ten lakh tonnes of nitrogen and 1.20 lakh tonnes of phosphate.

Hindustan Fertilizer Corporation Limited has five units in production three at Namrup in Assam and one each at Durgapur in West Bengal and Barauni in Bihar , Having total annual derated installed capacity of 4.24 lakh tonnes of nitrogen.

The Fertilizers and Chemicals Travancore Limited (FACT), Udyogamandal (Kerala), has at present three operating units, one at Udyogamandal and two at Cochin. Besides fertilizers, the company is engaged in the manufacture of chemicals . With the commissioning of a caprolactam plant in October 1990, the company has entered in the field of petro-chemical also.FACT Engineering and Design Organisation (FEDO) another division of the company is engaged in design, engineering procurement, supervision of construction and commissioning of fertiloizer./ chemical plants.

Madras Fertilizers Limited (MFL) is a joint venture, with the Governmnent of India holding 69,78 per cent of the equity share capital and the National Iranian Oil Company holding the remaining 30.22 per cent. The annual installed capacity of MFL is 1.76 lakh tonnes of nitrogen and 1.12 lakh tonnes of phosphate.

Pyrites , Phosphates and Chemnicals Limited (PPCL) set up in March 1960 is at present engaged in the exploration of pyrites deposits as well as production of single superphosphate at Anjhore in Bihar, exploration cum production mining of pyrites deposits as well as production of single superphosphate at Saladipura in Rajasthan and mining of rock phosphate ore from the Mussoorie phosphorite deposits.

Paradeep Phosphates Limited (PPL) was established in "December 1981 for setting up a phosphatic fertilizer complex of Paradeep in Orissa. The first phase of the project comprising 7.20 lakh TPW capacity DAP plant and allied facilities was commissioned in 1986 . The second phase of the project, comprising sulphuric acid and phosphoric acid plants went into commercial production in June 1992.

Projects and Development India Limited (PDIL) formerly known as Fertilizer (Planning & Development) India Limited is engaged in design engineering procurement and supervision of construction / commissioning of fertilizer and allied chemical plants. The company has played a pioneering role in developing the know how for manufacture of catalysts in India.

Cooperative Sector

Indian Farmers Fertilizers Cooperative Limited (IFFCO) incorporated on 3 November 1967 and *Krishak Bharati Cooperative Limited (KRIBHCO)* incorporated on 17 April 1980 are multi state cooperative societies under the administrative control of the Department of Fertilizer. IFFCO has five operating units one each at Kalol and Kandla in Gujarat and Phulpur, Aonla and Aonla Expansion in Uttar Pradesh. KRIBHCO has a gas based urea ammonia plant at Hazira in Gujarat with a capacity to product 14.52. lakh tonnes of urea per annum. The combined installed capacity of IFFCO and KRIBHCO is 18.65 lakh tonnes of nitrogen and 3.09 lakh tonnes of phosphate.

Constraints in Increasing fertiliser use

While adoption of modern HYN technology for increasing foodgrain production necessitated increasing fetiliser consumption, availability posed a serious constraint due to low domestic production.

Large scale import of urea and DAP is not possible because of foreign exchange limitations, on the one hand, and the higher international price of these products on the other. India being the second largest importer of fertilisers after China by its entry for procurement of any significantly higher quantities in the international market , also triggers higher international fertiliser prices.

Increase in domestic production of fertilisers is always preferable to havvy dependence on imports which leads to higher cost and consequently, higher subsidy payment apart from entailing serious problems of availability, foreign exchange problems and problems associated with handling and transportation of the imported material . However, efforts to augment the domestic production capacity have not kept pace with the demand due to the constraints listed below :

(1) *Raw Materials* : Inadequate supply of feedstock-Ammonia which is the most important raw material used in the manufacture of urea has not increased with the increasing demand . Thus a large part of the ammonia has to be imported. The industry is importing naphtha at present to meet Its fuel requirements as it is cheaper to do so than to build a system which can use either natural gas or fuel oil as a fuel. The Govt. has also announced significant increase in the price of gas.

(2) *Power* : Plants which do not have their own Captive power generation have suffered production loss due to power cut ranging from 40% to 70% in AP and 50% to 100% in Kerala.

(3) *Water Supply* : The plants especially located on the coastal areas have suffered due to shortage of water. Some of the plants have installed desalination facilities for treatment of water the cost of which is higher than that of treatment of raw water from conventional sources.

(4) *Movement* : Due to shortage of railway wagons movement of coal, fuel oil, phosphate, sulphur and finished goods of urea and DAP has been affected.

(5) *Market* : Artifical trade barriers created by certain State Govt. affects the market condition . As most of phosphoric and complex fertiliser plants are dependent on import of raw materials like sulphur, rock phosphate and intermediates like phosphoric acid and ammonia , a long term pricing policy is required so that the supply arrangement for these imported materials is not disrupted.

(6) *Low Nutrient Fertiliser* : The production of low nutrient fertiliser such as CAN (Calcium Ammonium Nitrate), ammonium sulphate and ammonium chloride is lost due to the fact that no subsidy support is available in these products.

(7) *Cumbersome Policies* : Increasing use of chemical fertiliser has been a vital factor in increasing crop productivity foodgrains production and overall agricultural production in the country. The overriding objective of various policies formuilated and implemented by the GOI from time to time, during the last three decades h as been to create an environment in which there are "incentives " as well as the "means" to increase fertiliser use. A review of these policies in necessary to analyse their impact on the industry.

STEEL INDUSTRY

Iron and Steel Industry is considered to be strength of Indian economy. There can be no two opinions about the urgent necessity of developing iron and steel industry for overall economic development of the country . The products produced by iron and steel industry is utilised by industries and agricultural for improving living condition of masses.

Origin and Growth

The production of iron and steel on large scale started in India in 1907 at Jamshedpur with the establishment of Tata Iron and Steel Company (TISCO) . Soon after some time the Indian Iron and Steel Company (TISCO) was set-up at Buranpur. Both these plants were established in the private sector. The first public sector unit was set up in 1923 at Bhadrawati when the Visvesaraya Iron and Steel works was set up. In the pre-independence period, the real development of the iron and steel industry was started in the second plan when Integrated Steel Plants were set up in the public sector.

Development During Plans

Since independence and more particularly during the five year plans , iron and steel industry in India have seen mushroom growth. In the following explanation, development of the industry during five year plan period is explained.

First Five Year Plan - In this plan several foreign agreements were took place for the integrated development of iron and steel industry in India. The production of steel which was 10 lakh tonne at the beginning of the plan has increased to 13 lakh tonne till the end of this plan.

Second Five Year Plan - Second five year plan of India accorded top priority to the development of industries in the country. The production steel in this plan has increased from 13 lakh tonnes to 25 lakh tonnes a sum of Rs. 431 crores were spent on the development of iron and steel industry in the country.

Third Five Year Plan - In this plan production capacity of all the public sector steel plants established till then were expanded . A new steel plant at Bokaro namely Bokaro Steel Plant was set up in this plan. A sum of Rs. 525 crores were provided to spent in this plan. The production of steel ingots has reached to 65 lakh tonne in this plan.

Three Annual Plans (1966-69)- In this period no new steel plant was established . In 1968-69, 65 lakh tonnes steel ingots and 47 lakh tones salable steel was produced.

Fourth Five Year Plan -The main objective of fourth five year plan in the steel sector was to maximum utilisation of steel making capacity in the country . The production capacity of Bhilai Steel Plant has been increased from 25 lakh tonne to 35 lakh tonnes. The production of steel ingot was of the order of 63 lakhs tonne during this plan.

Fifth Five Year Plan (1974-78)- In this plan production capacity Bhilai Steel Plant has been raised to 40 lakh tonne and to Bokaro to 47.5 lakh tonne. By the and of this plan production of steel ingot increased to 77 lakh tonnes. In this plan a sum of Rs. 1,622 crores was spent on the development of steel industry in public sector.

Two Annual Plans (1978-80)-. The production of steel during these two plans could not be increased as desired due to abnormal industrial relation and shortage of power and coal etc. During the year 1979-80 production of steel ingot was of the order of 82 lakh tonne.

Sixth Five Year Plan- During this plan a sum of 3,754 crores was proposed to spent on development of steel industry in the public sector but actual expenditure was tune to Rs. 4,800 crores only. The work of expansion of Bukaro and Bhilai Steel Plants was Completed in this plan. By the end of this plan production steel ingot reached to 108 lakh tonne and salable steel to 78 lakh tonne.

Seventh Plan - It was estimated that demand of steel by the end of seventh plan will reach to 138.6 lakh tonne. Keeping into consideration this fact plan for steel production was prepared .

Eighth Plan (1992-97) -The production steel ingots was 126.3 lakh tonne in 1991-92 has increased to 182.3 lakh tonne (except production of mini steel plants) in the last year of plan i.e. , 1996-97. To achieve this target Ministry Steel provided a sum of Rs. 14,589 crores in the public sector.

The Production and present position of Steel Industry anlongwith the development feature can be anticipated from Table 8

Table-8

Production Performance of Steel Industry.

Year	Production of Steel Ingots (Million Tonnes)	Production of Salable Steel (Million Tonnes)	Import (Rs. in Crore)	Export (Rs. in Crore)
1950-51	1.47	1.04	-	-
1960-61	3.48	2.39	123	-
1970-71	6.14	4.64	147	9
1980-81	10.33	6.82	852	70
1984-85	10.81	7.48	941	459
1989-90	13.72	13.00	2253	928
1990-91	12.15	13.53	2113	1049
1991-92	12.63	14.33	1970	1435
1992-93	13.25	15.20	2254	1104
1993-94	13.90	15.10	2494	1374
1994-95	-	17.82	2954	1297
1995-96	22.4	21.4	4,838	1,666
1996-97	23.8	22.7	6,866	1,922

Problem of Iron and Steel Industry in India and Suggestions

The Steel Industry in India faces variety of problem which have proved major hurdles in the way of achievement of production targets as well as fullest utilisation of production capacity. Some of the important problems facing by the industry discussed below :

1. *Lack of Cocking Coal* - In the production of steel best quality of coal is required for melting of iron. In India cocking coal is available less then demand. The country does not possess sufficient quantity of good quality coal. It is because of this reason that different mini steel plants have to face many problems which adversely affects the production of finised steel. It is suggested that not only production of cocking coal should be increased but new areas also be exploited.

2. *Lack of Expertise* - Development of steel industry in India remained confined to foreign technical collaboration . In India there not have adequate technical staff and trained workers. In these agreement the country has to pay every year crores of rupees in the form of fees, facilities and salaries to the foreign experts. The country required to take the services of foreign technical experts on attractive remuneration. To ease the problem the country should develop its own expertise.

3. *Transportation Problems* - Efficient, quick and cheap means of transport are needed for the development of iron and steel industry in India . Hence it is suggested that every type of means of transport should be developed.

4. *Industrial Unrest* - Industrial Unrest is the common features in all the steel plants of public sector . Due to single problematic factor, significant part of working hours lost. In order to remove this problem , top priority should be given to settle workers disputes etc.

5. *Lack of Capital* - Iron and Steel Industry in India also faces the problem of inadequate capital for modernisation and expansion. Development fund should be subscribed by the government for this purpose.

6. *Low Level of Capacity Utilisation* - There is problem under utilisation of production capacity in steel industry. Iron and Steel Industry in public sector could not utilised its installed capacity due to variety of problems . The ratio of capacity utilisation is quite high in private sector steel plant i.e. Tata Iron & Steel comapny.It is not even of the satisfactory level in public sector steel plants. Not only this but it has also varied from plant to plant and from year to year. The problem in the way of fullest capacity utilisation should be removed.

7. *Product-Mix and Wastes* - Further , there is the need to reorient the product mix of the industry and to use the waste material, namely slag. In view of the contemplated changes in the economy, the production of this industry will have to be increasingly consumer oriented, besides providing material for rural infrasture and basic capital goods for small industries.

8. *High Cost of Production* - Indian steel technology is largely based on open hearth system rather than electric are furnaces. Hence it is not most modern even yet. This has led to the high cost of production of steel. Truly speaking, SAIL is a sick giant.

9. *Rapidly Increasing Demand.*- Demand for steel is increasing very fast under the impact of the Five Year Plans. This requires that the output of the industry should be increased rapidly to cope with the ever increasing demand.

10. *High price of Steel* - Steel prices in India are quite higher in comparison to foreign countries . Steel prices have been raised several time frequently upto untorable hike. This has mode Indian steel quite costlier and affected our competitiveness adversely in the world market. Hence imports of steel is much preferred. Further our engineering industry has also been affected adversely due to steep rise in steel prices. Efforts should be made to bring down cost in steel production in India.

PAPER INDUSTRY

Paper is a vital and core industry for any country and per capita paper consumption can be taken as a measure of growth and progress in areas related to industrial cultural and educational activities. Per capita consumption of paper in India is less than 3 kg as against more than 300 kg in highly developed countries.

The origin of the paper industry could be traced back to 1812 when first paper mill was set up at Serampur, West

Bengal. In the beginning of First Five Year Plan in 1950, 1,60,000 tonnes of paper was manufactured and about 90,000 tonnes imported. Production expanded rapidly from the Second Plan onwards and by early 1980 , imports were down to 60,000 tonnes and production was almost ten fold. At present there are more than 379 mills in the country with an annual installed capacity of around 37.79 lakh tonnes. A significant aspect of the paper industry is strong presence of smaller paper mills with an installed capacity of 33,000 tonnes per annum or less. They accound for nearly 50 per cent of the total installed capacity and contribute about 50 per cent to the production of paper and paper board in the country.

Capacity utilisation of the paper industries has declined from 96.35 per cent in 1952 to about 60 per cent in 1995. Various reliefs and concessions have been extended in recent years to help the industry to improve its capacity utilisation and financial viability. These include libersalisation facility for import of raw materials, low excise on use of minimum 75 per cent non- conventional raw materials delicensing the manufacture of certain varieties of peper etc.

At present the country is self-suficient in respect of common varieties of writing and printing paper and paper board and only certain special varieties of paper are being imported. The import of paper has been brought under OGL and customs duty on import of paper has been reduced from 65 per cent to 20 per cent in this year. The demand of paper and paper board during 1995-96 was about 27.78 lakh tonnes which is expected to go beyond 40 lakh tonnes by the end of the century. The production of paper and paper board during 1995-96 has been reported around 27.10 lakh tonnes. The increased requirement of paper and paperboard upto the end of the Eighth Plan is likely to be met by some new mills, revival of some of the closed mills, and modernisation and expansion of some of the existing units. In order to encourage use of non-conventional raw materials, paper units based on use of minimum 75 per cent pulp derived from bagasse, agricultural residues and other non-conventional raw materials have been exempted from industrial licensing subject to locational policy.

Problem of Paper Industry

Although the development of the Indian paper industry has been very rapid, yet this rapid growth itself has given rise to several problems. The main problems of the industry are :

(1) *Raw Material Problem :* There is lack of sufficient raw material of the requisite quality for the paper industry. At first, *Sabai* grass and 'moonj' were used as raw materials. Later, bamboo pulp came to be used for making fine paper. The raw material is bulky and weight losing. It was uneconomical to carry it to long distances where the mills were situated. The transport costs were added to the cost of production and made Indian paper dearer as compared with the imported paper. In India, there is no dearth of raw material for paper industry. The Himalaya abound in spruce and fir trees; bagasses is also cheap and it can be used for making paper, as has been done in Philippines. The industry must explore the use of new kinds of raw materials, readily available in the country like bagasse, rice straw , paper waste, etc.

(2) *Problem of Location* - Since the raw material of the paper industry is quite bulky, the mills have to be located in the proximity of raw material. But most of the mills were located on the river Hooghly in Calcutta area, which was also away from the coal mines. This has made the location very uneconomical. Only when bamboo came to be used as raw material, the mills came to be located in Madhya Pradesh near the source of raw material. But they were still away from coal mines. Development of Hydro-Electricity has improved the location of this industry.

(3) *Shortage of Newsprint* - The Indian paper industry is unable to meet domestic demand for finer varieties of paper and for newsprint. Seventy per cent of our requirement of newsprient were met by imports. The paper is always in short supply and consequently, restrictions have to be imposed on the use of paper from time to time.

(4) *Poor Quality* - As already pointed out, the quality of paper made by the Indian paper industry is poor and compares unfavourably with imported paper.

(5) *High Cost of Production* - Another factor which places the Indian paper industry at a disadvantage is comparatively higher cost of production so that it is unable to face foreign competition. Higher cost of production is due to locational factors, lack of modern machinery and lower efficiency of labour.

(6) *Uneconomic Size of the Mills* - Most of the Indian paper mills are of uneconomic size. 100 tonnes per day is considered to be an economic size, but many mills are of a smaller size than this.

(7) *Lack of Balance Between the Pulp making and Paper making Equipment* - This has forced a part of the equipment to remain idle and has made the working of the mills quite uneconomical in India.

SUGAR INDUSTRY

Sugar industry is one of the major industries of India. It ranks second among the agro based industries. It provides employment in mills and in the production of sugarcane. Its contribution to the revenues of both the Central and the State Governments in the form of various taxes is quite high.

Sugar industry is one of the oldest industries of India. When the British came to India , the condition of this industry was not quite satisfactory. The first modern type of sugar mill was established in 1903, but the real development of this industry started from 1932 , when the industry received tariff protection against foreign competition. After the Second World

War, the prices of sugar started rising and the Government had to adopt the system of price control and rationing of sugar. The production of sugarcane as well as sugar increased rapidly.

The number of sugar factories rose from 138 in 1950-51 to 396 in 1990 . The trend in the production of sugar has been as follows :

Table-9
Growth of Sugar Industry
(October-September)

(lakh Tonnes)

Year	*Production*
1950-51	11.3
1991-92	132.8
1992-93	105.6
1993-94	96.6
1996-97 (target)	155.0

The total production of sugar during 1993-94 was 96.6 lakh tonnes only which was 36.2 lakh tonnes lower as compared to 1991-92 . This created serious shortage of sugar in the country. The Government had to resort to imports of sugar to meet the domestic shortfall. But due to problems of management in imports of sugar, retail prices or sugar short up considerably and the government had to face public criticism due to sugar scam or sugar muddle in in India.

The policy of partial control was reimposed on sugar industry since 1980 . The normal rati between levy sugar and free sugar is 45 : 55 at present. Hence, the industry has adopted dual pricing policy for better distribution of sugar and as an incentive for increased production.

The target of production for sugar for 1996-97 has been fixed at about 1.5 crore tonnes. Production or sugar has increased in 1994-95 as compared to the previous year.

Problems of Sugar Industry

(1) *Centralisation* - Most of the sugar mills of our country are situated in Uttar Pradesh and Bihar, whereas the area in the south is more suitable for the establishment of sugar mills, because of the fact that climate and other factors in the south are more suitable for the production of sugarcane.

(2) *Problem of Uneconomic Units* - Most of the sugar mills of the country are of uneconomic size, and they cannot be expected to produce sugar on a very large scale. As a result of this, the production cost of these mills is quite high.

(3) *Problem of Sugarcane* -The productivity of sugarcane in India is very low. It is much less than that of Cuba , Java and Hawali Islands, Further, the quality of sugarcane produced in India is not quite satisfactory.

There is a demand for sugarcane from the manufactures of Khandsari, gur, etc. also. There is problem during the period of short supply ofr sugarcane in the country.

(4) *Use of By-products*- When sugarcane is converted into sugar, several by products such as molasses, etc. are also produced. These by products are put to many uses such as bagasse is used as fuel and molasses are used to make alcohal, etc.

(5) *Problem of Modernisation* - Most of the sugar mills of our country possess outdated machines. The machines are to be replaced to increase the productivity and to reduce the cost of production.

(6) *Increase in Internal Consumption of Sugar* - The internal demand for sugar is increasing due to rise in population greater use of beverages and rise in the incomes of the people.

As a result of this, in spite of a remarkable increase in the production of sugar the price of sugar has increased at the retail level to a significant extent.

(7) *Burden of Excessive Taxation* - The industry has to face the burden of heavy taxation. Central excise duties and canecess have been imposed by the Central and State Government respectively . All this adds to the total cost of production.

New Sugar Licensing Policy

It was announced on June 1,1990. The main changes are as follows :

(i) The requirement of a minimum spatial distance of 40 km between the existing mill and the proposed new one has been removed.

(ii) Minimum economic size of crushing capacity has been raised from 1,750 tonnes to 2,500 tonnes a day.

(iii) Preference in licensing will be given to cooperative and public sector , rather than to private sector.

(iv) Liberal licences will be given for the manufacture of industrial alcohol.

The Sugar Development Fund was set up under the Sugar Development Act, 1982, in which proceeds of sugar cess are transferred. The fund is utilised for advancing loans on soft terms for the rehabilitation and modernisation of sugar industry and development of sugarcane in the factory area.

ENGINEERING INDUSTRY

Over the years, engineering industries in the country have registered a phenomenal growth to generate a strong base in a wide range of heavy and light engineering industries covering a broad spectrum of capital goods and consumer durable products. Bulk of capital goods required for power projects, fertilizer plants, cement plants, steel plants, mining equipment and petrochemical plants are being met from indigenous production. Construction mechinery and equipment for irrigation projects, diesel engines, pumps and tractors for agriculture, vehicles, etc, transport are also being met from within the country . Engineering industries have also demonstrated their capacity to manufacture large size plants and equipment for various sectors such as power generation , fertilizers and cement.

Major manufacturers of machine tools have now developed CNC machine tools such as machining centres, milling centres, turning centres etc. the machine tool industry has also commenced production of high productive machines such as industrial robots, flexible manufacturing system, etc. Indigeneous industry is not only exporting, general purpose machines to advanced countries but have also commenced export of CNC machine tools. Overall production of machine tools has increased from just under Rs one crore in 1950-51 to over Rs. 1,052.8 crore in 1995-96.

HEAVY ELECTRICAL INDUSTRY

Heavy electrical industry comprises equipment used for the generation, transmission, distribution and utilisation of power. It includes items such as generators, boilers, turbines, transformers, switchgears etc. The indigenous industry is equiped to meet the entire domestic requirement. The established capacity in the country for manufacture of thermal and hydro-power generating equipment is around 4,500 MW and 1,345 MW respectively. Most of these capacities are in the public sector, in companies such as BHEL . The entire industry has been delicenced under the new industrial policy announced by the Government of India. Also under the new policy , these items quality for automatic approval as regards foreign collaborations.

Steam and hydro turbines are manufactured both in the public and private sector. The total capacity is over 7,000 MW. The public sector undertaking BHEL has the largest capacity. Steam turbines upto 500 MW unit rating are being manufactured by BHEL , BHEL also manufactures gas turbines.

Boilers of both the categories, namely for industrial and power applications are being produced in the country. BHEL is capable of making boilers for super thermal power plants and M/s ABL, Durgapur, is a major unit manufacturing power boilers. There are 19 manufacturers of industrial boilers in the country . There are 33 units i n the organised sector manufacturing power and distribution transformers. The technology and design of power transfacturing manufactured in the country are comparable with the international standards. Indigenous industry is technology sufficient in transmission system upto 400 KV reactive compensation system upto 220 KV and is in the process of indigenisation of HYDC technology and development of 800 KV class equipments. A total switchover to All Aluminium Alloy Conductors (AAAC) , realising its techno economic benefits, would give a boost to this sector.

The electrical industry covers a wide range of products. The installed capacity is considered adequate to meet the domestic demand as well as exports . Under the new industrial policy, the entire industry has been delicensed. Many of the electrical items like electric motor, jelly filled cables, optic fibre cables and pumping sets also qualify for 51 per cent foreign equity and automatic foreign collaboration under the new industrial policy.

In the field of telecommnuication capacity has also been created for manufacture of optical fibre cables. Hindustan Cables Limited, a Government of India undertaking, and the Madhya Pradesh State Electronic Development Corporation, an undertaking of the Government of Madhya Pradesh, have been permitted to establish capacities for the manufacture of OFC to the extent of 40,000 and 20,000 fibre km per annum respectively.

The need for energy conservation has ensured greater focus in the manufacture of energy efficient electrical lamps. The industry is receiving adequate encouragement from the Government. A number of foreign collaborations have already been approved for manufacture of energy efficient lamps. Besides substantial concessions by way of reduction on the rate of excise duty on high pressure sodium vapour lamps and in the rate of import duty on the components required for manufacture of lamps have been given.

In the storage battery industry, some new units are coming up. The process of upgradation of technology in this industry is continuously benefiting the customers. The industry has started providing batteries to Maruti, Premier 113 NE and Contessa Classic apart from light commercial vehicles

The crane industry is de-licensed. By and large the indigenous manufacturers are capable of meeting the demand.

At present there are eight units in the country engaged in the manufacture of lifts and escalators. The present installed capacity of these units is of the order of 3,000 Nos per annum. A new range of lifts know as Sky Climbers has been/is under manufacture indigenously. These lifts are being produced for the first time.

With the increasing industrialisation and growth all round , the demand for electrical energy would correspondingly increase. As elsewhere in the world , there is an increasing shift in India to have large power houses particularly super thermal power stations. consequently, while there would be fewer but large power generating stations, the demand for transmission line towers for transmission of energy would grow substantially. There are at present over 25 manufacturing units reporting production to Ministry of Industry. There is sufficient capacity available in the country for manufacture of different types of transmission line towers. The industry is delicensed subject to locational angle.

AUTOMOBILE

The manufacture of all types of automobile vechcles is delicensed. There has been a significant growth in the production of automotive vehicles during 1994-95 as compared to that in 1993-94 . The automotive industry has presently the turnover Rs. 25,000 crore. The production of commercial vehicles during 1995-96 has been 2,59,131 as against 1,94,999 in 1994-95 . Production of cars has gone up from 2,64,368 in 1994-95 to 3,48,242 in 1995-96 . Production of jeeps during 1995-96 has been 67,679 while in 1994-95 it was 49,371 . The production of three wheelers has gone up from 1,33,193 in 1994-95 to 1,73,412 in 1995-96 . The production of tractors during 1995-96 was 1,91,149 as compared to 1,62,900 during 1994-95.

Problem of Large Scale Industries

Though large scale industries have a key role in India economy , even these industries have not yet acquired a expectable place in the economy . The growth of these industries can be possible only if the problems being faced by these industries are solved, some of the important problems being faced by these industries are as under-

1. *Problem of Finance* - The very first problem faced by large scale industries of our country of finance. These industries require very heavy amount of capital for their establishment but they do not get proper credit facilities.

2. *Problem of Under Uilisation of Capacity :* A great problem faced by large scale industries is the non-use of large part of their installed capacity under utilisation of resources implies wastage of precious capital resources.

3. *Relations with Small and Cttage Industries :* Relative roles of large scale, small scale and cottage industries in our economy always keep on changing. These changing relations create obstacles in the way of development of large

scale industries . Government policy towards small and cottage industries have been positive, that towards large industries has not been certain.

4. *Problem of Monopoly* : It has been the experience that in many case large scale industries belonging to private sector create monopolistic situation. Monopoly is associated with may evils.

5. *Problem of Obsolete Machines and Tchnology* : Many a large number of large scale industries continue to use obsolete machinery and old technique due to this problem , the production and productivity of these units remain much lower ..

6. *Industrial disputes* : In many large scale industries the relations between labour and management are not satisfactory. Huge wastage of manpower results from strikes , lock-outs etc.

7. *Difficulty of Management* : As the size of large scale industries is very big, the problem arises of management. Bigger the size of industry, more serious will be the problem of management. There is lack of skilled and trained managers also in adequate number.

8. *Infrastructural Problem* : Development and growth of an industry depends upon the development of infrastructural facilities in the country. Unfortunately, the development of these facilities has not been adequate in our country. It causes serious problems in the way of development of large scale industries.

****

9

Cottage and Small Scale Industries

Meaning of small scale and cottage industries

Small scale and cottage industries have been defined in India in many way from time to time . According to latest definition a small scale industry is one having investment in plant and machinery (fixed capital) upto Rs. 60 lakh. For ancillary unit (the units which supply parts and equipments to large scale industries) the limit of capital investment is Rs. 75 lakh. Tiny industry is or having investment in plant and machinery up to Rs. 2 lakh. It is important to mention here that capital investment for this purpose means the investment in plant and machinery and excludes the investment in land and building . A cottage industry is one which is run as full time or part time occupation mainly with the help of family members . Cottage industries are known as household industries also.

Importance of small scale and cottage industries

An important feature of Indian economy since independence is the rapid growth of small scale and cottage industries. Industrial policies of 1948, 1956, 1977 and 1994 of our country give special role to the small sector for creating additional employment with low capital investment . Importance of small scale ad cottage industries in Indian economy can be explained as given on next page.

1. *Vast employment* : Small scale and cottage industries use mainly labour- intensive technique which provides more and more employment even with low capital investment , in 1996,715 lakh persons were employed in small scale and cottage industries.

2. *Helpful in exports-* Contribution of small scale and cottage industries in the exports of our country has also been handsome. In 1976-77 , share of these industries in the exports of country was 14.9% . It has increased to 25% in 1995-96.

3. *Less Dependence on imports* : Small scale and cottage industries are based on the resources and technique available in the country itself. It minimises the need of imports and thus, saves valuable foreign currency.

4. *Suitable to the economic structure of the country* : India is a country having abundant labour force but facing the lack of capital small scale and cottage industries are suitable to this structure because these industries require more labour and less capital.

5. *Essential for the production of artistic goods* : these industries are essential for the production of artistic goods like handlomm, Banarasi sarees, Ivory products, silk sarees, showpieces etc.

6. *Helpful in equitable distribution of Income* : a great advantage of small scale and cottage industries is that these are helpful in just and equal distribution of income. It checks the concentratin of income and wealth in the hands of few persons because the ownership of these industries remains in the hands of lakhs of persons and families.

7. *Helpful in industrial decentralisation* : As small scale and cottage industries are scattered in all the corners of the country, these are helpful in achieving industrial decentralisation.

8. *Free from industrial problems* : Small scale and cottage industries are generally free from industrial problems like strikes, lockouts, etc. If at any time, any such problems arises, that is solved with mutual negotiations.

9. *Complimentary to large scale industries* : Small scale industries are not important for themselves only, but also for large scale industries. These industries supply raw materials and semi-finished goods to large scale industries in many forms.

10. *Need of less capital and technical knowledge* : Another very important advantage of small scale and cottage industries is that these industries need very little amount of capital and technical knowledge. For this reason , those industries can be established easily.

11. *Quick production* : In small scale and cottage industries production can be started immediately or within very short time of their establishment. Producers have not to wait for a long time for getting production.

12. *Cottage industries* : As such of rural prosperity cottage industries can contribute a lot towards rural prosperity ad economic well being of the people living in rural areas. As these industries are set up in rural areas, they can provide part time job to the people engaged in agriculture and whole time job to the village artisans and craftsman. Development of these industries offers a solution to all the problems of rural unemployment , poverty and economic oppression.

13. *Mobilisation of capital and entrepreneurial skill* : Small scale and cottage industries help in mobilising the capital and entrepreneurial skill of rural areas where it remains unutilised. There is large amount of concealed saving potential and untapped entrepreneurial skill in our village which can be utilised by setting up of small scale and cottage industries in rural areas.

14. *Helpful in checking migration of population to urban areas* : Development of small scale and cottage industries is helpful in checking migration of population from rural areas to urban areas by providing employment to rural people in their own areas. Thus over-crowiding in urban areas is also checked.

Small scale and cottage industries occupy an important place in Indian Economy. These industries provided employment to 113 lakh person in 1995-96 . Share of these industries in the total output of manufacturing sector is about 50% . Share of these industries in Gross National Product is 13% and in export 29%.

Importance of Cottage and Small-Scale Industries in India

Small-scale and cottage industries play an important role in the State economy. Their significance can be judged from the facts given in the following explanation:

The small and cottage industries contribute significantly to the total industries production and provide employment to largepart of population in the State. In this regard *Pt. Nehru* ones said, *"Cottage and small industries have great importance in the economy of India. These must be developed in all respects." Mahatma Gandhi "once observed that the salvation of India lay in the development of cottage industries."*

The case for the development or small and cottage industries rests on the following grounds:

1. *Employment-oriented–* The most important argument in favour of Small-scale industries is that they have a potential to create large employment opportunities. There is widespread unemployment and underemployment in Rajasthan resulting in more than one-fourth of the population living below the poverty line. These industries required more of labour and less of capital. Therefore, in a state where labour is surplus and capital scarce, production should be divided into small units.

2. *Decentralisation of Industries–* These industries can be started easily all over the country in villages and towns. Thus, their growth helps in the decentralisation of industries structure. On the other hand, large industries have a tendency to concentrated and locate only in few developed areas within the country.

3. *Equitable Distribution of National Income–* Since these industries are general established by middle and low income groups of the society, income is more equitably distributed. Large scale industries in the other hand lead to inequalities of income and concentration of economic power.

4. *Quick Production–* These industries can be set up in a short span of time. Thus these industries started giving quick production and returns to their owners. In this way, these help in controlling inflation.

5. *Contribution to Exports–* These industries plays an important role in State's export trade. Their products like gems and jewellery, ready-made garments, canned and processed fish, leather sandals and chappals, food products, hosiery etc.

6. *Less Pressure of Population on Land–* In India, the pressure of population on agriculture is fast increasing. As a result, our agricultural holding are becoming smaller and smaller day by day. This growing pressure of population on land can be reduced only when more and more small and cottage industries are developed in Rajasthan.

7. *Check of Large Scale Migration of Rural Population–* The development of small and cottage industries in the rural sector will check the migration of rural population to the already congested urban areas. Thus will help in maintaining healthy environment in urban areas.

8. *Complementary to Large Industries–* These industries are complementary to large industries as they produce a variety of goods like accessories an parts of cycles, machines etc. Their products are widely used by large industries.

9. *Less Industrial Disputes*– Large industries are ridden with industries disputes. These are mere prone to strikes and lock-outs. Small industries on the other hand, are freeform such hazards because they employ lesser number of workers which re generally unorganised.

In short, Small-scale and cottage industries offer a pattern of industrial development which is most suitable for a state like Rajasthan where capital is scarce factor and cheap labour is available in abundance. They must therefore be given a vital place in any scheme of economic planning. However these industries need to be developed along with large industries. Inefficient small enterprises should not be allowed to grow in the long run.

Several concrete measures have been adopted by the government to encourage the development of small scale and cottage industries. Some of the important steps taken up by the government are as follows :

1. *Establishment of Boards and Corporation* : A number of institutions has been set up by the Government to provide most of its help and support of small scale and cottage industries. These institutions are of various types and render different types of facilities to these industries to meet their various and peculiar needs. Some of the important organisations are

(i) National Small Industries Corporation

(ii) Small-ScaleIndustries Development Organisation

(iii) All India Handloom and Handicrafts Board

(iv) The Coir Board

(v) Central Silk board.

(vi) khadi and village Industries commission

(vii) State Khadi and village Industries boards etc.

All these industries /institutes have framed an infrastructure of the development of these industries.

6. *Priority inGovernment Purchases* : Government helps these industries by giving them priority in Government purchases , Government makes some of its purchases exclusively from small scale and cottage industries. The number of such commodities has gone up from 16 in 1956 to 404 in 1995.

7. *Tax and other Concessions* : Government has exempted many products of these industries from excise duty. On many other products negligible duty has been imposed . Some more concessions has also been announced line concession in Freight , power-rate etc.

8. *Organisation of Exhibitions* : Exhibitions are organised from time to time at different places of the country to make the products of small scale and cottage industries popular among public.

9. *Establishment of Industrial Co-operatives* : Government is encouraging co-operative organisation in this sector. At present over 45,000 industrial co-operative societies are working in 1996, National Federation of Industrial co-operative was set up with a view to provide help to these industries the marketing and export.

10. *National Institute for Entrepreneurship and Small Business Development* : This institute was set up in July 1983 the object of this institute is to provide training for small enterpreneurs and to co-ordinate the activities . This institute holds examination and confers certificates and diplomas on tranees. It conducts seminars, workshops and conferences for officers. It undertake research also.

11. *National Award* : To give recognition and encouragement to entrepreneurs in small scale sector , a scheme for National Awards has been introduced from the year 1983-84 . First three awards carry a cash prize of Rs. 25,000 and Rs. 15,000 respectively.

Above discussion makes it clear that Government has taken various steps for the development of small scale and cottage industries . The need is to implement all these programs and schemes effectively.

SMALL INDUSTRIES DEVELOPMENT ORGANISATION

A new Department called Small Scale Industries and Agro and Rural Industries (SSI & ARI) has been created in the Ministry of Industry headed by a Secretary to the Government . As part of this the Small Industries Development Organisation (SIDO) headed by the Development Commissioner (Small Industries) functions as the nodal agency for formulating, co-ordinating and monitoring the policies and programmes for promotion and development of small scale industries in the country. It provides a comprehensive range of facilities and services through a network of 28 Small Industries Service Institutes (SISIs) , 30 branch institutes, four regional testing centres , two central footwear training centres, one production centre and eight field testing stations in areas of concentration of specific types of industries. In addition, there are also specialised institutes which provide technical and managerial training and consultancy services in specialised fields.

INTEGRATED INFRASTRUCTURE DEVELOPMENT (IID) SCHEME

Pursuant to policy measures for promoting and strengthening small tiny and village entrepreses announced from 6 August 1991 the Scheme of Integrated Infrastructural Development (IID) (including technology backup) for Small Scale Industries in Rural/ Backward areas has been prepared. The scheme envisaged to set up about 50 IID Centres in backward districts / rural areas in the country, excluding those districts covered under the Scheme of growth centres to promote cluster of small scale and tiny units, to create employment opportunities and develop export. The Scheme also aims at promoting stronger linkage between agriculture and industry and to provide common facilities services and technological facilities like power , water, communication etc. in the new/existing centres/ industrial areas.

As per the financing pattern approved each centre is to cost around Rs. five crore. Out of which Rs two crore would be grant from Government of India to the implementing agencies and Rs. three crore will be loan from SIDBI . In the first instance the state government is required to identify the site of the IID Centre in a backward district and prepare a project report for the IID Centre and submit to SIDBI , who in turn will appraise the proposal and send it to High Powered Comittee(HPC) for sanction

So, far 32 centres have been approved by HPC to be set up in the backward districts of various parts of the country. During the Eighth Plan period an outlay of Rs. 50 crore was approved . The Central grant released so far is Rs. 12.56 crore. The Ninth Plan proposals for IID is for Rs. 250 crore and Annual Plan 1997-98 has been agreed for an amount of Rs. 15.0 crore.

TECHNOLOGICAL UPGRADATION / MODERNISATION

Under the scheme for promoting ISO 9000 certification, SSI units are given financial support by way of reimbursing 50 per cent of their expenditure to obtain ISO 9000 certification subject to a maximum of Rs. 75,000 . The scheme envisages providing financial support to first 100 SSI units for obtaining ISO certification on first come first serve basis. Now it has been extended to 200 units. A plan scheme has been approved for providing grants-in-aid assistance to Technology Development

Funds to be created in varius states with the involvement of state governments and industry associations. Total outlay of this scheme is Rs. 150 lakh during Eighth Plan period. The contribution to such funds is to be made in the ratio of 40: 40:20 between Centre, state and industry associations. Assistance to such fund is restricted to Rs. 30 lakh per fund. Modernisation of industries has been taken up on cluster basis in joint collaboration with State Bank of India and Small Industries

Development Bank of India.

Following the announcement in the Union Budget 1995-96 of the setting up of a technology development and modernisatin fund with an initial corpus of Rs. 200 crore, SIDBI has set up technology development and modernisation fund scheme for direct assistance to small scale industries to modernise their production facilities and to adopt improved updated technology so as to strengthen their export capabilities.

From 1996 , commercial banks and SFCs have also permitted to grant loans for projects upto Rs. 50 lakh broadly on same terms and conditions that are extended by SIDBI under direct assistance scheme.

The development of village and small industries as an integral part, in the expanding national economy, has been one of the key programmes under the five years plans. This is expected to lead to fuller use of local resources, meet a significant part of the expanding demand for consumer goods, form a vital link between agriculture and large scale industries and provide increasing opportunity for employment.

During the first three year plans in India , a sum of Rs 42 crores, Rs. 187 crores and Rs. 241 crores as , actually spent on village and small industries respectively. During the annual plans and fourth five year plan, the actual sum incurred on the development of village and small industries was Rs. 126 crores and Rs. 243 crores respectively. The following Table 1. gives the actual expenditure on promotion of village and small industries during planning in India .

Table -1

Expenditure on Development of Village and Small Industries

(Rs. crores)

Plan Period	*Expenditure*
1st Plan	42
2nd Plan	187
3rd Plan	241
Annual Plan	126
4th Plan	243
5th Plan (1974-78) estimated expenditure	388

Among the facilities extended to the village and small industries during the planning in India mention may be made of the following :

(a) Direct financial aid;

(b) Institutional credit;

(c) Supply of scarce raw materials;

(d) Expansion of training programmes;

(e) Subsidy on power supply;

(f) Organisation of cooperatives;

(g) Reservation of industries for small sector ; and

(h) Granting suitable reliefs from excise duties on the product o f village and small industries.

Sixth Five Year Plan (1980-85) - : Promotion of village and small scale industries will continue to bvve an important j element in the national development strategy particularly because of its very favourable *Capital output ratio* and high employment intensity. The *objective of the Sixth Plan* with respect to development programmes of village and small industries included the following :

1. Improvement in the levels of production and earning , particularly of the artisans, through measures like *upgradation of skills and technologies and producer oriented marketing etc,,*

2. Creation of additional employment opportunities on a dispersed and decentralised basis;

3. Significant contribution to growth in the manufacturing sector through , *inter alia, fuller utilisation of existing installed capacities;*

4. Establishment of a wider entrepreneurial base through *appropriate training and package of incentives;*

5. Creation of a viable structure of village and small industries sector so as to progressively reduce the role of subsidies; and

6. Expanded efforts in export promotion.

In the sixth five year plan 1980-85 , a *public sector* outlay of Rs. 1,780 crores was provided . Besides the public sector investment , it is estimated that private sector investment in this sector would be of the order of Rs. 12,600 crores which would be forthcoming from financial institutions, promoter's own resources and non-institutional sources. The industrial policy of 1980 provided the guidelines for the development of industries in small sector during the plan period. The policy measures adopted to promote the growth of small scale industries included the following :

(i) integration of the promotional programmes in the small sector with area development programmes;

(ii) restructuring the organisation base at the district level to make it more effective and result oriented;

(iii) development of approrpriate technologies and skills- their effective extension and transmission;

(iv) increased availability of raw materials including creation of buffer stock particularly of critical raw materials;

(v) increased flow of institutional funds specially in favour of artisans, village industries , and tiny units;

(vi) selection reservation of items for exclusive production and purchase from the cottage and small industries;

(vii) strengthening and extension of cooperative form of organisation particularly for the cottage and tiny units;

(viii) building up of a sound data base to facilitate proper policy formulation and evaluation.

As a result of the measures outlined above, the production in the small sector was expected to increase at the rate of 8.7 per cent annum during the sixth plan period . Employment was expected to go up to 89 lakh persons, while exports were expected to increase from Rs. 1050 crores to Rs. 1850 crores.

The small scale industry has registered an impressive performance and the targets set for the Sixth Plan have been achieved. This has been possible due to a large range of policy/programme support in the nature of *reservation of items* for exclusive production and purchase , *priority in the disbursement of loans by the financial institutions, concessions in the import of a raw materials and machinery,* and direct assistance like consultancy training etc., through a wide net work of promotional bodies namely Small Industries Services Institutes, and the District Industries Centres.

During the period 1973-74 to 1984-85 and number of small scale units have increased from 4.16 lakhs to 12.75 lakhs, employment from 39.7 lakh persons to 90.0 lakh persons, and the value of production at current price, from Rs. 7,200 crores to Rs. 50,520 crores. Exports during the period have registered a significant increase from Rs. 538 crores, to Rs. 2350 crores. The range of items being produced in the sector has diversified remarkably, and today the small scale industry produces anything from basic wage good to the most sophisticated electronic items. Out of the nearly 5000 items manufactured in this sector about 873 items have been reserved for exclusive manufacture by the small scale industries and 404 products reserved for exclusive purchase under the government purchase scheme.

Seventh Five Year Plan (1985-90) -The objectives of promoting small scale industries determined as follows :-

(i) to assist in the growth and widespread dispersal of industries ;

(ii) to increase the levels of earnings of artisans;

(iii) to sustain and create avenues of self-employment;

(iv) to ensure regular supply of goods and services through use of local skills and resources;

(v) develop entrepreneurship in combination with improved methods of production, through appropriate training and package of incentives;

(vi) preserve craftsmanship and art heritage of the country.

The strategy for achieveing the above objectives included:

(i) improvement in productivity enhancement in quality, reduction in cost, and re-structuring product mix through up gradation of technology and modernisation;

(ii) Optimum utilisatin of existing capacities through supply of adequate inputs including c redit, power and raw materials etc.;

(iii) Increase in share of VSI product in the domestic market through, publicity, standardisation, market support and increased participation in the government purchase programmes;

(iv) Promoting specilisatin in production and export-oriented industries;

(v) Strengthening and enlarging of skill profile and entrepreneurial base and management practices to increase opportunities for self-employment; and

(vi) Lastly , improving general levels of welfare of workers and artisans through better working conditions, welfare measures and security of employment.

During the Seventh Plan period the production in small scale sector was targeted to increase from Rs. 50,520 crores to Rs. 80,220 crores at 1984-85 prices, exports from Rs. 2350 crores to Rs. 4,140 crores; and employment from 90 lakh persons to 119 lakh persons.

Though the overall output of SSI sector during the plan period was targeted to increase from Rs. 65730 crores (at 1984-85 prices) in 1984-85 to 1,00,000 crores by 1989-90 , registering an annual growth rate of 8.8 per cent. The employjment during the same period was estimated to increase form 315 lakh persons to 400 lakh persons. The target for export by 1989-90 was set at Rs. 7444 crores, envisaging an annual growth rate of 10.2% during the plan period.

Against the 6th plan outlay of Rs. 1780.45 crores, (expenditure Rs. 1979-80) crores) the outlay for the 7th plan in respect of Centre . States and Union Territories stands at Rs. 2752.74 crores.

Eighth Plan (1992-97) -The 8th Plan aims at a growth rate of 5.6 per cent. The growth rates for the manufacturing sector and exports have been kept at 7.3 per cent and 13.6 per cent respectively. While *No growth rate has been indicated for the village and small industries sector* it is likely to be higher than that of manufacturing sector. As the plan emphasises on generation of adequate employment as one of the priority areas, development of small sector is geared towards that. Several activities pertaining to small sector like processing of agricultural produce , agriculture and allied activities have been identified as critical to development of the sector. Measures are adopted to solve credit and raw materials problems of the small scale industries. In order to upgrade technology, emphasis is laid on the establishment of tool rooms and provision of training facilities.

A sum of Rs. 6334.20 crores is provided for development of small scale industries during 8th plan as public sector outlay.

The small scale industries (SSI) which currently contributes about 40% of the gross turnover in the manufacturing sector and more than 30% of exports , *recorded a growth rate of 7.1 per cent in 1993-94* as against 5-6 per cent in *1992-93 and 3-1 per cent in 1991-92.*

The total number of small scale units in the country in 1997-98 was 30.14 lakh compared to 28.57 lakh in 1996-97 Value of production of small Scale units in 1997-98 aggregated Rs. 4,65,171 crore. The volume of employment in small scale sector stood at 167.2 lakh as of end-March 1998 . Exports emanating from the SSI sector account for abour thirty five per cent of the country's total exports. In 1997-98 , SSI exports valued at Rs. 43,946 crore registered an i ncrease of twelve per cent over 1996-97 Table-3

Table-3
Overall Performance of SSI Sector

Year	No. of Units (in lakh)	Output (at current prices) (Rs. crore)	Employment (lakh nos.)	Export (at current prices) (Rs. crore)
1991-92	20.82	1,78,699	129.80	13,883
	(6.9)	(15.0)	(3.6)	(43.7)
1992-93	22.46	2,09,300	134.06	17,785
	(7.9)	(17.1)	(3.3)	(28.1)
1993-94	23.81	2,41,648	139.38	25,307
	(6.0)	(15.5)	(4.0)	(42.3)
1994-95	25.71	2,93,990	146.56	29,068
	(8.0)	(21.7)	(5.2)	(14.9)
1995-96	27.24	3,56,213	152.61	36,470
	(6.0)	(21.2)	(4.1)	(25.5)
1996-97	28.57	4,12,636	160.00	39,249
	(4.9)	(15.8)	(4.8)	(7.6)
1997-98	30.14	4,65,171	167.20	43,946
	(5.5)	(12.7)	(4.5)	(12.0)

Note : Figures in the brackets give the increase over previous year.

Recognising the importance of the small scale sector, in the Union Budget for 1998-99 , the exemption limit for excise purposes available to small industrial undertakings was raised from Rs. 30 lakh to Rs. 50 lakh. The Budget also provided for a flat nominal rate of 5 per cent excise for clearances between Rs. 50 lakh and Rs. 100 lakh. The ceiling for the purpose of working capital determined by banks at the rate of 20 per cent of annual turnover was doubled for small scale units from the existing Rs. 2 crore to Rs. 4 crore. Pursuant to the announcemtn in the Union Budget, commercial banks have been advised by RBI to moderate cost of credit to the SSI sector by lowering spreads over PLR for units with good track record. Powers of bank managers of specialised SSI branches have been enhanced for disposing credit decision at the branch level . The Budget also announced delinking of SIDBI from IDBI and transfer of IDBI shareholding in providing credit to small units . Necessary steps are being taken for amending the SIDBI Act and the SFCs Act for implementing the announcement . RBI has also been asked to strengthen the existing mechanism available for discounting bills of small scale industries for reducing delays in payments to SSIs. Commercial banks have been directed to give greater weightage to overdue outstandings that large units have in respect of SSI suppliers, while appraising credit proposals.

A High Powered Committee set up by RBI for improving credit system to SSIs and simplification of procedures thereof, has submitted its report in June 1998. Some of the recommendations of the Committee have already been accepted by the RBI. These include, enhancement in limit of composite loan from Rs. 2 lakh to Rs. 5 lakh , delegation of more powers to branch managers for granting ad-hoc facilities to the extent of 20 per cent of sanctioned limit, strengthening of recovery mechanism opening of more SSI bank branchews, meticulous implementation of Nayak Committee recommendations etc. Other proposals are under examination by RBI.

Small Industries Development Bank of India (SIDBI)

SIDBI was set up a subsidiary of IDBI and it commenced its operations from April 2, 1990.

Its immediate thrust will be on :

(i) Technological upgradation of existing units;

(ii) expansion of marketing channels of SSI products; and

(iii) employment promotion in semi-urban areas.

The financial assistance of SIDBI to small units will be channelised through SFCs, SIDCs, Commercial banks, Cooperative banks and RRBs. Their total number now is 869.

The authorised capital of SIDBI is Rs. 250 crore, which can go upto Rs. 1,000 crore. Its activities are as follows :

(a) Refinancing of loans and advances extended by the primary lending institutions to small scale units.

(b) Discounting and rediscounting of bills arising from sale of machinery to small units.

(c) Extension of seed capital/soft loan under National Equity Fund (NEF), etc.

(d) direct financing and refinancing for export of goods.

(e) to provide factoring, leasing and other services to small units.

(f) to extend financial support to State Small Industries Development Corporations for providing scarce raw materials and marketing of end-products of SSI units.

(g) to extend financial support to National Small Industries Corporation for providing, leasing hire purchase and marketing support to SSI units.

During 1993-94, the sanctions of SIDBI were Rs. 4,014.1 crore, while the disbursement were Rs. 3,331.1 crore. Under sanctions, refinance constituted a major portion of the total sanctions. Rediscounting of short term bills and bills rediscounting scheme to help manufactures in offering deferred payment credit facilities for purchases were the other forms of financial assistance to small industries by SIDBI.

These come under indirect assistance provide by SIDBI. It provides direct assistance, also in the form of direct discounting, marketing scheme, assistance to leasing companies, infrastructural development, factoring services, etc. It provides equity support for seed capital, Mahila Udyam Nidhi (MUN) Scheme and Special Scheme for Ex-servicemen. It provides resource support to National Small Scale Industries Corporation Ltd., and State Small Industries Development Corporations.

Thus SIDBI has become an important central financing institution for the development of SSIs in India and its role will increase with the passage of time.

New Small Sector Industrial Policy, 1991

On August 6, 1991, the government of India announced its new small scale industrial policy entitled "Policy Measures for providing and strengthening small. Tiny and village enterprises". The following are some of the salient features of this new policy.

1. **Charge in investment limits**: Under this policy the government has changed the investments of small industries and ancillary industries. Capital investment limit has been raised from 35 lakh to 60 lakh for small industries and from Rs. 45 lakh to 75 lakh for ancillary units. Investment limit for tiny units has been extended from Rs. 2 lakh to 5 lakh.

2. **Infra-structural Facilities**: A technology development cell (TDC) in the Industries Development Organisation (SIDO) will be set up for providing technology inputs for improving productivity and competitiveness of the products produced by the small sector.

3. **Marketing and exports**: National small Industries Corporation will sell on large scale consumer goods under a common Brand name. An export Development Center in small Industries Development Organisation (SIDO) will be established.

4. Promotion of Entrepreneurship : Government will help new entrepreneurs through training. Trainers and motivators will be appointed, female entrepreneurs will be helped through special training programmes.

5. Equity Participation : Limited Partnership Act will be introduced to limit the financial of new and non-active partners/entrepreneurs to allow foreign companies upto 24%.

6. Financial Support : The sphere of National Equity Fund has been extended. It includes projects upto Rs. 10 lakh (15% equity support) simple window loan scheme is extended upto 20 lakh rupees. Efforts will be made to ensure adequate and regular flow of credit of special monitoring aency will be established in order to look after the genuine credit needs for the small scale industrial sector.

7. Village Industries : Handloom sector, Handicrafts sector and other village industries will be promoted.

As a consequence of above measures, a massive growth have taken place in the small scale sector. This sector now contributes 40% of the gross turnover in the manufacturing sector and 34% of the total exports. New Small Scale Industrial Policy 1991. Under this policy investment limits for small and annually units have been raised from Rs. 35 lakh to 60 lakh and Rs. 45 lakh to 75 lakh respectively. Investment limit for tiny units was raised from Rs. 2 lakh to Rs. 5 lakh. The new policy proposed a separate package for the promotion of tiny units. The 1991 policy provided equity participation by other industrial units in the small scale units not exceeding 24% of the total shareholding. Another important feature of this policy was the introduction of a new legal form of organisation of business in form of restricted or limited partnership. In this form, the liability at least one partner is unlimited. Government will help new entrepreneurs through training. Female entrepreneurs will be helped through special training programmes.

The performance of the Indian economy in 1998-99 measured in terms of GDP growth rate was better than the previous year. The GDP growth was 5.8 per cent during 1998-99 compared with 5.0 per cent during 1997-98. The major contribution to good performance was from the agricultural and allied activities which demonstrated a turnaroudn output growth of 5.3 per cent in 198-99 compared with a negative growth of 1 per cent in the previous year. However, growth in the industrial sector decelerated to 3.8 per cent in 1998-99 from 6.6 per cent during 1997-98. The lower growth of the industrial sector has been ascribed to, among other things the slackening of aggregate demand on account of falling export growth and infrastructure bottleneck. Subdued demand for Indian exports massive and competitive depreciation of currencies of many Asian countries lower export realisation due to consistent fall in international prices of products and more importantly, the economic sanctions imposed on India in the wake of nuclear tests accentuated the pressure on sector during 1998-99 hs also been lower at 6.7 per cent compared with the growth of 8.2 per cent during the previous year.

The exports in US dollar terms reportedly showed a comparatively higher growth of 3.7 per cent during 1998-99 as against the growth of 2.6 per cent during the previous year and the imports recorded a growth of 7.9 per cent during 1998-99 compared with the growth of 5.8 per cent during the preceding year. The ratio of gross fiscal deficit to GDP was 6.5 per cent during 1998-99 as against the budgeted figure of 5.6 per cent. The inflation, measured by wholesale price index on a point-to-point basis, was lower at 5.0 per cent at March 1999 compared with 5.3 per cent at March 1998. The inflation rate has been showing a general downward trend during the latter half of 1998-99 after having reached a level of 8.8 per cent in

September 1998 on account of sharp rise in prices of certain primary products. As at end-March 1999 the foreign exchange reserves were of the order of US$ 32.5 billion as against US$ 29.4 billion as at end-March 1998.

Policy Environment For SSIs

Revision of Investment Ceiling

The Government had enhanced the ceiling on investment in plant and machinery for SSIs and ancillaries to Rs. 300 lakh from Rs. 60 lakh for SSIs and Rs. 75 lakh for ancillary and export oriented units. Simultaneously, investment ceiling in respect of tiny units was also raised to Rs. 25 lakh from Rs. 5 lakh. However, the Government of India is contemplating to reduce the investment ceiling to Rs. 100 lakh for SSIs, with the investment ceiling for tiny units continuing at Rs. 25 lakh.

Dereservation

The Government of India carried forward the policy of dereservation during the year and removed 9 more items from the reserved list for SSIs, thereby reducing the number of reserved items to 812.

Budget Announcements relating to SSIs

While presenting the Union Budget 1998-99 in June 1998, the Hon'ble Finance Minister had announced the delinking of SIDBI from IDBI and transfer IDBI shareholding in State Financial Corporations (SFCs) to SIDBI so as to equip SIDBI to play its apex role in SSI credit dispensation more effectively. The matter is under consideration of Government of India.

The other initiatives proposed in the Budget 1998-99 included doubling of the limit on working capital requirements of SSI units from Rs. 2 crore to Rs. 4 crore in the context of computation of working capital limits by banks on the simplified basis of 20 per cent of the projected annual turnover, enhancement in the powers delegated to branch managers of specialised SSI branches of banks and strengthening the existing mechanism available to SSIs for discounting of bills. It was also proposed to take steps to make provisions in the legislation on delayed payments more effective to reduce the handicap of SSIs on account of delayed payments from large companies. Accordingly, the Interest on Delayed Payments to Small Scale and Ancillary Indstrial Undertakings Act, 1993 was amended in August 1998.

With a view to providing inducement for increasing production, the Budget 1998-99 had raised the exemption limit on turnover for levy of excise duty on SSIs and tiny units from Rs. 30 lakh to Rs. 50 lakh with clearneces between Rs. 50 lakh and Rs. 100 lakh attracting tariff at a flat rate of 5 per cent.

In order to accelerate the pace of growth in small scale sector, the Government of India initiated certain important measures through the Budget 1999-2000. The budgetary measures include ; a) increase in the limit of composite loan scheme from Rs. 2 lakh to Rs. 5 lakh to ease operational difficulties of the small borrowers by providing term loan and working capital through a single window, b) raising the limit on working capital requirements from Rs. 4 crore to Rs. 5 crore in the context of calculaton of working capital requirements for SSI units by banks at 20 per cent of the projected annual turnover, c) reckoning of lending by banks to non-banking financial companies (NBFCs) or other financial intermediaries for purposes of on-lending to the tiny sector as priority sector lending and, d) devising a new credit insurance scheme for small scale units to provide adequate security to banks and to improve recovery. For flow of funds to the micro enterprises the Budget also proposed that SIDBI and National Bank for

Agriculture and Rural Development should ensure coverage of at least 50,000 Self-Help Groups during the course of 1999-2000.

The package for SSI sector in the Budget 1999-2000 consisted of following provisions;

a) Under specific excise duty concession schemes for units manufacturing cosmetics, refrigeration and air-conditioning equiptment , the turnover under the eligibility criteria was doubled from Rs. 50 lakh to Rs. 100 lakh, duty free exemption limit was increased from Rs. 15 lakh to Rs. 30 lakh and clearnces eligible for duty at half the normal rates was increased from Rs. 15 lakh to Rs. 20 lakh.

b) The benefit of the SSI exemption limits was extended to small scale units producing cotton yarn.

c) Small job workers engaged in printing of glazed tiles were exempted from the incidence of excise duty.

d) SSI exemption was extended to goods bearing brand name of another manufacturer, when produced by units located in the rural areas.

e) Permission was granted to SSIs to pay excise duty on a monthly basis with effect from June 1999.

Credit Delivery to SSIs

Over the years, the Government of India and the Reserve Bank of India (RBI) have been constantly endeavouring to strengthen the credit delivery system for SSIs. In December 1997, RBI appointed a one-man Committee under the Chairmanship of Shri S.L.Kapur, former Secretary to Government of India, Ministry of Industry, Department of SSI and ARI to ;

a) review the working of credit delivery system for SSIs with a view to making the system more effective, simple and efficient to administer, b)make suggestions for simplification and improvements in systems and procedures, and

c) consider the ways and means of strengthening the existing internal mechanism in banks for redressal of customer grievances.

In its report submitted to RBI in June 1998, the Committee made 126 recommendations. The important recommendations having direct implications for SIDBI include : augmenting lendable resources of SIDBI at soft rates by the Government of India and RBI, according to SIDBI the role of stake holder and resource provider to the state level institutions, merging SIDBI's Mahila Udyam Nidhi Scheme with its National Equity Fund Scheme, covering at least 25,000 rural women per annum by SIDBI under Mahila Viaka Nidhi Scheme, giving a big push to the utilisation of SIDBI's Technology Development and Modernisation Fund Scheme setting up of (i) Reconstruction Fund' by SIDBI with the initiative coming from the Government RBI to provide margin money and (ii) Small Industries Infrastructure Development Fund' by RBI with the initial corpus of Rs. 1000 crore to be kept with SIDBI opening up of more branches by SIDBI in areas where SFCs are weak, delinking SIDBI from IDBI and setting up of a new Credit guarantee Corporation.

Out of the 126 recommendations of the Committee, RBI accepted 40 recommendations for implementation. Subsequently, banks were advised by RBI to :

a) delegate more powere for sanctioning the ad hoc limits up to 20 per cent of sanctioned loan limits to the branch manager,

b) meticulously implement the Nayak Committee recommendations on the norms of fixing eligible working capital limits,

c) open more specialised SSI branches or, as the case demands, to convert the existing branches at clusters having high concentration of SSI units as specialised SSI branches,

d) dispose of the loan applications up to Rs. 25,000/- within a fortnight and those above Rs. 25,000/- within 8-9 weeks,

e) introduce loan application form in tri-lingual format and

f) assess the credit to SSIs on the basis of disbursement rather than outstanding balance. RBI has enhanced the limit of composite loans from Rs. 2 lakh to Rs. 5 lakh.

RBI also advised the sponsor banks of REgional Rural Banks (RRBs) and SIDBI to provide crash training programme to the staff of RRBs for serving SSIs in a moe effective manner.

Credit Policy

In the monetary and credit policy policy announced by RBI in April 1998 , the Bank Rate was reduced from 10 per cent to 9 per cent and it was specified that interest rates on loans below Rs. 2 lakh should not exceed Prime Lending Rate (PLR) of the bank concerned. It was also proposed to bring forth a 'Discussion Paper' aiming to arrive at greater clarity in the roles of banks and financial institutions. At the time of mid term review of monetary and credit situation by RBI in October 1998, the industrial slow down was still persisting and overall inflation was higher than what was expected. The international experiences, particularly of South East Asia and Japan, brought to the fore the arguments for strengthening the financial sector. The thrust of the policy, therefore was on furthering the financial sector reforms in phases over a period of time. In the post-Budget announcement in March 1999, the RBI initiated measues to spur credit demand, revive the sagging economy and move interest rates in the country closer to global rates. RBI slashed the Bank Rate by one percentage point from 9 percent to 8 per cent effective March 1, 1999, the repo rate by two percentage points from 8 per cent to 6 per cent effective March 3, 1999and the cash reserve ratio (CRR) requirement of banks by 0.5 percentage point from 11 per cent to 10.5 per cent effective the fortnight beginning March 13, 1999. Consequently leading banks slashed the interest rates.

The monetary and credit policy for the year 1999-2000 announced in April 1999 , framed within the challenge of conflicting objectives of restraining the overall growth of liquidity in order to ensure price stability, and at the same time facilitating flow of adequate bank credit for productive sectors to improve growth, also intended to carry forward the direction of financial reforms initiated in the earlier years. The credit policy further reduced the CRR from 10.5 per cent to 10 per cent effective May 8, 1999 and introduced Interim Liquidity Adjustment through repos and collateralised lending facility. Thus RBI made its intentions clear that financial institutions and non-bank participants need to gradually move out of call money market. The freedom to operate loans with maturity-based PLRs and fixed rate loans has been given to banks by RBI with regard to micro credit, discretion has been bestowed on banks to decide the interest rate on loans to micro credit organisations or ultimate beneficiaries, subject to adherence to interest rate prescribed by RBI in respect of loans below certain levels. The credit policy also qualified incremental lending by banks to NBFCs for on-lenging to small road and water transport operators and tiny units to be priority sector lending.

Technology Upgradation Fund for Textile Industry

In spite of strong fibre and production base the textile industry in the country suffers from severe technological obsolescence and lack of economies of scale, for various historical reasons. Considering the fact that one of the important factors impeding the technological progress is high cost of capital the Government of India launched the Technology Upgradation Fund Scheme for the textile and jute industries with effect from April 1, 1999 for a period of 5 years.

The main feature of the scheme is 5 percentage point reimbursement on the interest actually charged on loans provided by the identified financial institutions for technology upgradation projects. Cover for adverse exchange rate fluctuation not exceeding 5 per cent in respect of foreign currency loans would also be provided. SIDBI has been appointed as the nodal agency for SSI textile sector and cotton ginning and pressing sector.

Amended Exim Policy 1999-2000

The modified Export-Import Policy for the year 1999-2000 announced on March 31, 1999 has further liberalised foreign trade by cutting down the negative list of imports, expanding the free and special import licence list and proposing to convert all existing Export Processing Zones {EPZx} into free trade zones. The new policy has moved 1308 items from the restrictive list (including 894 items from the current negative list) to the Special Import Licence (SIL)/Open General Licence (OGL). The threshold limit for zero duty Export Promotion Capital Goods (EPCG) Scheme has been brought down from Rs. 20 crore to Rs. 1crore for chemicals, plastic and textiles, enabling these sectors to upgrade themselves technological and become globally competitive. The policy has also announced duty-free import of consumables up to certain limits for gems and jewellery, handicraft and leather sectors.

The policy changes introduced for gems and jewelly industry include permission to export jewellery through courier or through personal carriage, introduction of 'Diamond Imprest' licence with a view to allowing import of cut and polished diamonds for mixing with local cut and polished diamonds or for export in the same condition with 10 per cent value addition and permission to import consumbales to the extent of 1 per cent FOB value of exports of the previous the country for the year 2003 when all quantitative restrictions on imports will be droppd by India as per the World Trade Organisation norms. The impact of the present amended Exim Policy on high growth sectors, such as gems and jewellery, information technology, agricultural products, plastics, chemicals, textiles, etc. with perceptible presence in the SSI sector, is expected to be significant.

Bank Credit to SSIs

As at the end of March 1998, outstanding bank credit to SSIs from public sector banks, private sector banks and foreign banks in India aggregated Rs. 46,041 crore accounting for a share of 17.3 per cent in the net bank credit. During 1997-98, the outstanding credit to SSIs had increased by Rs. 7909 crore, i.e. by 20.7 per cent.

Specialised SSI Branches of Commercial Banks

The policy of operationing specialised commercial bank branches for SSIs continued during the year. The cumulative number of specialised commercial bank branches for SSIs stood at 379 as at December 1998.

Performance of Small Scale Sector

Against the backdrop of subdued industrial scenario in general, the performance of small scale sector by far remained satisfactory during 1998-99. The number of SSI units is estimated to have increased to about 31.21 lakh in 1998-99 from 30.14 lakh in 1997-98. The estimated real growth in production of modern SSIs at around 9.9 per cent in 1998-99 is higher than the growth of 8.4 per cent achieved in 1997-98.

The production of Village and Small Industries (VSI) Sector in 1998-99 is estimated to have increased to Rs. 6,31,463 crore from from Rs. 5,46,547 crore during 1997-98. The production of modern SSIs is estimated to be Rs. 5,38,357 crore in 1998-99 as against Rs. 4,65,171 crore in 1997-98. The employment in the VSI sector is estimated to have increased to 585 lakh persons as at the end-March 1999 from 562 lakh persons as at end-March 1998 creating an additional employment of 23 lakh during the year . The estimated exports from SSIs at Rs. 49,481 crore in 1998-99 reflects a growth of 11.4 per cent during the year and accounts for a share of 35.8 per cent in the total exports of the country for the year at Rs. 1,38,211 crore. The estimated aggregate exports from VSI sector at Rs. 90,730 crore in 1998-99 account for a share of 65.6 per cent in the country's total exports. (Table-3).

Prospects

At the threshold of the next millennium, two sets of issues have come to the fore. First, the role and functions of Development Financial Institutions (DFIs), including SIDBI, in the context of ongoing financial sector reforms which have entered into a more challenging phase, and the second, institutional orientation to support the diverse needs of SSIs which in turn, are changing in the dynamic environment.

following the recommendations of the Khan Working Group, RBI in consultation with Government of India, brought out a discussion paper in January, 1999 containing draft proposals for bringing more clarity in respective roles of banks and financial institutions and for greater harmonisation of facilities and obligations applicable to them.

The discussion paper highlighted gradual blurring of traditional functions of banks and DFIs and emphasised that the evolutionary process of universal banking should be guided both by international experience and domestic requirements. The process of enabling, both by banks and DFIs, the provision of diversified services, either in-house or through the subsidiary route as a conglomerate, should continue, albeit in a gradual and orderly fashion, subject to appropriate regulartion and supervision.

Table-1

Performance of Village and Small Industries Sector

	Production (Rs. Crore)		*Employment (Lakh Nos.)*		*Exports (Rs. Crore)*	
	Achievement 1997-98	*Anticipated 1998-99*	*Achievement 1997-98*	*Anticipated 1998-99*	*Achievemen t 1997-98*	*Anticipated 1998-99*
A. Modern SSIs						
SSIs	4,65,171	5,38,357	167	172	44,437	49,481
Powerlooms	23,365	21,108	38	40	4,520	4,856
Sub-total	4,88,536	5,59,465	205	212	48,957	54,337
B. Traditional Industries						
Khadi	624	708	15	16	Neg.	Neg.
Village Industries	3,895	4,447	46	48	12	13
Handlooms	16,200	23,389	153	160	1,855	2,003
Sericulture	1,542	1,766	61	64	926	1,036
Handicrafts	34,650	40,538	77	80	26,688	33,059
Coir	1,100	1,150	5	5	239	282
Sub-total	58,011	71,998	357	373	29,720	36,393
Total	**5,46,547**	**6,31,463**	**562**	**585**	**78,677**	**90,730**

Note: Figures for 1998-99 are provisional based on estimates made by respective authorities and SIDBI. Neg. Negligible.

Sources: DC (SSI), Office of the Textile Commissioner, Cotton Textile Export Promotion Council, KVIC, DC-Handlooms, Handloom Export Promotion Council, Central Silk Board, DC-Handicrafts, The Gem and Jewellery Export Promotion Council and Goir Board.

While recognising the special role of DFIs in the present institutional infrastructure, the discussion paper advocated that a DFI should have the option to become a bank subject t fully conforming to all prudential, regulatory and supervisory norms as applicable to banks, or evolve as an NBFC. However, the question of transformation of a DFI into a bank should ideally be considered after a period, say of five years from now, in view of the following reasons:

Firstly, DFIs will continue to be an important source of finance for the capital needs of the industries till the capital market, especially debt market, is fully developed.

Secondly, DFIs have project appraisal capabilities, which other financial intermediaries are yet to develop.

Thirdly, the financial sector has to develop along with financial markets to provide adequate competitive services by all financial intermediaries.

Fourthly, DFIs themselves will have to plan for and acquire necessary expertise in offering various banking services in-house and develop an appropriate branch network.

Finally, the policy environment as well as regulatory and supervisory framework should also be evolved for such a transformation of DFIs into banks. Considering the above, the harmonisation in the working of banks and DFIs into banks. Considering the above, the harmonisation in the working of banks and DFIs should be at their own initiative, with RBI available for guidance and consultation. SIDBI has initiated measures to reposition itslef in this changing scenario.

Historically, the small scale sector has been consistently outperforming the large scale sector. Nevertheless, the sector has to overcome a number of daunting challenges thrown up by a liberalised, fast changing and highly competitive environment. The challenges are of varying nature and degree, encompassing those orignating from within the domestic sector as well as from the international sector.

In the wake of globalisation and intensified competition from both domestic and foreign companies, the most important challenge before the SSIs is to effect, at the earliest both embodied and disembodied technological upgradation. The small scale enterpreneurs have to be made aware of the gravity and impending nature of these issues and in some cases supported to bridge the technology gap. A number of problems continue to besiege the sector on the technology front such as lack of proper co-ordination among SSIs, R &D institutions and Government, lack of information network regarding the availability of new and suitable technology, cumbersome procedures in transfer of technology, difficulties in proper evaluation of new technology, etc. All these issues need to be suitably tackled and concerted efforts need to be initiated by theSSIs, SIDBI and other institutions involved, for this sector to make a quantum leap towards the next millennium.

If Indian SSI sector has to become globally competitive, the main issues which would need immediate attention are setting up of technology information exchange with regular display of latest technologies, simpler procedures for technology transfer, availability of soft funding for upgradation and modernisation, competitive R & D facilities, better industry orientation of national research laboratories, good facilities for export of Indian technologies, etc. Further, the growing complexity of world economic structure characterised by customs unions, trade blocks and increasing recourse to non-tariff barriers by developed countries are other roadblocks for faster growth of SSI exports from India. In addition, as the global trade is expected to be increasingly channelised by World Trade Organisation, the costs thereof have to be borne mainly by industries of the third world countries, including Indian SSIs. Such challenges, however, also provide vast opportunities for SSIs to attain self-sustained growth in future.

Yet another problem pertains to the availability of adequate and timely assistance to the smaller of the SSIs. The issues which need to be addressed in this regard include introducing a scheme for credit insurance or credit guarantee so that collateral security is not insisted upon for smaller loans, providing tax benefits to financial intermediaries, opening of more specialised branches, developing the bills culture and more importantly, providing low cost funds to SIDBI as already recommended by major committees, to enable it to discharge its obligations towards SSIs more effectively.

The SSIs at the upper end of the spectrum can gain through changing their organisational and structural form. Certain impediments to adjust themselves to the changing environment emanate from the present form and structure of a vast majority of SSI units. They ae either proprietorship concerns or partnership firms. To facilitate them to emerge as corporate enities, what may be needed is a set of definite policies with adequate incentives to motivate and induce them to adapt to the changing times these SSIs should also be encouraged to increase their capital base through mergers, amalgamations, takeovers, etc. and to go in for credit rating. Alongside, SSIs also need to upgrade their managerial capabilities and technological skills which would call for training the small scale entrepreneurs on frontier areas of technology and greater interaction of the entrepreneurs with the specialised academic, R&D and training institutions. Aboveall, SSIs should lay greater emphasis on in-house R&D for technology upgradation.

In the current transitionary process of integrating India with the world economy, the SSIs require strong institutional support in therms of effective marketing and information about international markets to enable them to strengthen their competitive advantage. As the S.L. Kapur Committee report on credit to SSI pointed out, SSIneed "to develop a global vision, respond to more demanding standards of the customers, identify the patterns of shifting value and craft the key strategies that will leapfrog them ahead of competition." Clearly this is a gigantic task which necessitates coordinated and concerted efforts with a sense of urgency from various banking and financial institutions, promotional agencies, entrepreneurs and, more importantly, the Government. Only then will the SSIs in India be able to successfully meet the onslaught of the challenges of the emerging economic environment in the twenty-first century.

The year that has gone by has been by and large a strainful year for the economy in general and the industrial sector in particular. The small scale industries had to bear, perhaps in the greater measure, the hardship arising out of diverse pulls and pressures in the operating environment . SIDBI as an institution for the SSIs at the apex level, readjusted its approach, refined its process and adopted certain business strategies so as to reduce the intensity of the adverse impact on SSIs in this situation. The thrust of SIDBI, besides ensuring higher flow of credit to SSIs, has been to forge technology adoption and upgradation through its 'Techno-mission and to foster, through a multi agency participation process, specialised venture funds and institutions to meet the needs of high growth SSI sub-sectors such as information technology, food processing and bio-technology and at the same time empower women and rural youth through provision of micro credit. The wide canvas of the small scale industries in the country requires SIDBI to adopt a balanced approach to meet the demands of every segment of SSIs. The chapters which follow discuss the policy initiatives, operations and the promotional and developmental services provided by SIDBI to support SSIs to maintain their overall effectiveness and performance.

Problems of small Scale and Cottage Industries

Small scale and cottage industries are very important for Indian economy. But they can play right role if they are free from problems unfortunately, at present , these industries face many difficulties and inadeuqacies . Some of the problems being faced by these industries are as follows :-

1.*Problem of Raw Materials* : Small scale and cottage industries face the following problems in respect of raw materials (i) Raw materials available to these industries are of inferior quality because large scale industries through their better capacity commers the materials of high quality (ii) As small scale industries are unable in buying in bulk they have to pay the higher prices. (iii) Generally, these industries do not get raw materials on time.

2. *Problem of Technique* : In most of the cases the method and techniques of production adopted by small scale and cottage industries are old and of low technological level. The entrepreneurs are neither able to buy new equipments , nor do they know much about new methods and technology.

3. *Problem of finance* : Another difficulty of small scale and cottage industries is of finance. Adequate and cheap credit facilities are not available to them . Banks and other financial institutional still hesitate in granting loans and advances to these industries. The result is that many small producers are handicapped for want of finance.

4. *Problem of Marketing* : A very serious difficulty faced by small producers is in the field of marketing. They do not have any proper marketing organisation to sell their output at remunerative prices. Besides these producers find it very difficult to complete with large scale producers in the sale of their products.

5. *Competition from large Scale Industries* : Large scale industries organised on modern lines, they use latest technology and they get many facilities. The result of which is that they produce goods and services of high quality at low cost. On the other hand, small scale and cottage industries are not properly organised they use out-dated technology and they do not get high quality and their cost of production is high. Therefore, small producers cannot stand up against them in the market.

6. *Problem of under -utilisatin of Capacity* : In many cases , is has been the experience that industries are useing only about 50% of their installed capacity.

7. *Inadequacy of Power* : Small scale and cottage industries do not get adequate power. As a result , their production remains much less than their capacity.

8. *Lack of Efficient Management* : Most of small scale and cottage industries are managed by their owners themselves who are not necessarily efficient managers. The result is that these industries are managed in traditional manner.

9. *lack of Standardisation and Gradation* : These industries do not adopt the technique of standardisation and gradation. As a result they do not get high prices for their products.

10. *Lack of Research information and Data* : There is lack of research facilities in the field of small scale and cottage industries. Besides , these entrepreneurs do not get complete information of their industry in time. The result is that they are unable in introducing new products in their line.

Steps Taken by Government to encourage small scale and Cottage Industries

Several concrete measures have been adopted by the government to encourage the development of small scale and cottage industries. Some of the important steps taken up by the government are as follows :

1. *Establishment of Boards and Corporation* : A number of institutions has been set up by the Government to provide most of its help and support of small scale and cottage industries. These institutions are of various types and render different types of facilities to these industries to meet their various and peculiar needs. Some of the important organisations are (i) National Small Industries Corporation (ii) Small Scale industries Development Organisation (iii) All India Handloom and Hnadicrafts Boards (iv) The Coir Board (v) Central Silk board (vi) Khadi and village Industries commission (vii) State Khadi and village Industries boards etc. All these industries /institute have framed an infrastructure of the development of these industries.

2. *Financial Assistance* : Measures have been adopted to provided large credit to these industries on liberal terms through several agencies like commercial bank, co-operative banks, Regional Rural Banks, State Financial Corporations etc. These agencies are providing credit both for short terms and log term purposes at liberal terms and concessional rate of interest. These industries have been included in priority sector for commercial bank lending. All the possible efforts are being made to reduce the dependence of these industries on money-lenders and traders.

3. *Technical Assistance* : Adequate technical facilities have been provided by the government to these industries . Small Industries Development organisation is providing technical assistance and consultation to small producers. This organisation is running 26 service institute , 40 extention centres, 7 training centre 2+2 = 4 regional test centres and 1 product and process centre . This centre provided technical assistance to 7.41 lakh small entrepreneurs in 1982-83.

4. *Marketing Facilities* : Central Collage Industries Emporium was setup up by government of India in 1949. This emporium provides help in the marketing of products of cottage

industries within and outside the country. In addition to this several co-operative marketing societies have also been established . These societies are making great contribution in the marketing of goods produced by these industries.

5. *Licencing concession* : Small Scale Cottage industries have been granted many concessions in licence policy. according to licence policy of 1970, the production of some commodities has been reserved for this sector . At present the number of such commodities is 873.

6. *Priority in government Purchases :* Government helps these industries by giving them priority in Government purchases. Government makes some of its purchases exclusively from small scale and cottage industries. The number of such commodities has gone up from 16 in 1956 to 404 in 1995.

7. *Tax and other Concessions :* Government has exempted many products of these industries from excise duty. On many other products neglibible duty has been imposed. Some more concessions has also been announced line concessions in Freight power rate etc.

8. *Organisation of Exhibitions* : Exhibitions are organised from time to time at different places of the country to make the products of small scale and cottage industries popular among public.

9. *Establishment of Industrial Co-operatives :* Government is encouraging co-operative organisation in this sector . At present over 45,000 industrial co-operative societies are working in 1996 , National Federation of Industrial co-operative was set up with a view to provide help to these industries the marketing and export.

10. *National Institute for Entrepreneurship and Small Business Development* : This institute was set up in July 1983 the object of this institute is to provide training for small entrepreneurs and to co-ordinate the activities of various institutes and agencies engaged in training activities. This institute holds examination and confers certificates and diplomas on trainees. It conducts seminars workshops and conferences for officers . It undertake research also.

11. *National Award:* To give recognition and encouragement to entrepreneurs in small scale sector, a scheme for National Awards has been introduced from the year F198_84 . first three awards carry a cash prize of Rs. 25,000 Rs. 20,000 and Rs. 15,000 respectively.

Above discussion makes it clear that Government has taken various steps for the development of small scale and cottage industries . The need is to implement all these programms and schemes effectively.

****

10

Public Sector in India : Its Growth and Problems

State intervention in the economic activities is no longer an economic anathema or political taboo, as it was in the past. It is now regarded as an inescapable part of the obligations of present-day governments to redress economic imbalances, to safeguard the interests and welfare of the community as a whole, to plan for overall rapid progress and prosperity and to undertake and execute scheme and projects vital to the needs of the nation. There is very little doubt that the future of a developing country and its ability to meet national aspiration or removal of poverty and faster improvement in living standards would largely depend upon the role assigned to public enterprises there. These enterprises have been developed there out of necessity and not on account of any dogmatic approach and, in fact, there has been no choice before the government of such economics. Hanson rightly stated that, "Whatever the ultimate perspective may be, the country anxious to develop economically has no alternative but to use public enterprise on a considerable scale, at the very least in order to get things going."[1] He has also gone to the extent of saying that "Public enterprise without a plan can achieve. something, a plan without public enterprise is likely to remain on paper."

The Concept of Public Enterprise

Often, there is a misconception or confusion about the term 'public enterprise'. Such a confusion arises as these enterprises are called by a variety of names. For instance, they are stated as 'Public sector undertakings', 'Nationalized industries'. 'Socialised industries', 'State-owned industries', 'State enterprises', 'Government concerns,' etc. The annual report regarding the working of public enterprises, published by the Bureau of Public Enterprises, uses the term 'industrial and commercial undertakings of the central government'. The Administrative Reforms Commission has used the term 'public sector undertakings' in its report. The Standing Committee of Parliament calls them as 'public undertakings'.

In foreign countries the term has been used in conformity with their political and administrative structures. They are known as Public Corporation (Great Britain), Crown Corporation (Canada), Statutory Corporation (Australia), Government Sponsored Corporation (Pakistan), Government Corporation (USA). In Italy, the term is used to refer public corporations, municipalities and autonomous government departments. In France, the term is used to a restricted sphere, i.e., industrial and commercial undertakings of the government.

Definitions

In order to do away with the difficulty of terminology, the definitions given by the authorities on the subject have been examined below :

A. H. Hanson states that "Public enterprises mean state ownership and operation of industrial, agricultural, financial and commercial undertakings."The term has been used here in a more familiar sense and the coverage of enterprises is very specific.

Encyclopedia Britannica— "The term usually refers to government ownership and active operation of agencies engaged in supplying the public the goods and services which alternatively might be supplied by privately owned profit motivated firms (private enterprise)" The definition has laid emphasis on government ownership and absence of profit motive.

N. N. Mallya has laid more emphasis on the autonomous character and stated as follows: "Public enterprises are autonomous or semiautonomous corporations and companies established, owned and controlled by the state and engaged in industrial and commercial activities."

S. S. Khera contends that "By public enterprise is meant the industrial, commercial and economic activities carried on by the central government or by a state government or jointly by the central government and a state government and in each case either solely or in association with private enterprise, so long as it is managed by a self-contained management." The definition has stressed the following points:

(i) It covers the industrial, commercial and economic activities.

(ii) State ownership whether by the Center or by the state forms the basis for a state enterprise.

(iii) It is managed by a self-contained managerial cadre.

Fridman defines public enterprise as "an institution operating a service of an economic or social character, on behalf of the government, but as an independent legal entity, largely autonomous in its management, though responsible to the public, through government and Parliament and subject to some direction, by the government, equipped on the other hand with independent and separate funds of its own and the legal and commercial attributes of a commercial enterprise."[6] The definition is comprehensive and has covered almost all the important features of PE, i.e., government ownership, autonomous functioning, accountability to public through government and Parliament, separate financial system, etc.

Main Characteristics

The analysis of the above mentioned definitions reveals following main characteristics of public enterprises:

1. *Government Ownership*— The public enterprises should either be wholly owned by the central government or state government (s) or local authority or jointly owned by two or more of them. Government ownership means that more than 50% of the equity is being held by a public authority. If the enterprise is owned by the government and private persons, the state must have the predominant share (at least 51%) in the ownership of such enterprises. Section 617 of the Indian Companies Act clearly specifies that 'Government company means any company in which not less than fifty one per cent of the paid up share capital is held by the central government or by any state government or central government partly and partly by one or more state governments." Further, the public corporations and the departmental undertakings and fully owned by the government. It has to be kept in mind that the public enterprises do not include the enterprises functioning under co-operative sector. Recently, the state government of Uttar Pradesh has included the co-operative enterprises under public sector fold.

2. *Government Control and Management*— Public enterprises are managed by the government or the public authority. If a public enterprise is operating under the management of private institutions, it does not mean that it has become a private enterprise. The essential condition for a PE is that the government has got a right to manage and control the affairs of the enterprise. In the USA, the Atomic Energy Commission is managed by private institutions and even then it is called a PE.

3. *Public Accountability*— The enterprises are provided funds from the public exchequer. It becomes imperative that they should be accountable to the public through Parliament, whose funds are invested to carry on the activities of the enterprises. This goal is achieved through ministers, government, Parliament, audit bodies, etc.

4. *Constituent of Political and Administrative Structure*— The establishment and continuance of PE is a political decision and its operations are controlled at strategic

points by a system where the politicians have the final say. Though efforts have been made to insulate PE from the pernicious external effects the result has not been encouraging, particularly in developing countries. Thus, these enterprises at present are considered as constituent of political and administrative structure.

5. *Public Purpose*— The private enterprise is essentially a business proposition in which public purpose finds a subsidiary or peripheral position and in no case supersedes business considerations. In PE, social aspects can well precede, supersede and even completely engulf business considerations. The public interest in various forms and shape provides as under-current for all its strategic decisions.

6. *Wide Coverage a Activities*— The public enterprises are not established for a specific line of activity of manufacturer. They cover varied range of activities. 'If we exclude agriculture, home trade, and a few other areas, mostly in the unorganized sectors like lorry transportation, it pervades the economy world today.' In India, specially after independence, the PEs are operating in almost every ara, viz, contruction, marketing, agriculture, finance, development, mining, etc.

7. *Economic Enterprise*— In a public enterprise, the price charged for its goods and services is expected to cover the cost. In some cases, the price charged may not cover the cost, but the aim is that in the long run the enterprise as a whole would at least break even. Hospitals, universities and a few public utilities like railways, posts and telegraphs charge a fee for their service, but as it does not cover, and it is also not intended to cover the cost, such activities are not PE, though owned and managed by the state.

8. *Autonomous Functioning*— In spite of the initial huge investment made by the government, the PEs are provided sufficient autonomy to mange their affairs in their own fashion. The self-contained management has the right to manage the affairs on the basis of sound business considerations

and prudent commercial practices. The government does not interfere in their day-to-day activities. The finances of these enterprises are kept separate from the public exchequer. Departmental undertakings are exception to this financial autonomy.

Thus, public enterprise can be defined as "an activity of the government, whether central, state or local, involving manufacturing or production of goods including agriculture, or making available, it has a sound blending of public purpose, public accountability, autonomous functioning and inherent right to manage and control the enterprise by the government."

Role of the Public Sector in Economic Development

It is experience of all developing nations that the public sector plays a very important role in economic development. Indeed its role has to be a dominant one if economic development is to be accelerated. The public sector in India is also intended to fulfil some of the specific objectives of planning. These includes as follows:

Main Points of Difference	*Public Enterprise*	*Private Enterprise*
1. Motive	Service motive	Profit motive
2. Nature of Industry	Capital Intensive and Risky Industries	Comparatively little requirement of capital and lesser amount of risk
3. Performance	Surplus generation, Cost of Production, Productivity andContribution to Exchequer	Profitability mainly
4. Secretary	Except in defence,secrecy is not maintained	Secrecy is maintained
5. Autonomy	Comparatively lesser autonomy is given to top officials	They are autonomous units.

6. Risk	risk is not personal in nature	Risk is personal by nature.
7. Market Condition	Monopolistic inmajority of the case	Competitive in majority of the cases.
8. Pricing	Administered pricing	Not so.
9. Public Accountability	government and Parliament facilitate public accountability.	It is not so in the case.
10. Audit control	Audit by CAG is must	It is not compulsory.
11. Social overheads	They have to act as model employer	It is not so in this case.
12. Flexibility	Lack of flexibility ofbureaucracy and governmental interference.	This attribute is present in decision-making and control
13. Role in Industrial Policy	Prime role has been assigned.	Secondary role hasbeen assigned.

1. *Achieving Socialistic Pattern*— The achievement of the object of a socialistic pattern of society in India has made it necessary for the Government to assume direct responsibility for developing certain industries. "In an under-developed country, a high rate of economic progress and the development of a large public sector and a co-operative sector are among the principal means for effecting transition towards socialism". Expansion of the public sector is expected to counter the tendency towards monopolies and concentration of economic power which is socially undesirable.

2. *Building Industrial Base*— The Planning Commission observes: "The public sector is expected to provide specially for the further development of industries of basic and strategic importance or in the nature of public utility services, other industries being also taken up by the Government to the extent necessary".

The public sector has to pioneer some of the key but difficult projects where gestation periods are very long and full output can be reached only after several years of operation. Thus the role of the public sector has been confined to industries of growth-generating and infrastructure type. In fact, the public sector has assisted their expansion from Plan to Plan.

3. *Capital Formation*— It is now realised that capital formation is the key to economic growth. By creating opportunities for investment, the Government encourages the people to save and invest. The Government can also increase collective savings through taxation and borrowing. The Government can also resort to deficit financing. In these ways it ca mobilise resources required for speedy economic development.

4. *Social Overheads*— It is for the public sector to create social overheads like Institutions for reached and general and technical education, hospitals, etc. The private investor cannot be expected to put his capital in such projects where no money return can be expected. The returns in the form of better health and higher education and technical skills accrue to the whole society rather than to the individual investors.

5. *Economic Overheads*—The investment in economic overheads too is too large to be within the reach of any individual investor. Moreover, the return from such investment is not only low but it is realised only after a long time. Only the public sector can, therefore, make investment in economic overheads like roads, railways and ports. Economic overheads create external economies for other industries and accelerate economic growth.

6. *Optimum Allocation of Resources*— The public sector-plays an important role in bringing about optimum allocation of resources in the community so that economic development is promoted. The resources are likely to be misallocated by private enterprise guided by profit motive. For instance, private investment may be directed to the production

of non-essential goods for the rich, whereas the production of essential goods for the masses may be neglected. It is only the public sector which can be guided by considerations of social welfare.

7. *Balanced and Unbalanced Growth*— The Nurkesian doctrine of balanced growth requires investment simultaneously in capacity of private entrepreneurs. Similarly, planned unbalanced development as propounded by Prof. Hirshcsman will be out of the question in a purely private sector, because investment has to be made in some specific fields to generate maximum external economies. Public sector has, therefore, necessarily to step in to accelerate economic development.

8. *Balanced Regional Development*— The private sector will not hazard investment in backward and comparatively under-developed regions. But the development of such regions is considered socially desirable. Only the public sector can be relied upon to do this. The Government can create infrastructure in these regions and quicken their growth.

9. *Social Objectives*— There are several desirable social objectives for which Governments in the under-developed countries can only rely on the public sector will prevent the concentration of income and wealth in a few hands. Profits of public enterprises can be utilised for promoting general social welfare. Then there is he removal of disguised unemployment by diverting surplus labour from agriculture to productive spheres.

10.*Creation of Investible Surpluses*— The profits in the private sector are squandered away in conspicuous consumption, but the profits of public enterprises can be ploughed back in business.

Thus the role of public sector in promoting economic development cannot be over-emphasised. In the words of Prime Minister, Mrs. Indira Gandhi, "We advocate public sector for three reasons : to gain control of the commanding highest of the economy; to promote critical development in terms of social gains or strategic value rather than primarily on consideration of profit; and to provide commercial surpluses with which to finance further economic

Growth of Public Enterprises

The growth of PEs over the years could be traced to the declaration of the industrial policy resolutions and decisions to embark on the path of planned economic development.

The first industrial policy resolution was declared in 1948, which laid heavy emphasis on the setting up, growth, development, and acquisition of industries in the public sector. On account of socio-economic and political compulsions, the 1948 Industrial Policy Resolution was altered in 1956. The 1956 Industrial Policy Resolution demarcated certain industries for both the public and private sectors; and the Company-existence of the public and private sectors was acknowledged as a major thrusts of industrial policy. The aim of establishing a socialistic society was to be achieved through the control of private industry, on the one hand, and the progressive growth of public sector, on the other. The 1977 Industrial Policy Resolution, which was adopted by the Janta government, attempted to reduce the stronghold of the public sector on the national economy. This trend was, however, reversed in 1980 when the Congress (I) was voted back to power, which restored to the public sector the place it had in the Industrial Policy Resolution of 1956. The present government at the center has re-endorsed its policy of following this resolution in the future. it is, however exposing the PEs to the private sector in India and also to the international economy, which is a part and parcel of its *economic liberalisation process,* designed to make the public and private sectors competitive and stand on their own ground.

After deciding to follow the path of planned economic development in 1951, eight five-year plans and three annual plans have been completed and presently we are in the ninth five-year plan period. The plan outlays indicate that on an average two-thirds of the plan allocations have gone in favour of the public sector. The development strategy during the plan periods has been one of extensive growth of heavy industrial base combined with the green revolution which were risky areas for the private sector in terms of investment. Greater emphasis has been laid on the expansion of infrastructural facilities.

There has been a considerable growth of PEs in terms of the number and investment as indicated in Table 1.

Causes of Growth

In view of the important role that the public sector plays in economic development, it is only natural that it should have progressively expanded since we launched planned development in India in 1951. The following are the main reasons for the expansion of the public sector in India:–

1. *Accelerated Economic Growth*— It has been realised that unless Government actively participates in carrying out development programmes, the rate of growth will continue to be painfully slow. The rate of economic growth as measured in national income has been much faster during the last 15 years (about 65 per cent) when the public sector participated than in the previous 50 years (about 10 per cent) when the private sector remained supreme. Obviously the private entrepreneurs cannot be expected to exercise sufficient forethought; they will pickup rich quick schemes and will not be bothered about the overall rate of growth of the company. "In the scheme of development, while making full use of all available agencies, the public sector is expected to grow both absolutely and in comparison and at a faster rate than the private sector".

2. *Even Distribution of Economic Power*— The public sector has been enlarged progressively with a view to bringing about more even distribution of economic power. If the economic enterprise is left entirely to private entrepreneurs they will

Table 1

Growth of Investment in PEs

Period	Total investment (Rs. in crores)	Number of enterprises
1	2	3
At the Commencement of the First Five Year Plan (1.4.1951)	29	5
At the Commencement of the Second Five Year Plan (1.4.1956)	81	21
At the Commencement of the Third Five Year Plan (1.4.1961)	953	48
At the Commencement of the Forth Five Year Plan (1.4.1969)	3,902	85
At the Commencement of the Fifth Five Year Plan (1.4.1974)	6,237	122
At the Commencement of the Sixth Five Year Plan	18,150	179
At the Commencement of the Seventh Five Year Plan (1.4.1985)	42673	215
At the end of Seventh Five Year Plan (31.3.1990)	99329	244
At the Commencement of the Eighth Five Plan (1.4.1992)	135445	246
At the end of Eighth Five Year Plan (31.3.1997)	206655	242
As on 31.3.1998	221987	240
As on 31.3.1999	230140	240

Source : Bureau of Public Enterprises, *Public Enterprises Survey*, 1998- 99, Vol. I, Government of India, New Delhi, p. 168.

enrich themselves at the expense of the community. The rich people become richer still. But in the case of public enterprises the profits go to the State and can be utilised to promote general economic welfare. Labour can also be more generously treated. Prices can also be so fixed as to benefit the poor. In these and several other ways the public sector can be used as a powerful instrument for narrowing the gulf between the rich and the poor and for reducing disparities in income and wealth which are otherwise accentuated from generation to generation.

3. *Socialistic Pattern*— The Indian constitution lays down the establishment in India of a socialistic pattern of society as a fundamental objective of State Policy. Obviously movement towards socialism necessitates the setting up of State enterprises or expansion of the public sector. Under socialistic pattern, private enterprise cannot be left free to operate unfettered over the entire economic field. Naturally, the public sector has expanded to take the country towards the goal of an egalitarian society.

4. *Pattern of Investment*— The desired pattern of investment has also resulted in the expansion of the public sector. In some spheres of industry, it becomes essential for the State to come forward, make investment and take over the entrepreneurial risks. For instance, projects requiring huge outlay like the iron and steel plants, projects requiring long gestation period like the steel plants and the multipurpose river valley projects public utilities and other enterprises which have to be run on no-profit, no-loss basis or the basic and the heavy industries which are necessary for helping other industries are all such enterprises which have to be taken up by the State.

5. *Balanced Regional Development*— The public sector has also expanded to bring about a balanced development of the country. Local resources being inadequate or the prospects

not being otherwise bright, private entrepreneurs generally neglect backward areas. The State being the custodian of general welfare of the community cannot adopt such a callous attitude. The development of under-developed regions is, therefore, more a special responsibility of the public sector.

6. *Resource Mobilisation*— Effort to resource mobilisation has led to the expansion of the public sector. Income from public sector enterprises is an important source of funds required for development. The private entrepreneurs are keen on getting higher dividends but the public enterprises are in a better position to plough back profits into business.

7. *External Aid*— We need foreign assistance for economic development and we are lucky enough to secure it from both the capitalist and the socialist blocs. But the aid from the socialist countries is given only for the public sector. Foreign aid so obtained has resulted in the expansion of the public sector.

Conclusion— Thus to give speed and direction to our economic development, to prevent concentration of economic power, to bring about balanced regional development and to bring about a more desirable pattern of investment, it has been found necessary to expand the public sector in India.

Problems & Suggestions

An unbiased scrutiny and analysis of the working of PEs in India reveal a glaring fact that their failures outweigh the achievements. Their contribution in the form of strengthening infrastructural base; enhancement of employment opportunities, reduction in regional imbalances, increase in production, etc., lose their significance when we focus our attention to certain glaring lapses observed in their functioning. This brings us to ponder over the manifold diversified, though complex marginal problems which our PEs are facing on the threshold of twenty-firs century and highlight those problems along with the suggestions, wherever necessary.

1. Political Interference in Choice of Location

In many instances, it has been found that political interference has influenced the decisions concerning the location of projects. Powerful Ministers in the ruling party make promises about future location of project in a state irrespective of the results of the feasibility study about costs. This approach leads to considerable wastage of capital resources

2. Ambiguous Government Policy

The Government has not yet laid down the criteria for selecting one form of organisation or the other for the various PEs. In the Industrial Policy Resolution of 1956, no categorical statement was made regarding the choice o the form of organisation. The pronounced Government philosophy in favour of public corporations has not been changed in other policy documents and declarations.

3. Ineffective Government Control

The ARC found that while the span of Government control was wider than it need be, the effectiveness of control was not adequate. It added : "Ineffective control is worse than no control because it inhibits the operational initiative by an external control apparatus. It fails in its objective of regulating matters in those areas where regulation is essentially required". It is, therefore, necessary that Government control is not diffused and dispersed over a wide area, but is confined to basic things and key points, and is planned carefully.

4. Conflicting Objectives

PEs India have been set up with multidimensional objectives which are conflicting in nature. The objectives unlike that of private enterprises, economic as well as non-economic, are often not possible, in practice, to fulfil both simultaneously. Late smt. Indira Gandhi had said that a public sector is advocated to promote critical development in terms of social gains or strategic value rather than primarily on considerations of profit as well to provide commercial surpluses with which to finance further economic development. These two objectives are conflicting with each other-one emphasises social and strategic importance and the other recognises the urgent need of internal resource generation.

5. Problem of Autonomy

The PEs must be delegated effective authority and be encouraged to take decisions for which they are held responsible. The effort should be that PEs stand on their own rather than continue to remain tied to the Government which would frustrate the basic purpose of creating autonomous units. Under no circumstance should the Government try to take over the functions of the enterprise itself in its anxiety to bring it on the track or increase the overseeing function to the point of making the enterprise feel cramped.

6. Lack of Initiative and Operational Autonomy

In almost all the forms of organisation, initiative and operational autonomy, so essential for effective operations of industrial and commercial enterprises, are lacking. For departmental form of organisation, the First Five Year Plan had stated that, "The drawbacks of departmental management of PEs are well known. Successful conduct of such enterprises required a great deal of initiative and power o take quick decisions on the past of the executive incharge, and these can hardly be secured if the enterprise is under Government department". The public corporations, set up by the statutes enacted by Parliament, do not have any operational autonomy as the modifications, if desired, can only be made by Parliament itself. Even the company form of organisation does not assure autonomy in the real sense as "the extent of autonomy that it provides for can be materially affected or altered by executive agencies of the Government".

7. Competition with Private Sector Enterprises

Stiff and cut-throat competition in case of elastic products increases the advertising expenditure. The unit, if it is in a monopolistic position for an inelastic product, can enjoy a good market for its sale operations. Bakeries at Kanpur is facing the competition from private local bakeries. The Triveni Structurals Ltd. is facing competition with Jessops & Co. Ltd. and other small entrepreneurs. The Scooters India Ltd. is facing the toughest competition from the makers of Bajaj Autos. Almost all the important products of Bharat Pumps and Compressor Ltd. have tough competition from private manufacturers. The products of National Textile Corporation of India are not accepted by the customers mainly because of the good quality products offered by private entrepreneurs.

8. Unsound Production Organisations

It has been found that the production organization of many PEs is not very sound. It has a number of loopholes. PEs should, in particular, examine their existing production organisation in the light of factors such as changes in market standards of performance and quality, production diversification, and product development. It has been observed that highly sophisticated plants and machinery were being operated on obsolete and outmoded techniques of planning and control of production.

9. Technical Know-how Problems

The aspect of choice of technology is not given due importance. Further, the PEs purchase the equipments through the collaborator when the require equipment of good quality is available from indigenous sources. The collaboration agreements also include training of Indian personnel, preparation of detailed project reports and preparation of drawings for which the collaborators charge excessive fees by way of remuneration.

10. Underutilisation of Capacity

It was suggested by several committees that "Government should immediately analyse the reasons for this persistent underutilisation of capacities in various undertakings and take remedial measures in respect of each of them". Out of 235 manufacturing units surveyed during 1991-92, 52 PE units operate in the capacity utilisation range of below 50 per cent while 60 PE units operate in 50 to 75 per cent capacity utilisation range. These two categories constitute a percentage share of 52 during the year as compared to 45 per cent during 1990-91. This is certainly not an optimum situation. In a country with limited capital resources, it is inexcusable for PEs to sub-optimally utilize their resources of men, materials and machines. The main factors affecting capacity utilisation are power shortages, inadequacy of demand, equipment breakdowns, lack of balancing equipments, inadequacy of raw materials and managerial inefficiencies.

11. Poor System of Quality Control

PEs generally have "stage to stage" inspection starting from incoming material to the finished product. Some enterprises also hold quarterly review meetings to discuss unfavourable trends in quality and also to fix targets for reduction of off-grade reduction. A large number of PEs follow the statistical quality control technique for regulating the quality of their products. In spite of all these, the products of PEs are not of desired quality and specifications. Customers, generally, rely very little on the products manufactured by PEs. Scooters, footwears, clothes, etc., produced by PEs are not popular in consumers' market. The main reason advocated for such rejection is poor quality of PE products.

12. Problem of Efficient Materials Management

It has been found that cost of materials accounts for nearly two-third of the total cost of production in Indian industries and hence the importance of efficient and effective materials management. PEs in India do not follow the scientific materials management practices. This results in the wastage of materials as well as improper storage, care and custody of materials. In PEs, by and large, materials management has not been given the important it deserves both in terms of the status in the organisation hierarchy and effective functioning. That a large number of PEs do not care to attend such elementary requirement as fixing the minimum and maximum limits of stores proves this point.

13. Problems of Raising Financial Resources

PEs today are extremely dependent on the Government's budgetary appropriation because the surpluses generated by them are poor. The major problem in generation of internal resources for expansion is the basic nature of most of our PEs, where prices are kept low due to social, political and overall economic considerations. A large part of the internal resource is at present generated through provision of depreciation only. Amongst the external sources, the PEs are not getting adequate support from the capital market for loans, public deposits and foreign investment. Recently, the Government has permitted the PEs to issue bonds for strengthening their resource position. This source of found is attracting huge investments. The bonds, however, were issued by the profit-earning PEs only.

14. Poor Profitability and Lower Returns

A review of the working of PEs reveals that either the profits in them have been deplorably low or that they have been making losses. The return on investment of PEs in India is very low from the point of view of an investor. It is very low in the light of reasonable expectation of return of 10 per cent in PEs.

15. Inefficient Planning and Budgeting

Many PEs continue to follow the traditional pattern of budgetary forms and procedures. The system of classification of expenditure adopted in the budgets does not link expenditure to activities and end results. The detailed budgets are not prepared. The budgets for PEs serve as a base for obtaining funds, and an instrument of controlling expdnditure levels. These budgets do not serve other managerial requirements.

16. Heavy Burden of Social Overheads

Heavy expenditure is often incurred on social overheads, such as building of townships, schools, hospitals and theaters. While these are necessary, the question is whether the expenditure on such items could have been avoided or reduced, and whether the country could afford such expenditure. The investments in the townships of steel sector have constituted one-third of the total township investment. The gross expenditure on township maintenance, administration and social overheads has increased over the years. This puts excessive burden on the budgets of PEs.

17. Problem of Extravagant Expenditure

PEs are often accused of lacking in cost consciousness. This may be partly due to the lack of result-oriented approach and profit consciousness and overemphasis on procedures.

18. Poor Manpower Planning

No scientific personnel policy was worked out, nor was there scientific and accurate estimate of manpower requirements. It has been brought out that manpower is in excess of actual requirements in most PEs. The man reasons for this state of affairs are (i) employment under pressure to construction staff and (ii) the employment of helper for every job.

19. Problem of Low Labour Productivity

Labour welfare increases the productive efficiency of the workers and infuses in them a new spirit of self-realisation and consciousness. In the initial yeas of operation, public sector units are not in a position to provide all fringe benefits and welfare amenities which are provided by and enterprise of decade or so. The new employees with high aspirations compare themselves with the emoluments and benefits of well-established units. They concentrate little on their duties. Job security in PEs also results in lower productivity of employees.

In a survey about 10 per cent of the managers clearly indicated that they would be better motivated if their job security is reduced.

20. Lack of Professionalism in Management

It has been observed in several studies that personnel managers in PEs were often not professionally qualified and personnel departments more or less resembled the establishment sections of Government departments with their activity often decaying into a lifeless routine. It recommended recognition of personnel management as a staff function of the highest importance and the department dealing with it to be equipped with the requisite expertise in industrial engineering, manpower planning and labour relations. The Government still favours the continuance of bureaucracy in the management of PEs. The bureaucrats are not in a position to evolve a management culture specially suited to the requirements of industrial and commercial enterprises. They simply follow the procedures and are not prepared to take risks and cultivate dynamism in the organisation as we find in the professional management culture.

21. Low Morale of Public Sector Employees

PEs are also facing a big challenge regarding toning up the morale of the PE executives and employees. Motivation has little role to play in this sphere. In PE management culture, the incumbent, after the initial experience, comes to know the price which he has to pay if his risk fails to give benefit to the enterprise. He also knows that there is absolutely no system of rewarding him if his risk rings good results to the concern. In this managerial culture successes are taken for granted and are treated as a part of normal functions of management. However, the failure lead to comments like "who asked you to do this?" This clearly infers that one should do only when one is asked to do.

22. Fight of Talent

It is argued that there is flight of personnel from PEs to private enterprise. In a study made by the Indian Institute of Public Administration, this was considered as a potentially threatening problem. The departmental undertakings, particularly ordnance factories, were affected by it more than corporate undertakings; and older undertakings were affected more as compared to newer undertakings. Migration was generally more significant among graduate engineers with some years of experience engineers with some years of field experience.

23. Lack of Confidence in Younger Managers

A study of the age composition of the executives manning top-level posts in different PEs reveals that the number of managers holding top posts in the age group below 45 years is insignificant. Moreover, nearly 60% of the cadre strength at this level consists of persons who are more than 50 years. Younger in age and buoyant with energy, the younger managers can play a more effective role in deciding the density of the organisation in which they are working.

Limitations of Public Enterprises

PEs have, at present, emerged all over the world as a fact o economic life but they are not free from limitations.

In this context the following points deserve special consideration:

(i) PEs are required to fulfil a large number of objectives, economic as well as non-economic. they are *conflicting* with each other. The objectives are not made clear and often there is a *lack of policy clarification* on various matters.

(ii) PEs in general face the shortage of skilled, experienced and competent managers because of relatively lower salary and perquisites, etc. This has led to the *inefficient management* of these enterprises.

(iii) Theoretically, PEs are provided autonomy in their working. In practice, the government, the ministers, the politicians and other government agencies *constantly interfere in their day-to-day activities.* This results in inefficient functioning and poor performance of the enterprises.

(iv) The *management* of these enterprises, even if they are competent enough, *do not show keen interest in their efficient working as they do not have any incentive or financial stake.* Moreover, unlike private enterprises, they do not fell insecure about their jobs also. So, neither they have incentive of reward nor fear of losing their jobs.

(v) PEs do not believe in individual decisions. Committees are formed to take decisions relating to the operational requirements. This process leads making, so essential for a business enterprises, are not availed of.

(vi) Often, in practice the decisions, in PEs are based *on political rather than economic grounds.* Their very location is decided on political basis rather than economic expediency.

(vii) PEs do not function purely on the basis of commercial considerations. *Lack of commercial approach* by their executives leads to wastages, inefficiencies and resultant lower productivity.

(viii) Often, in practice, *bureaucratic style of management* is followed in PEs which leads to rigidity, strictness, adherence to rules and procedures and impracticability. This leads to inefficient functioning of these enterprises.

(ix) In the enterprises, there is *lack of concern about cost control, avoidance of waste, improvement of efficiency or increasing the capacity utilisation,* Even if they are incurring losses, no special concerted efforts are made to reduce that or improve the situation.

(x) PEs are often very *weak in labour relations.* For several reasons, the employees' aspirations go on increasing, even though they may be better placed, and even on petty issues, they resort to undesirable practices creating hurdles in production and sales.

****

11

Commercial Policy of India

Export-Import Policy

The external sector has a very important role in the process of economic development of a country. Developing economies have to evolve a suitable commercial policy mix which may create export outlets and as well may supplies of essential imports. In its simplest sense, commercial policy refers to the policy of the Government related to operating of external sector may be termed as commercial policy or trade policy or Export Import (EXIM) policy.

The Commerical and Trade Policy are synonymous term. Trade Policy is a relatively comprehensive term as compare to commercial policy. It is because under commercial policy includes only matters related to export and import , whereas , under trade policy, besides export and import, all other matters relating to international trade are also included. The trade or commercial policy has impact not only on the volume and composition of foreign trade of the country, but as well on the pattern of investment and direction of development, entrepreneurial and business behaviour, consumption pattern etc.

COMMERCIAL POLICY

International trade plays an important role in the economic development of developing countries. The volume and composition of international trade along with the terms of trade have significant influence on the rate and nature of development of developing countries. The main features of the India's Commercial Policy announced in 1991 are explained below :

1. *Freedom in the Field of Foreign Trade*— The policy considerably reduces licensing, quantitative restrictions and other regulations along with discretionary controls. Quantitative restrictions on imports of most intermediate inputs and capital goods have been eliminated. In order to provide more freedom in the sphere of foreign trade, the following measures have been included in the policy

- By formulating the negative lists of exports and imports, licences and administrative controls have been withdrawn in most cases.
- The negative list of imports has been classified in *three* categories *viz.,* (a) Prohibited item, (b) Restricted Items, and (c) Canalised items
- The restricted list of exports has been pruned. It has been classified into *four* categories *viz.,* (a) Prohibited items, (b) Restricted items, (c) Canalised items and (d) Regulated items.

2. *Export Promotion*— One of the most important highlight of the present trade policy is the widening of the scope of the Export Promotion of Capital goods (EPCG) Scheme to provide for zero duty import of capital goods. The policy more emphasise on export promotion rather than import restriction. Special schemes have been launched for export promotion.

3. *Export Earnings*— In order to make international trade policy allowed Indian exporters retain 30 per cent of their export earnings. They have also been allowed to sell that amount of foreign exchange in open market in India (to the highest bidder).

In the budget announcement of February 1992, Indian rupee was made partly convertible. By this provision, Indian exporters are required to hand over 40 per cent of their export earnings to government at official rate of exchange while 60 per cent of India's imports would be finance through sale in open market of export earnings.

4. *Devaluation of Rupee*— With the intention of make Indian rupee cheaper in terms of hard foreign currencies and make foreign currencies dearer in term of India rupee, in he first week of July 1991 Indian rupee was devaluated. It was expected that this step will help India to push up exports and reduce her imports.

5. *Cash Compensatory Allowance*— The Indian rupee was devaluated with the expectation to make Indian goods cheaper by 80 per cent in foreign market. Since these cash compensatory allowance hereto given to Indian exporters for exporting their goods was discontinued.

6. *Import Licensing System*— The system of import licensing has been stopped except in the case of some specific commodities of strategic significance. Further, restrictions on imports of industrial raw material and capital goods hereto were in operation have also been cancelled.

The procedural difficulties faced by value-based advanced licence holders with reference to MODVAT has been minimised by enabling such licence holders to claim MODVAT or drawback, as the case may be, in most of the cases.

The Duty Free Licensing Scheme has been made more domestic supplier-friendly. The holder of such a licence may now avail of the facility of Back-to-Back Letters of Credit through the banking system to access goods from indigenous supplier without applying for an advance release order.

7. *Encourage Private Bonded Sharehouses*— In order to facilitating easier access to imported inputs for exporters, private bonded sharehouses has been allowed to be opened.

8. *Open General Licence*— To ensure adequate availability of goods of mass consumption at competitive price, a detailed review of the Restricted List of imports has been undertaken. Many such goods are being made freely improtable popularly known as OGL.

Special Import Licence in the case of goods, other than he restricted list, the approach is to allow realisation in a posed manner through the Special Import Licence (SIL) route. A number of additional items are being permitted for import under SIL.

9. *Re-defined Consumer Goods*— The definition of consumer goods has been modified to allow free import of components, parts and spares of consumer durables. The definition of consumer goods has been changed to suit the needs of the importer, so as to allow them to freely import parts, components and spares of consumer goods as well.

These were earlier restricted to the extent that these could be imported without a licence only by actual uses. With the charges made, any person can import parts or components of consumer durables freely without licence and without actual user conditions.

Critical Assessment of the Policy

The present Trade Policy of the government announced by the then commerce Minister Mr. P. Chidambaram is a appreciable efforts. The policy emphasised on protection of imports of certain items linked to exports by enlarging and liberalizing the replenishment licence system. In order to achieve this objective major trade reforms have been announced from time to time. However the critics point out the following against the liberal Trade Policy of 1991.

1. *Protection to Domestic Industries*— Liberal import policy will have adverse effect on the growth of domestic industries. In the situation of liberal imports of foreign goods, Indian industries will find themselves in a very miserable position to stand fierce competition with highly developed industries in developed countries namely the USA, Japan and Germany.

2. *Open General Licence (OGL)*— Some 208 Capital goods have been included in the system Open General Licence. This means, hereafter capital good can be imported without licence from the government. Rates of custom duties on many capital goods have also been reduced in the budget for 1992-93.

No doubt , policy of liberal import of capital good from developed countries will put Indian industries in trouble as it will be very difficult for them to successfully stand competition.

3. *Liberal Import Policy*— The provision of liberal import policy seems more in the favour of large multinational companies. These companies have entered in the Indian capital and consumer goods industries found it very difficult to compete with such foreign goods.

THE NEW EXPORT-IMPORT POLICY (1992-97)

The Government on March 31, 1992, announced the new export-import policy coinciding with the Eighth Plan for a five year period i.e., April 1, 1992 to March 31, 1977 . For the first time after the Independence , the trade policy has been formulated for a five year period objectives. The major objectives of the new export import policy are as follows :

1. Accelerating the pace of country's exports;
2 New incentives for export promotion;
3 Liberalised duty-free import for export;
4. Reducing the number of items in the negative list of export; and
5 Establishing a self-reliant dynamic economy

Highlights :

The major highlights of the new export import policy are as given on next page :

(i) For the first time the trade policy will be co-terminus with the Five Year Plan. It is of five year duration.

(ii) By formulating the negative lists of exports and imports trade has been made free. Licences and administrative controls withdrawn in most cases.

(iii) All item except petroleum products, edible oils, fertilizers , food, etc., have been decanalised.

(iv) The negative list of imports has been classified in three categories :

(a) Prohibited Items : These include three items, viz. (i) tallow fat and oils of any animal origin, (ii) animal rennet, and (iii) unmanufactured ivory.

(b) Restricted Items : These include 68 items. The important items included in the restricted list are consumer goods and sports material and equipment camera, precious and semi precious stones, defence material , seeds and seeling, animal , insecticides and pesticides etc.

(c) Canalised Items : These include 8 items. The important items in the Canalised list are petroleum products , medicines, edible oils, chemical fertilizers , seeds saplings etc.

(v) The restricted list of exports has been pruned, It has been classified into four categories :

(a) Prohibited Items : These include seven items. These include all kind of wildlife such as exotic birds, all items of wild flora, beef, human skeletons, tallow , fat and oils of animal origin , etc.

(b) Restricted Items. These include 62 items.

(c) Canalised Items . These include 10 items. The major items in the canalised list are petroleum products, butter, gum, mica-dust , specified mineral ores, etc.

(d) Regulated Items : No licence is required to export these items but certain rules and procedures shall have to be followed.

(vi). The formality of obtaining licence for the import of second-hand capital goods has been done away with the import list of such items will be made public through a government notification.

(vii) .The new policy places more emphasis on export promotion rather than import restrictions. Special schemes will be launched for export promotion.

(viii).Basides quality - Based advance licensing value -based advance licensing will also be adopted so as to widen the scope of duty.-free , scheme. It will give more flexibility to exporters to import essential raw materials , components, equipment, etc.

(ix).Export house, trading houses and star business houses will have the facility of automatic -certification under the advance licence scheme.

(x).The capital goods export promotion scheme (EPCG) has been made more liberal. Now, there will be two avenues for the import of capital goods at the concessional custom duties. Export liabilities will also be different according to the concessional custom duties.

(xi).In case the domestic producers of the capital goods need any import component , they will also be entitled for 15 per cent concessional custom duty rates under EPCG.

(xii).Export promotion scheme of diamonds and precious stones will continue with certain modifications.

(xiii).Under the new policy, 100 per cent EOUs and EPZs will not only be allowed to install their own machinery but will also be permitted to install machinery procured on hire -purchase. They will also be allowed to export their products through export house, trade houses and star trade houses.

(xiv).EOU/EPZ schemes will be extended to agriculture, horticulture, animal husbandry , paultry farming, etc.

(xv). Deemed exports have been defined and the concessions and advantages attached to them will be available to manufacturers.

(xvi) Some exports and exporters of specific category will be eligible for special import licence. These include deemed exports, export houses trading houses and producers having quality certificates of ISO 9,000 (category) or BIS 14,000 (category).

(xvii). The rules and regulations relating to export -import producer will be postfied on May 1, 1992.

Evaluation

The new export-import policy is a firm and dynamic step in the direction of liberalisation. The most important feature of the new policy is its long duration. Frequent changes in the trade policy create an atmosphere of uncertainty for the entrepreneurs and traders. The two tier system of concessional custom duty exports will promote exports, however, will discourage new entrants in the field of exports, because the concessions would be available to the extablished exporters. It is also feared that reduction in the number of canalised items will put pressure on foreign exchange , allocation of foreign exchange in 60 :40 ratio for the private sector would prove to be indequate.

In brief , the new export import policy is likely to help economy to come over the balance of payments crisis.

EXPORT IMPORT POLICY
1997-2002

The government announced the current Export-Import Policy (1997-2002) on 31st March, 1997. The new policy seeks to consolidate the gains of the previous policy (1992-97). The policy also further carry forward the process of liberalisation coincide with the Ninth Plan.

Objectives

The principal objective of the Exim Policy 1997-2002 are described below:

1. To accelerate transition of the country to a internationally vibrant economy with a view to derive maximum benefits by the expanding of global market opportunities.

2. To stimulate sustained economic by providing access to essential raw materials, intermediates, components, consumerables and capital goods required for augmenting production.

3. To enhance the technological strength and efficiency of Indian agriculture, industry and services, thereby improving their competitive strength while generating new employment opportunities, and to encourage the attainment of internationally accepted standards of quality.

4. To provide consumers with goods quality products at reasonable prices.

Salient Features

The salient features of the Exim Policy are as follows:

(1) *Liberalisation*–The most notable feature of the new trade policy is liberalisation or freedom. As a liberalisation measure, licensing, quantitative restrictions and other regulatory and discretionary controls have been substantially eliminated. All goods, except those coming under the negative list, remaining may be freely imported and exported.

(2) *The Negative List of Imports*– The negative list consists of goods, the import or exports which classified the items into three broad categories as follows:

(i) *Prohibited Items*– The prohibited goods shall not be imported or exported. As per policy, there are three prohibited items of import (tallow, animal rennet, wild animals including their parts).

(ii) *Canalised Items*– These include petrol products, all types of nitrogenous phosphatic and potassic fertilisers, coconut-oil, RBD palm oil, seeds, all other non-edible oils (excluding tung oil/china wood oil) palm sterin, cereals, cloves, cinnamon and casia.

(iii) *Restricted Items*– These include consumer goods precious and semi-precious and other stones, safety, security and related items, ammunition, chloro fuloro hydro carbons, seeds, plants and animals, insecticides and pesticides, drugs and pharmaceuticals, chemicals and allied items, etc.

(3) *Negative List of Export*– Negative list of items classifies the items into three broad categories as follows:

(i) *Prohibited Items*– These include all forms of wild animals, exotic birds, all items of plants, human skeletons, beef, tallow, fat and oils of any animal origin, wood and wood products in the form of logs, timber, stumps, chemicals, sandal-wood in any form, Red sandalwood in any form.

(ii) *Canalised Items*– These include petroleum products, gum karaya, micawaste, mineral ores and concentrates, nigr seeds, onions, etc.

(iii) *Restricted Items*– These include cattle, chemical fertilizers, dress materials/readymade garments, fur of domestic animals, hides and skin, fodder, minerals, ores, milk, pulses, paddy, rice, seeds and planting materials, sea shells, ses weeds, silk worms vintage motor cars, etc.

It is important to mention here that any goods, the export of which is restricted through licensing may be exported or imported only in accordance with a licence issued in this regard. However a licence may include such items and conditions as may be specified by the licensing authority.[1]

(4) *Duty Entitlement Pass Book Scheme (DEPB)*– A new scheme–Duty Entitlement Pass Book Scheme (DEPB)- introduced in the current policy. It combines the positive aspects of both Value Based Advance License as well as Old Pass Book Scheme.

Under the proposed scheme, exporters, on the basis of notified entitlement rates, will be granted duty credits, which will entitle them to import goods duty free.

(5) *Export Promotion*– Duty on capital goods has been reduced from 15 percent to 10 percent under the Export Promotion of Capital Goods (EPCG) Scheme.

(6) *Zero Duty Scheme*– Under the scheme, the threshold level has been reduced from Rs. 20 crores to Rs. 5 crores for agriculture and allied sector.

(7) *Special Licence Facility*– Special Imprest Licence Facility (SILF) is being extended to domestic capital good supplies for supply under zero duty EPCG scheme.

(8) *Deemed Export Benefits*– These have been extended to oil and gas sector in addition to power sector.

(9) *EPZ/EOU Units*– In agriculture and allied sectors these units can now sell 50 percent of their production in Domestic Tariff Area (DTA), without stipulation of any valueaddition and have only value addition and have only to ensure positive net foreign exchange earning.

(10) *Limit Raised*– The SIL entitlement in case of exporters holding ISO 9000 series for IS/ISO 9000 series is being raised from 2% of 7.0.b to 5% 7.0.b.

(11) *Recognition of Export House–* The following criterion has been prescribed for recognition of export houses:

Table-1

(Rs. in Crores)

Category	FOB Criterion		NFE Criterion	
	Average FOB value of exports made during the preceding 3 years	FOB value of exports made in the pre-cedng year	Average Net foreign exchange value of exports, made during the preceding 3 years	Net foreign exchange value of exports made during the preceding year
Export Houses	20	30	16	24
Trading Houses	100	150	80	120
Star Trading Houses	500	750	400	600
Super Star Trading Houses	1500	2250	1200	1800

1. These includes (i) The quantity, description and value of the goods; (ii) Actual user condition, if any; (iii) Export obligation if any; (iv) The value addition to be achieved, if any; (v) The minimum export price, if any; (vi) The country of origin and destination of the goods.

(12) *Free Export-Import–* All items, except those in negative list may be freely exported and imported.

(13) *Import of Capital Goods–* Capital goods of both type– new as well as second hand may be imported under EPCG scheme. Capital goods including spares can be imported at a concessional rate of custom duty subject to an export obligation to be fulfilled over a period of time as prescribed given on next page:

Table-2

Duty	Export Obligation		Period
	FOB Basis	NEF Basis	
10%	4 times	Not applicable	5 years
Zero duty (in case c.i.f. value is Rs. 20 crore or more)	6 times cif	5 times cif	8 years
(in case cif value is Rs. 5 crore or more for agriculture and allied activities)	6 times cif	5 times cif	6 years

(14) *Duty Exemption Scheme (DES)–* The scheme has been introduced for the exporters. The scheme consists of (i) Duty Free Licence, and (ii) Duty Entitlement Pass Book. A brief description of each one of them is as follows:

(i) *Duty Free Licence–* The scheme includes the following:

(a) *Advance Licence–* An Advance Licence is granted to a manufacturer exporter for the import of inputs required for the manufacture without payment of basic custom duty.

(b) *Advance Intermediate Licence–* Is granted to a manufacturer-exporter for the import of input required in the manufacture of goods to be supplied to the ultimate exporter holding an advance licence.

(c) *Special Import Licence–* The licence is granted to a manufacturer-exporter for import of input required in the manufacture of goods to be supplied to EOUs units located in EPZs, STPs, or EHTPs, to projects financed by multilateral or bilateral agencies, to fertilizer plants, to power, oil and gas sectors etc.

(ii) *Duty Entitlement Pass Book Scheme*– Under this scheme, an exporter is entitled to claim credit in the form of specified percentage of f.o.b. value of exports made in freely convertible currency. The credit will be available against such export products and such rate as may be specified by the Director General of Foreign Trade.

(15) *Duty Free Imports*– All EOU, units in EPZs, EHTP units and STP unit are allowed duty free import of all types of goods including capital goods required by them for manufacturing provided these are not prohibited items in the negative list of imports.

(16) *Quality Awareness*– Emphasis has been laid down on quality awareness in the Exim Policy. It has been proposed under the new policy to encourage manufacturers and exporters to attain internationally accepted standards of quality. In this regard, industry and trade with the support and assistance of the government will also provide help in modernisation and upgradation of test houses and laboratories with a view to bring them at par with international standards.

(16) *Import-Export Code Number*– No imports or exports allowed to any person without an Import-Export code number issued by a competent authority.

It is clear from the above explanation that, the new policy emphasises on certain important aspects of India's foreign trade, *e.g.*, openness, transparency, quality awareness, international competitiveness and globalisation. No doubt, the changes introduce in the new Exim policy will open new avenue for Indian publishers in the international market. It will also help in promoting export-growth, accumulate large forex reserves and will case the balance of payment crisis.

* * * * * * * * * * *

12

Trends in India's Foreign Trade:

Volume, Composition & Direction

India's foreign trade was confined with a colonial and agricultural country till 1947. The bulk of the country's foreign trade was confined to Britain and other common wealth countries. India had a pattern of trade consisted of few agriculture-based commodities like, the cotton textiles. Jute and Jute goods, Tea, Spices and hides skias and mining products like mica and maganese ore. The imports were also restricted to and consisted mainly of manufacture articles. There was a favourable balance of trade which resulted in a low level of industrial production and development.

Foreign Trade has an important place in the economy of a country. According to *Robertson, "foreign Trade is an engine of economic growth"*. Because of foreign trade : (i) A country can make efficient use of its natural resources. (ii) It can export its surplus production. (iii) It can obtain technical know-how foodgrains and other goods from abroad and (iv) Much needed foreign capital, machines and essential raw materials can be imported to facilitate industrialisation. Further, through effective regularisation of foreign trade, employment, output, prices, industrialisation and economic development of a country can be properly influenced. It is because of these reasons that Planning Commission of India has laid so much emphasis on the development of foreign trade in the Five Year Plans.

Table 1
Volume of India's Foreign Trade

(in crore Rs.)

Year	*Import*	*Export*	*Total*
1950-51	608	606	1,214
1960-61	1122	642	1762
1970-71	1634	1535	3139
1980-81	12549	6711	19260
1985-86	19658	10895	30553
1989-90	35416	27681	63097
1990-91	43198	32553	75757
1991-92	47851	44041	91892
1992-93	63375	53688	116763
1994-95	89971	82674	171645
1995-96	122678	106353	229031
1996-97(P)	138919	118817	257736
1997-98(P)	151554	126286	277840

Source : Economic Survey 1996-98 and others.

Foreign Trade after Independence

India's Balance of Payments

Unfavourable balance of payments of India has been a matter of grave concern. Before we undertake a detailed study of the problem, it is necessary to know the meaning of the balance of payments.

Meaning— Balance of payments refers to that account which records all economic transactions between the residents of a country and the rest of the world, during a given period of time. *Balance of payments of trade is just a part of balance payments: it is the difference between exports and imports of the goods and services.* Balance of payments has two accounts

(1) Current Account It includes :

(i) The difference between the value of import and exports of goods, that is, *Visible items* and

(ii) Services, that is , *Invisible items* like insurance, banking etc. and

(2) *Capital Account which includes capital receipts and payments. Favourable or unfavourable balance of payments refers to favourable or unfavourable balance of payments on current account.*

Unfavourable balance of payments in India means that the total value of imports of visible as well as invisible items is greater than the total value of exports of visible as well as invisible items. Favourable balance of payments means that India's foreign trade is profitable, that is, visible and invisible exports are greater than visible and invisible imports.

Trends of Balance of Payments

Since Independence, India's balance of payments has been unfavourable. During World War II, India's balance of payments became favourable. During war period, India supplied large amount of goods to U.K. and allied nations. Consequently, UK had to pay Rs. 1,733 crore (called sterling balances) to India by way of payments of these goods. But immediately after partition India's imports increased much more than its exports landing the country into balance of payments difficulties.

Table 2 indicates that except during the period of Fifth Plan, India's balance of payment on current account has remained unfavourable.

Table 2
India's Balance of Payments

Period	*Balance of Payments Rs. (Crore)*
First Plan (1950-56)	– 151
Second Plan (1956-61)	– 1,838
Third Plan (1961-66)	– 2,360
Annual Plan (1966-69)	– 2,150
Fourth Plan (1969-74)	– 1,781
Fifth Plan (1974-78)	+ 3,803 (Favourable)
Sixth Plan (1980-85)	– 11,385
Seventh Plan (1989-90)	– 38,284
1990-91	-10,640
1991-92	-3,809
1992-93	-9,686
1993-94	-3.352
1994-95	-7,296
1995-96	-16,325
1996-97	-19,319
1997-98	-2,5268

Source : Statistical Outline of India

The deficit in the current accounts is met by an equivalent surplus on capital account. it consists of the following (i) Loans from foreign governments (ii) Private foreign investment and loans (iii) Movement of funds by the banks. If the inflow of funds from all these sources falls short of the current account deficit, the balance is financed by utilising the foreign exchange reserves of the country.

Causes of Unfavourable Balance of Payments

Main causes of India's unfavourable balance of payments are as follows:

(1) *Import of Machinery*— After Independence, imports of machines in India increased due to two causes : (1) During World War II machines worked over-time causing lot of wear and tear and depreciation. In order to replace the same, new machines were imported from abroad. (2) During Five Year Plans, machines were imported to facilitate industrialisation of the country. Machines being costly items resulted into unfavourable balance of payments.

(2) *Import of War Equipments*— In order to strengthen her defence against the hostile attitudes of neighbouring countries, India had to import war equipments on a large scale. It also rendered our balance of payments adverse.

(3) *More Demand of Consumption Goods*— In the post-World War II era, demand not only increased of foreign goods but also of domestic goods increased. Previously, tea, oilseeds, iron used to be exported on a large scale, but now their domestic demand has increased so much that exportable surplus has declined.

(4) *Price Disequalibrium*— According to Fiscal Commission Report, after 1945 there occurred wide differences in the price of domestic goods and goods entering into foreign trade. After the war inflation rate has continued to be alarming. Due to rise in the prices of foodgrains, the prices of other goods also rose. This rendered our exports relatively costlier in the international market causing a fall in demand.

(5) *Foreign Competition*— India mainly exports jute, tea and cotton textiles, but there is increasing foreign competition in these goods. For instance, India has to compete with Bangla Desh for the export of jute, Sri Lanka for tea and East Africa for cotton textiles. Over time our competitive power has generally tended to decline.

(6) *Increase in the Price of Petrol*— Price of Petrol has been rising in the international market for the last so many yeas. Consequently, the value of our imports has increased

considerably. In 1973 price of Petrol was 2 dollars per barrel. It increased to 36 dollars per barrel. Hence the value of imported petrol has increased tremendously. In 1970-71 petrol worth Rs. 136 crore was imported. But in 1995 its value increased to Rs. 18,613 crore, About 24 percent of our total export-earning is spent on the import of petrol.

(7) *Payment of Interest on Foreign Debt*— Government of India is indebted to other countries to the tune of 3,11,792 crore. it paid in 1995, about rupee 40,924 crore. as interest on these debts. It also resulted into unfavourable balance of payments.

(8) *Less Growth of Exports*— Till 1976, exports of India increased less than her imports, causing disequilibrium in the balance of payments. The same situation obtained at the beginning of the Seventh plan. The gap between exports and imports has further widened only to compound the problem of balance of payments.

Direction of Foreign Trade

Direction of India's foreign trade has also undergone considerable change after Independence.

(a)*Change in the direction of Export Trade*— Prior to 1950-51 most of India's export trade was with UK., commonwealth countries and USA. Of the total exports of India in 1951-52, about 27 percent used to go to UK., 18.6 percent to USA and 2.2 percent to Japan. The share of the former USSR was just 1.2 percent, that of European Union 5.9 percent and to Germany just 1.0 percent. In 1994-95, India's exports to UK, decreased to 6.4 percent but to U.S.A., Japan and USSR increased to 19 percent, 7.3 percent and 3 percent respectively. Share of EU countries, that is, Belgium, France, Luxembourg, Germany, Netherlands, U.K., Italy, Denmark and Ireland increased to 26.4.

Table -3

Direction of India's Foreign Trade

Country	*Percentage of Imports*			*Percentage of Exports*		
	1951-52	1970-71	1996-97	1951-52	1970-71	1996-97
Britain	17.0	7.8	5.4	25.9	11.1	6.1
U.S.A.	20.4	27.7	8.8	18.1	13.5	19.8
Canara	2.0	7.2	0.8	2.2	2.1	1.1
France	1.2	1.3	2.0	1.6	1.2	2.2
Germany	3.0	6.6	7.2	1.3	2.1	5.6
Russia	0.1	6.5	1.6	0.9	13.0	6.0
Japan	2.6	5.2	5.7	2.0	13.3	6.0
Oil Producing Countries	-	7.7	26.4	-	6.7	9.7
Total Inclucing Others	100	100	100	100	100	100

Composition of Foreign Trade

Composition of India's foreign trade after Independence and during five-year plans underwent a significant change. Goods that India used to export previously, *e.g.*, foodgrains, cotton etc., now figure in her imports. On the other hand, the share of finished goods; iron and steel, engineering goods, jewellery and gems increased significantly.

(a)*Change in the composition of Exports*— Since 1947, there has been significant changes in India's export trade. Before Independence India used to export mostly primary products like tea, jute, cloth, leather, iron, cashew and spices etc. Now variety of finished goods like capital goods (machines), engineering goods, chemicals, chemical products, ready-made garments, gems, processed foods, handicrafts etc. are on export list. Share of conventional exports like tea, jute, cotton textile in the total exports stood at 55 percent in the year

1950-51. It came down to just 16 per cent in the year 1994-95. On the other hand, the share of engineering goods increased from just 0.05 per cent in 1951 to 13.3 percent in 1994-95.

(b)*Change in the Composition of Imports*— After 1947, import of foodgrains, cotton, jute etc. had increased considerably. But now import of these primary products is on the decrease. Import of petroleum, fertilizers, steel, iron, non-ferrours metals, industrial raw materials, machinery, capital goods, edible oils, chemicals, uncut diamonds etc., has increased substantially.

Table 4

Principal Exports From India

(Rs.. in Crores)

		1950-51	*1960-61*	*1970-71*	*1980-81*	*1990-91*	*1997-98*
1.	Cotton and Cotton Fabrics .	138	NA	115	NA	6929	27793
2.	Engineering Goods	-	-	116	-	3,877	13,973
3.	Leather and Leather Mfg.	26	28	80	NA	2600	4,891
4.	Tea and Mats	80	124	148	426	1070	1505
5.	Coffee	0.4	7	25	214	252	1622
6.	Tobacco	14	16	33	141	263	1058
7.	Cashew Kernels	9	19	57	140	447	1384
8.	Fish & Fish Products	2.5	5	31	217	960	4313
9.	Iron Ore	0.2	17	117	303	1049	1763
10.	Gems and Jewellery	-	7	29	225	2924	19014
11.	Chemicals and Allied Products	-	7	29	225	1176	13500

Table 5
Principal Imports From India

(Rs.. in Crores)

Commodities	*1950-51*	*1960-61*	*1970-71*	*1980-81*	*1990-91*	*1997-98*
Capital goods Machinery -Equip-Mentsete	91	356	404	1910	10466	26532
Petroleum, Oil and Lubricants	-	69	136	5264	10816	30538
Iron and Steel	-	123	147	852	2113	5595
Non-Ferrous Metals	-	47	119	477	1102	3337
Paper, Paper Board Etc.	10	12	25	187	456	1844
Chemical elements and compounds	12	39	68	358	2289	12128
Pearls, Precious and Semi precious stones	-	2	25	187	3738	11680
Food and Food Products	99	-	213	-	182	-
Synthetic Yarn and other Threads	NA	-	9	97	56	459
Fertiliser and Chemical Products	12	88	217	1490	1766	3755

Principal Imports and Exports of India

About 7500 goods are on the import and export list of India. Both our exports and imports have been continuously rising.

Chief Imports— India mainly imports following goods from other countries—

(1)*Machinery*— To meet her needs of industrialisation, India imports machines on a large scale. these are imported from U.S.A., West Germany, Japan, U.K., Russia etc. In 1996-97 machines worth Rs. 19,360 crore were imported.

(2)*Iron and Steel*— India has not yet become self-sufficient in the production of iron and steel. Hence it imports steel from abroad every year. It is mostly imported from West Germany, USA, U.K., Italy and France. In 1960-61 iron and steel worth Rs. 47 crore were imported imports of which has increased to Rs.5595 crores in 1997-98.

(3)*Non-ferrous Metals and Metal Products*-Non-Ferrous metals like, zinc, copper, tin and products made of these metals are imported from abroad. These metals are imported from Malaya, Brazil, U.S.A. etc. In 1996-97 metal products worth Rs.3,024 crore were imported imports of which has increased to Rs. 5595 in 1997-98.

(4)*Petrol and Petroleum Products*— India imports 35 percent of its petroleum requirements from abroad. India gets petroleum from Iran, Kuwait, Iraq and Saudi Arabia. In 1996-97 petrol and petroleum products worth Rs. 25,174 crore were imported.

(5)*Transport Equipments*— Efficient means of transport are most essential for the economic development of the country. Motor vehicles, ships, aeroplanes etc. are therefore, imported from abroad. Transport equipments are largely imported from West Germany, Italy, Japan, U.S.A. and Britain. In 1960-61 transport equipments worth Rs. 25 crore were imported from abroad imports of which has increased to Rs.3368 crores in 1997-98.

(6)*Chemical Fertilizers*— In order to increase the productivity of land, use of fertiliser is most important. Hence

India imports large quantity of chemical fertilizers from U.S.A., Russia and East Europian countries. In 1996-97, fertilizers worth Rs. 5,629 crore were imported.

(7)*Foodgrains*— India faiced acute shortage of foodgrains after partition. This shortage was met through imports from U.S.A., Australia, Canada, Burma and Argentina. In 1975, foodgrains worth Rs. 1058 crore were imported. As a result of Green Revolution in India, imports of foodgrains have almost stopped. However, in 1997-98 food and food products worth Rs. 1017 crore were imported under bulk import. .

(8)*Wool*— India imports wool from New Zealand, Australia, etc. In 1960-61, India imported wool worth of Rs. 182 crore which has increased to Rs. 593 crores in 1997-98.

(9)*Cashewnuts*— India imports raw cashew from abroad. After processing, it is re-exported. In 1970-71 cashewnuts worth Rs. 29 crore were imported. In 1997-98 the cashewnuts worth Rs. 749 crores were imported.

(10)*Paper Boards etc.* — India imports paper from Sweden, Czechoslovakia etc. The import of paper and paper boards etc. has increased from mere Rs. 10 crores in 1950-51 to Rs. 1844 crores in 1997-98.

(11)*Chemicals*— India imports from abroad, variety of chemicals, medicines, dyes etc. In 1994-95, chemicals worth Rs. 7,344 crore and medicines worth Rs. 624 crore were imported.

(12)*Edible Oils*— Imports of edible oils and oil-seeds have increased considerably for the last few years in India. In 1996-97, India imported oils worth Rs.2,262 crore from U.S.A., Canada etc.

(13)*Precious Stones*— Import of precious stones has also increased significantly. After cutting the same are re-exported. These stones come from Belgium, America etc. In 1996-97 precious stones worth Rs. 7,045 crore were imported by India.

Main Exports

Since Independence, special efforts have been made to increase exports. The main exports are as follows:

(1) *Jute Products*— Jute occupied the first place in India's exports. But in 1990-91, it dropped to 21st position. Jute products are largely exported to U.S.A., Japan, Belgium, Russia, Britain and Canada. In 1960-61 Jute products worth Rs. 135 crore were exported Which has increased to Rs. 621 crore in 1995-96. However in recent years its exports, declined miserably to Rs. 552 crores in 1996-97 and further to Rs. 362 crores in 1997-98. .

(2) *Tea*— India is the largest exporter of tea in the world. In 1950-51, tea worth Rs.80 crore was exported to other countries.The exports of tea and mate has increased significantly and reached to Rs. 1505 crores in 1997-98. Principal buyers of our tea are Britain, U.S.A., Canada, Egypt, Iran, Japan and Germany. Tea is also exported to Russia these days. Maximum quantity of tea from India is exported to Britain.

(3) *Cloth and Apparels*— India exports cotton cloth and apparels. In 1994-95 cotton cloth worth Rs. 7,014 crore were exported to other countries. Ready-made garments worth Rs. 10,305 crore were exported.

(4) *Metallic Ores*— India exports metallic ores, like manganese, mica and iron to other countries. These ores are exported to USA and Japan. In 1970-71, iron ore worth Rs. 117 crore and in 1997-98 worth of Rs. 1763 crores were exported , Mica worth Rs. 16 crore in 1970-71 , Rs. 25 crores in 1997-98 and manganese worth Rs. 15 crore in 1994-95 were exported to other countries.

(5) *Spices*— Variety of spices, like black pepper are exported from India. These are exported to U.K., Germany, Italy, Japan, Russia, Saudi Arabia, USA etc. In 1960-61 spices worth Rs. 17 crore and in 1997-98 worth of Rs. 379 were exported.

(6) *Leather and Leather Products*— India exports leather, shoes and leather products to other countries. The main customers being UK, USA, France, Germany, Russia, Italy etc. In 1960-61 , leather worth Rs. 28 crore and in 1997-98 worth of Rs. 5461 was exported.

(7) *Oil Cakes*— India also exports oil-cakes in large quantity to Japan, Netherlands and Britain etc. In 1960-61 oil-cakes valuing Rs. 14 crore and in 1997-98 worth of Rs. 3,404 crore were exported.

(8) *Tobacco*— India exports tobacco to U. K. Japan, Russia and Nepal. In 1960-61 tobacco worth Rs. 16 crore and in 1997-98 worth of Rs. 1058 crores was exported.

(9) *Coffee*— Export of coffee from India has been on the increase. It is exported to USA., Italy and Yugoslovakia. In 1960-61 coffee worth Rs. 7 crore and in 1997-98 worth of Rs. 1622 crores was exported.

(10) *Gems and Jewellery*— Of the various items showing increase in exports over time, the gems and jewellery, occupy the principal status. These are exported to countries like Hong Kong, U.S.A. and Belgium etc. In 1994-95 gems worth Rs. 14,131 crore were exported.

(11) *Cashew Kernels*— India earns considerable profit from the export of cashew kernels to Russia, USA and Japan. In 1960-61 cashew kernels worth Rs. 19 crore and in 1997-98 worth of Rs. 1384 were exported.

(12) *Engineering Goods*— India exports engineering goods to Sri Lanka, Saudi Arabia, Egypt, Burma, Malaysia, Indonesia. In 1996-97 engineering goods worth Rs. 13,922 crore were exported.

(13) *Handicrafts*— Handicrafts made of Indian cottage industries, like ivory goods are exported to USA., Germany, Saudi Arabia and Middle east countries. In 1997-98 handicrafts worth Rs. 1740 crore were exported.

Main Features of India's Foreign Trade

Main features of India's foreign trade after Independence are as follows—

(1) *Increasing Share of Gross National Income*— Foreign trade has a significant role in India's national income. In 1950-51, India's foreign trade (Imports and exports) accounted for 12 percent of net national income. In 1994-95 it increased to 23 percent of net national income.

(2) *Less Percentage of World Trade*— However, share of India in world trade has been diminishing. In 1950-51, India accounted for 1.8 percent of world's total import and 2 percent of world's total exports. In 1995 India's share in total world imports went down to 0.6 percent and in total world exports to 0.5 percent.

(3) *Oceanic Trade*— Most of India's foreign trade is through sea routes. India has very little trade relations with her neighbouring countries like, Nepal, Afghanistan, Pakistan, Burma and Sri Lanka etc. About, 68 percent of India's foreign trade is oceanic trade.

(4) *Dependence on a few Ports*— India's foreign trade is mainly through Bombay, Calcutta and Madras ports. These ports are therefore, always crowded. After Independence more ports have been developed especially in kandala, Cochin, Vishakhapatnam etc. to cope with heavy cargo traffic.

(5) *Increase in Volume and Value of Trade*— Sine Independence the volume and value of India's foreign trade have increased substantially. Compared to the past, the volume and value of India's imports and exports have increased manifold. In 1939, her imports were worth Rs. 152 crore and exports Rs. 169 crore. Thus, the total value of India's foreign trade was Rs. 321 crore. Immediately after independence, that is in 1948-49 the value of foreign trade had gone up to Rs. 792 crore. In 1997-98 it increased to Rs. 2,77,840 crore; of it the exports were of the value of Rs. 12,6,282 and imports of the value of Rs. 1,51,554 crore.

(6) *Change in the Composition of Exports*— Significant changes have taken place in India's export trade since 1947. Prior to Independence India used to export mostly primary products like, tea, jute, cloth, leather, iron, cashew and spices etc. Now several types of manufactured goods are being exported, such as engineering goods, chemicals, chemical products, ready-made garments, gems and jewellery, electronic goods, handicrafts, processed foods etc., in addition to conventional items like tea, jute, cotton textile etc.

(7) *Change in the Composition of Imports*— Prior to 1947 India's imports were composed of consumers goods, like medicines, textiles, electrical goods, motor vehicles, iron and steel etc. Now, the imports of essential raw materials and capital goods have increased tremendously. Our imports are now composed of petroleum, steel, fertilizers, iron, non-ferrous metals, industrial raw-materials, machines, edible oils, chemicals, uncut diamonds etc.

(8) *Direction of Foreign Trade*— Direction of foreign trade refers to those countries with which trade relations are established. Prior to Independence, India's foreign trade was mainly confined to U.K. but now the tables have turned. At present, India has maximum imports from and exports to European Union. Role of Japan, U.S.S.R. USA and Organisation of Petroleum Exporting countries (OPEC) in India' foreign trade has increased substantially.

(9) *Balance of Payments*-Prior to Independence India's balance of payments used to be favourable. After Independence it became unfavourable, that is, imports exceeded exports. In 1944-45, India's balance of payments was favourable to the tune of Rs. 42 crore but from 1946 onwards it turned unfavourable year after year. In 1994-95 balance of payments on current account was adverse to the extent of Rs. 6,534 crore. During the period of planning only two years *i.e.* 1972-73 and 1976-77 witnessed favourable balance of trade.

****

13

Export Promotion Schemes

India is a developing economy. It has adopted the course of planned economic development to accelerate the rate of economic growth. India's export were totally stagnant throughout the sixties. It was only when the Second Plan ran through a serious foreign exchange crisis and the Third Plan was forced with a serious shortage of foreign exchange resources that export promotion attracted the attention of our planners.

Rationale of Export Promotion : There is an imperative necessity to promote export in Indian economy. The following arguments can be advanced to justity the need for export promotion :

1. The import needs of the economy are likely to increase in future. The bill on account of direct oil imports and the investment-induced imports of foreign technology and capital put together, is likely to assume an enormous magnitude in the future . We must have sufficient exportable surplus to pay for our imports.

2. It is not a wise policy to depend upon external assistance to finance essential imports. Instead we should create exportable surplus for financing our imports.

3.There are certain capital goods, machinery and industrial raw materials which the country would not be able to produce in the foreseable future. Till such time the country is able to produce these goods we shall have to depend upon foreign supplies. To pay for such imports the country will have to promote its exports.

4. Export earnings need to be raised for creating substantial purchasing power to import essential consumer goods.

5. In order to expand the capacities of the existing units and find market for the products of new units , we will have to explore possibilities in the foreign markets.

6.We have not tapped fully our export potentials. The Indian economy has certain inherent comparative strength like price stability, low wages and allow industrial base to increase its exports.

7. The deficits in India's balance of payments are being plugged through foreign assistance. Our debit servicing has already assumed serious proportions and projected to grow more serious . It is not advisable any more to contract new credits to pay of the old loans instead, we must create repaying capacity by promoting the exports.

Export promotion measures initiated to step up exports from the country could be divided into three broad categories.

Export Production : In order to step up export production, sharpen competitive edge and bring about quality and technology upgradation, following measures have been initiated –

Liberalisation : Trade and industrial licensing policies have been reoriented towards exports.

Supply of Raw Materials : License free import of capital goods raw materials, intermediates, components, consumables, spares, part accessories, instruments and other goods is permitted provided imports of such items are not regulated by the Negative List of Imports.

Export Promotion Capital Goods (EPCG) Scheme

The objective of EPCG Scheme is to allow import of capital goods, both new and second hand, at concessional rate of 15% customs duty. A manufacturer-exporter can import capital goods (including spares upto 10% of the CIF value of the capital goods) at a concessional rate of customs duty of 15% subject to export obligation and other provisions as stipulated in the EXIM Policy. The EPCG Scheme has also been extended to the Services Sector.

Import of Second Hand Capital Goods : Import of second-hand capital goods having a minimum residual life of five years is allowed free of licence subject to actual user condition.

Duty Exemption Scheme : The scheme facilitates duty free import of raw materials, components, intermediates, consumables, parts, accessories, packing materials, and computer software required for the purpose of export production under various schemes of Advance/Special/Imprest/ Intermediate Licences and Self-Declared Pass Book Scheme as also Advance Customs Clearance Permit.

Investment in Plant and Equipment : Investment in plant and equipment beyond Rs. 75 lakhs is permitted to SSI Sector subject to provisions laid down in the EXIM Policy.

EPZ/EOU/EHTP/STP : Establishment of Export Processing Zones, Export Oriented Units, Electronic Hardware Technology Parks and Software Technology Parks to facilitate export production in the non-traditional sectors by exempting supplies of imports and machinery from customs/excise duties, and other terminal taxes.

Quality : To promote the concept of total quality management the Central Government assists in the modernisation and upgradation of test houses and laboratories in order to bring them at par with international standards so that certification by such test houses and laboratories is recognised within the country and abroad.

Export Marketing Assistance

Fully Convertibility : Full convertibility of Indian rupee is permitted whereby all foreign exchange receipts can be converted into rupees at market rate of exchange.

Retention Limit : Retention limit has been raised from 15 to 25 per cent of foreign exchange receipts in an account designated in foreign currency. In case of EOU/EPZ/EHTP and STP the retention limit is upto 50 per cent.

Lending Rate : Lending rates charged by the banks on term loans of three years and above have been reduced from 15 to 14 per cent.

Income Tax Exemption : Full exemption from income tax of export profits from merchandise trade has been granted.

Duty Drawback : Exporters are allowed to get refund/rebate of duty chargeable on imported materials or excisable materials used in export production.

Export Finance : Finance for pre-shipment and post-shipment is made available at reasonable rates of interest from Export-Import Bank and other commercial banks in Indian rupees and in some cases of post-shipment credit, in foreign currency also.

Export Credit Risk Insurance : Export Credit Risk Insurance is available from ECGC at a low premium to protect exporters from risks, both political and commercial, involved in extending credit to overseas buyers.

Cash Compensatory Support : CCS was granted to make Indian exports competitive in the international markets. This facility has been withdrawn with effect from 1992.

International Price Reimbursement Scheme : Reimbursement of difference between the domestic and international price of iron and steel to promote exports of engineering goods. The scheme has been withdrawn from 1.4.94.

Jute Marketing Assistance : Marketing assistance under the internal and External Market Assistance (IMA) and (EMA) Schemes cover those products which contain two or more fibres, in which jute is the dominant fiber by weight. While IMA provides market assistance @ 8 percent on sale of specified jute products, EM grants @ 10 per cent of FOB value realisation on export of specified diversified products. The benefit under EMA is available to both manufacturer-exporters and merchant-exporters. These schemes are valid till the end of the Eighth Planed period.

Export House/Trading House/Star Trading House and Super Star Trading House : Additional benefits are granted to exporters who have achieved the specified level of exports over a period of time as notified in the EXIM Policy. Such exporters are accorded a special status by the Government.

Import Replenishment : Grant of Import Replenishment Licence against exports to the exporters of gem and jewellery products listed in Appendix I of the EXIM Policy.

Deemed Exports : Supplies of goods and services to Five Specified Categories within the country which earn or save foreign exchange are treated as deemed exports. Such exports are eligible for facilities under duty exemption scheme, duty draw back, refund of terminal excise duty, and Special Import Licences @ 5% of FOR value of supplies made with effect from 1.4.94.

Institutional Framework

To strengthen infrastructural facilities required for export production and promotion, Government of India has set up a wide network of institutions/organisations in the country.

Transport : To provide support to carriage of goods by sea, air, rail and inter modal transport, Government has set up Inland Container Depots (ICDs). Container Freight Stations (CFSs) and Air Cargo Complexes (ACCs) equipped with container handling facilities at various places.

Board of Trade : To provide a forum for ensuring continuous dialogue with trade and industry in respect of major developments in the field of international trade, Board of Trade has been set up under the aegis of Ministry of Commerce.

States Cell : A State Cell has been created in the Ministry of Commerce to act as a nodal agency for interaction with State Governments/Union Territories, State Export Corporations, Associations of Industries and Commerce and Export Organisations like ITPO, FIEO and EPZs on matter concerning export from and imports into the State.

Market Development Assistance : This scheme, functioning under the Ministry of Commerce, was set up in 1963 with a view to stimulating and diversifying export trade along with the development of the marketing of Indian products and commodities abroad. financial support is provided for : market research, commodity research, area survey and research; product promotion and commodity development; export publicity and dissemination of information; participation in trade fairs and exhibitions; trade delegations and study teams; establishment of offices and branches in overseas countries; grants in-aid to export promotion councils and other approved organisations for the development of exports and promotion of foreign trade and any other scheme which is calculated generally to promote the development of overseas markets for Indian products.

Export Promotion Councils/Commodity Boards/Export Development Authorities : 19 Export Promotion Councils, six commodity Boards, two Export Development Authorities and Federation of Indian Export Organisations (FIEO) are functioning under the Ministry of Commerce to provide support to have exporting community.

Indian Institute of Foreign Trade : IIFT has been rendering useful service, since 1964, in the area of human resource development for international business, through need-based training programmes, seminars and workshops, interfaced with and supported by, continuous research on a variety of topical subjects in the field of foreign trade and international business.

India Trade Promotion Organisation : Established under the Ministry of Commerce, ITPO projects the image of Indian goods and services by organising trade fairs and exhibitions, buyer-seller meets, and conducting market studies both within the country and abroad.

Export Inspection Council : Export Inspection Council subjects a number of items meant for exports to compulsory quality control and pre-shipment inspection under the Export (Quality Control and Inspection) Act, 1963. However, items bearing ISI Mark/Agmark and goods being exported by recognised Export House/Trading Houses/ Star Trading Houses/Super Star Trading Houses are exempted from the purview of compulsory pre-shipment inspection.

Indian Council of Arbitration : The role of Indian Council of Arbitration is to amicably settle commercial disputes arising from the export transaction/contract between the exporter and the importer.

Directorate General of Foreign Trade : DGFT, formerly known as CCI&E, assists and advises Government of India in formulation of EXIM Policy and in the implementation of the policy through the mechanism of licensing.

Export Control

Government of India also exercises control/restriction on exports and imports of such commodities and services considered vital to the economy or those that effect the domestic industry. Effort is, however, made to limit such regulation to minimum number of items.

Exports in India are controlled/regulated under the provisions of Export (Control) Act, 1947 which has since been replaced by Foreign Trade (Development and Regulation) Act, 1992. Besides, exports are also regulated under the Customs Act, Coffee Act, Tea Act, Marine Produces Export Development Authority Act, minimum export price (MEP), quantitative ceilings, canalisation, export licensing, compulsory registration with EPCs/FICO etc.

Some of the important measures initiated to control/restrict export of items which are essentially needed in the country are as follows :

Negatives List of Exports : The Negative List of Exports as given in the EXIM Policy 1992–97 (as revised upto March 30, 1994) is divided into three parts, viz.:

Prohibited Items	10
Restricted Items	31
(subjected to Export Licensing)	
Canalised Items	9

(Different canalising agencies have been designated for different products).

Negative List of Imports : The Negative List of Imports as given in the EXIM Policy 1992-97 (as revised upto March 30, 1994) is also divided into three parts viz.:

Prohibited Items	3
Restricted Items	72
Canalised Items	7

Quantitative Ceilings on Exports : The following items are subject to quantitative ceilings as given in the EXIM Policy :

1. Brown seaweeds and agarophytes excluding G-edulis of Tamil Nadu coast origin in processed from ;
2. Cotton yarn;
3. Grain and flour, namely wheat, barely, maize, bajra, jowar (excluding hybrid jowar –feed grade) and ragi;
4. Meat of sheep and goat;
5. Peacock tail feathers including handicrafts and articles made thereof;
6. Manufactured articles and shavings of shed antlers of chital and sambhar;
7. Sunflower seeds;

8. Rape seeds and mustard seeds; and
9. Powder milk (skimmed or full cream) whole, and infant milk food.

Minimum Export Price : The following items are permitted for exports subject to minimum export price fixed from time to time :

1. Coir & coir products;
2. Grain and flour, namely wheat, barley, maize, bajra, jowar (excluding hybrid jowar – feed grade), and ragi;
3. Non-basmati rice.

****

14

Investment of Foreign Capital

The International flow of capital has facilitated development of the world's natural resources and has been instrumental in transmitting the direct effects of the industrial revolution from one region to another. A number of presently more advanced countries owe a good deal of their earlier industrial development to the influx of foreign capital. In fact , nearly every developed country had to lean on external sources to supplement its own meagre savings during the early stages of its development. England borrowed from Holland in the 17th and 18th centuries. The United States of America , now the richest country in the world, borrowed heavily in the 19th century for its development outlay. In the early days, russia had to rely mostly on the help of the Americans. China developed rapidly because the Soviet Union helped it liberally.

Role of Foreign Capital in Economic Development

Foreign capital combined with skill and enterprise is essential for the development of economic potentialities in under-developed or developing regions where the opportunities for the accumulation of capital are unequally distributed. The inflow of foreign capital serves various purposes. *First,* the rate of saving in an under developed country is too small to generate a self-sustaining rate of economic development. Under developed countries find it difficult on their own , to get out of the vicious circle of low income resulting in a low rate of capitaì formation. This, coupled with low productivity of labour, leads to low incomes. It is, therefore, very essential to augment the domestic savings by external resources, *Secondly*, an under-developed country is not only deficient in capital, but also deficient in skills and in trained and technical manpower. External assistance can, by bringing in technical experts and technbical ' know-how ', bridge the gap between the need for, and supply of , technical knowledge as well as of trained personnel to carry through the programmes of industrialisation. *Thirdly*, external assistance has a vital role in supplying to under-developed countries the fruits of years of scientific and industrial research, accomplished by the older industrialised countries. *Fourthly*, external aid makes it possible to run a deficit in the balance of payments, caused due to the import of capital goods and other equipment required for strengthening the industrial structure. *Finally*, external assistance enables to plan for quicker development without the inherent inflationary pressures of the developmental outlay. It is anti inflationary in character.

The lending countries are also benefited by the international investments because the economic structures of such highly industrialised countries are conditiooned to large exports of capital goods and to the purchase of a large part of their imports by means of their invisible exports. Moreover , investment in under-developed regions may offer more remunerative outlets to capital exporting countries than those available internally. Thus the "expanding world economy" cannot be fully realised without a continuous international flow of investment funds. Different countries are at different stages of economic development - some are more profusely equipped with savings available for investment while others have large and more urgent opportunity for the profitable investment of savings . If each country relies on its own capital resources for its further development, the savings of the world will not be put to their best use and the world will be less presperious.

Role in Economic Development

India is developing economy and has choosen the path of economic planning to achieve desired level of economic growth. Of course, natural resources and labour force in the country are available in abundance but certainly there is lack of capital. The technological knowledge though available in the country but the same is out dated and industrial productivity of the country is also very low. Under aforesaid circumstances, the importance of foreign capital need not be emphasised which can be explaned as follows :

(1) *Proper Exploitation of Natural Resources* - As mentioned at so many places in this book that the country possessed abundant natural resources but because of lack of technological know how and capital the natural resources may not be properly exploited . Therefore, foreign capital required necessary in order to accelerate pace of economic development.

(2) *Encouragement of Domestic Savings* - As what normally happens in a developing country, the level of domestic saving in India is quite low. It is mainly because of low income of the people. In these circumstances , the saving and investment level in the country may be pushed up with the help of foreign capital. In this way foreign capital prove boon in supplementing the growth of capital.

(3) *Availability of Foreign Technology and Managerial Technique* - Developing countries also suffer from lack of new technology and modern scientific managerial technique, India is also not exception of this fact. Foreign technology and managerial technique can easily be obtained with the help of foreign capital. Thus, foreign capital complete a process necessary for the economic development of the country.

(4) *Solve Un-employment Problem* - Un-employment and under-employment is a normal feature found in developing countries. In India too, unemployment is increasing constantly. With the help of foreign capital industries can be set-up and chances of expanding the old ones also increases.In this way foreign capital increase the level of employment opportunities.

(5) *Lack of Enterprising Spirit* - It is common phenomenon found in developing countries where enterprising spirit is lacking, Not only this but in these countries capital is also tends to be shy , capitalists are apprehensive of investing the capital in risky industries. Hence foreign capital is welcomed to face and tackle the initial hurdles in developing countries.

Foreign Capital and Assistance Policy

Policy Statement. - The change in outlook about the desirability of foreign capital culminated in the statement of Pandit Nehru in Parliament on April 6, 1949. He pointed out that " the stress on the need to regulate, in the national interest, the scope and manner of foreign capital arose from past association of foreing capital and control with domination of the economy of the country. But circumstances today are quite different. The object of our regulation should, therefore, be the utilisation of foreing capital in a manner most advantageous to the country. Indian capital needs to be supplemented by foreigncapital, not only because our national savings will not be enough for the rapid development of the country on the scale we wish but also because in many cases scientific technical and industrial knowledge and capital equipment can best be secured along with foreign capital".

The Prime Minister stated that the Government of India would expect all undertakings, Indian or foreing to conform to the general requirements of their industrial policy. In return assurance was given that there would be no discrimination between the Indian and foreing interests. Further, he pointed out that " as regards existing foreing interests Government do not intend to place any restrictions or impose any conditions which are not applicable to similar Indian enterprise. *Secondly*, foreign interest would be permitted to earn profits subject only to regulation common to all. *Thirdly* if and when foreign enterprises are compulsorily acquired, compensation will be paid on a faid and equitable basis..

The government of India have no desire to injure in any way British or other non-Indian interest in India and would gladly welcome their contribution in a constructive and co-operative role in the development of India's economy." Regarding the remittance of profits and repatriation of capital the Prime Minister said : " We do not forese any difficulty in continuing the existing facilities for remittance of profit and Government have no intention to place any restriction on withdrawal of foreign capital investments but remittance facilities would naturally depend on foreign exchange considerations. If, however, any foreign concern comes to be compulsorily acquired 'Government would provide reasonable facilities for the remittance of proceeds.

With the receipt of substantial amount of foreign assistance there has been a great change in the approach towards the significance of foreign capital in India economy. This change can be marked not only in the statements of the Government spokesmen but also in the attitude of capital exporting countries. Weightly pronouncements have been made by the Prime Minister , the Finance Minister and other Ministers to the effects that there would be no nationalisation of industries and services on doctrinnaire grounds. Assurances have been advanced to foreing investors in regard to remittance of profits and repatriation of capital.

The mind of the Indian Governments seems to be adapted to receiving private foreign investment not only in the private sector but in collaboration with certain public enterprises too. The continuing shortage of foreign exchange and the urgent need to push ahead with development plans, has made the Government look more and more to foreign entrepreneurs and investors.

The policy of the Government of India till 1991 is based on the same principles so far adopted by the Government in its earlier polices. In five year plan more importance was accorded to foreign aid. But gradually emphasis has been sifted towards control by the Government of India and training of personnel. Now foreign aid has been encouraged to use in new directions, export promotion and reduction of imports. A clear indication was given in the plan documents of Fourth Plan to get complete aid from foreign rid. No significant accomodation was given to foreign aid in fifth Five year plan till 1980-81 herculean efforts have been made achieve indepence in developmental activities without foreign aid.

Present Foreign Capital and Assistance Policy 1991

With a view to fulfill the need of foreign aid for successes of New Economic Policy and to tackle the problem of un-favourable balance payment, a librel and encouraging policy with regards to foreign assistance was adopted . The policy has been made liberal further after 1992-93 . The following are the unique features os present foreign capital and assistance policy 1991.

(1) Provisions have been made allow 100% foreign equity direct investment in 22 top priority industries,if foreign equity fulfill the need of foreign exchange for imports of gods.

(2) To impose binding for a balance between payment of dividends and imports. Restriction imposed by the Reserve Bank of India for remittance of dividends.

(3) Mainly by the companies , permission has been given for 51% foreign equity participation to those companies engaged in exports so that these companies may enter into international markets.

(4) Restrictions have been lifted if foreign technicians invited on remuneration. However the approval of payment is this regards will be within the purview of the Reserve Bank of India.

(5) Relexation will be given while making expansion 100% relxation will be given in areas of higher priority by existing companies.

VARIOUS SOURCES OF FOREIGN CAPITAL & ASSISTANCE

Normally foreign capital and assistance available to the nations in the following forms :

(1) Private Foreign Investment,

(2) Grants and loans from Foreign Governments ,

(3) Grants and loans from International Institutions, and

(4) External Commercial Borrowings.

Each one of the above mentioned source can be described as follows :

(1) *Private Foreign Investment* - Under this form of foreign assistance all types private foreign investment are included which are transferred in the forms through portfolio investment, direct investment and transfer of capital with the help of banks.

(a) Portfolio Investment - It is a form of form of foreign capital investment under which private foreign capitalist or institution purchase the bonds and securities of any firm or company working in the aid receiving countries.

(b) Direct Investment - Under direct investments shares of companies established in the aid receiving countries are purchased by foreing capitalists or private institutions. They may be partner in the ownership and management of such a company .

(c) Transfer by Commercial Banks - Under this mentord investment does not take place directly but takes place indirectly and through international institutions. These are termed as foreign commercial loans.

(2)*Grants and Loans from Foreign Government* - Foreign Government also extends loan, grants, technical assistance etc. at the level of the Government, under this category loans and grants also be extended in the form of exports of foodgrains. India could able to receiptionsit of assistance under this category from USA, UK, Russia, Japan, France and Germany etc. U.S.A. , Canada, Australia also externed foreign assistance in the form of foodgrains to India. India is regural receiver of technical assistance, services of experts and training facilities under Colombo plan.

(3) Loans and Grants from International Institutins - All most all the developing nations of the world approached International Financial Institutions to obtained foreing aid for their economic development. This tendency is becoming more vigorous now a days because it provides them get rid from political bindings. There have been established several international financial institutions namely the World Bank , International Development Association, International Financial Corporation, Asian Development Bank, International Co-operation Administration, Indian Aid Club etc. which encourage to economic development of developing countries by either granting loans or by providing gurantee.

(4)*External Commercial Borrowings* - India also obtained external trade loans from important segments of International Capital Market such as EXIM Bank USA, EXIM Bank, Japan and Export Credit Gurantee Corporation of U.K.

The role of foreign capital in India's economic development during the five year Plans may be examined from the following table-1

Table-1

Pattern of Investment and Finance During the Five Year Plan

(In Cores of Rs.)

	Public Sector Investment	*Private Sector Investment*	*Total*	*Domestic Saving*	*Inflow of Foreign Capital*	*Total*
First Plan	1,560	1,800	3,360	3,080 (92)	280 (8)	3,360 (100)
Second Plan	3,731	3,100	6,831	4,878 (71)	1,953 (29)	6,831 (100)
Third Plan	7,129	4,190	11,319	8,874 (78)	2,445 (22)`	11,319 (100)
Fourth Plan	13,655	8,980	22,635	19,991 (88)	2,644 (12)	22,635 (100)
Fifth Plan	15,700	11,200	26,900	21,100	3,700	26,100
Sixth Plan	14,530	12,500	27,130	20,500	3,650	24,160
Seventh Plan	12,550	8,450	21,000	17,200	3,800	21,000
Eighth Plan (Proposals)	53,200	8,500	61,700	42,000	19,700	61,700

The amount of foreign capital required for financing economic development has been increasing with each successive plan though percentage of foreign capital to total financing declined from 29 in the Second Plan to 22 in the Third Plan and 12 in the Fourth Plan. Until our economic reaches the stage of self-regeneration, reliance on foreing capital is inevitable under conditions of democratic planning.

RECENT TRENDS

1990s have ushered in a new era of globalisation . Interaction have become more and more common place during the last one and half decades, as a number of MNCs doing business throughout the world has increased rapidly . Today there are more than 3500 MNCs ,30,000 exporting manufacturers, 25,000 companies with overseas branches and affiliates and 40,000 firms operating abroad on adhoc basis. Free flow of capital goods and services across the world has come to stay . An abrupt shift in Political and Market Philosophy of Eash European countries has opened up new markets for the Western manufacturers. Unification of Germany and disintegration of USSR is likely to setup new aligments in business relations between various countries. A large number of developing countries are making all out efforts to lure foreing capital for their rapid economic development.

In this international economic backdrop, globalisation in India has also become a buzzword during the last couple of years. Along with others India is also moving in the lines of liberalisation and trying to woo foreing investors for its economic growth . The present chapter makes an attempt to analyse how far the liberalisation policies of India could actually attract foreign investment in its right perspective.

The Liberalisation Move :

After a long period of control and regulation , India has come out with a large number of relaxation and is heading towards an economic revolution. In the seventies and eighties, the national consensus was on the state control and the approach to foreign companies was one of extreme distrust. But soon after the present government set to work on reviving the economy, several initiativges have been taken towards deregulation and promote the resource of foreing investment including NRIs participation in the process. The policy initiatives towards foreign investment have become an integral part of the strategy of modernising the economy and establishing global linkages which are of crucial importance in the emerging world economy.

The important liberalisation measures implemented during the past few years are : abolition of industrial licensing for all but 18 industries : virtual removal of import licensing on all raw materials, components, intermediate and capital goods; hike in foreing equity holding limit upto 51 per cent in most of the industries (100 per cent in case of export oriented units and firms producing life saving equipments and drugs) : expedious clearing of foreign investment proposals by Foreing Investment Promotion Board (FIPB) and facillities for portfolio investment by foreign investment institutions. The liberalisation package is broadened in the 1993-94 budget by making the Indian rupee fully convertible and massive cuts in import duties. The latest in the liberalisation list is the Government's announcement that India will now allow Foreign Institutions (FIIs) to invest in Indian Stock Markets This exhaustive list relaxatin has made India quite attractive for foreign investors, very much comparable to the best of world's emerging economic powers.

Trend in Flow of Foreign Investment :

The world Investment Report 1993 says that India is now making its presence felt in the field of Foreign Direct Investment (FDI) by being able to attract noteable increase in flows. The real outcome of the liberalisation move is found to be relatively encouraging though it is too early to judge the actual inflow of foreign investment on this count.

The total volume of foreign investment approval at about Rs. 430 Crore during August 1991 to December 1992, is more than three times the Rs. 127 Crore of the total foreign investment approved in the last decade . About 1520 proposals of foreing collaborations have been approved during 1992. Direct foreign capital investment is usually accompanied by advanced technological inputs. During April to December 1992 , 1092 technology import agreements were signed as compared to 592 in the whole of 1989-90 . Still a better flow is expected since more alluring liberalisation packages are declared in the recent past.

The reform measures have encouraged several countries including UK USA and Germany who have expressed an interest in signing bilateral investment treaties. Britain and France power companies are convinced by the Indian government"s commitment on investment guiarantee for foreing investors keen to invest i n the power sector in India.

Foreign Investment

FDI inflows to developing countries are estimated to have gone up to U.S.$ 149 billion in 1997 from U.S. $ 130 billionin 1996. India's share of global FDI flows rose from 1.8 per cent 1996 to 2.2 per cent in 1997 Table-2 deficts the fact . On the other hand, India's share in net portfolio investment flows to the developing countries declined to 5.1 per cent in 1997 after increasing to 8.7 per cent in 1996. as depicted in Table-2.

Table -2

FDI by Host Region

(US $ Mllion)

Country	*1992*	*1995*	*1997*[e]
China	11156	35849	45300
India	233	1964	3264
Indonesia	1777	4348	5350
Korea,Rep.of	727	1776	2341
Malaysia	5183	4132	3754
Philipines	228	1459	1253
Thailand	2114	2002	3600
All developing countries including China	51108	105511	148944
Share of India in developing countries (%)	0.5	1.9	2.2

Source *World Investment Report , United Nations, 1998.*

'e' *estimates.*

Note *Figures for India in this tabel not be comparable with those in other tables because of differences in coverage and source of information.*

Table-3

FII net investment in India as a percemt of Portfolio investment in Developing Countries

(US$ Million)

Item	*1994*	*1995*	*1996*	*1997*
Portfolio investment in India #	5348	1361	4579	2816
Net Portfolio investment in developing countries @	85700	22200	52700	55500
India's share in developing countries(%)	6.2	6.1	8.7	5.1

\# Include FII net investment (SEBI data) and GDR (RBI data)

@ Data published in the world Economic Outlook, I.M.F.1998.

Foreign investment into India in 1997-98 was lower at U.S. $ 5,025 million compared to U.S.$ 6,008 million in 1996-97 because of a decline in portfolio investment as depicted in Table-4. Although foreign direct investment (FDI) increased by 18.6 per cent from U.S.$ 2,696 million in 1996-97 to U.S.$ 3,197 million in 1997-98 portfolio investment declined from U.S. $ 3,312 million in 1996-97 to U.S.$ 1,828 million in 1997-98 . This decline in portfolio investment is mainly attributable to the contagion from the East Asian crisis, which adversely affected capital flows to all emerging markets.

Table-4

Foreign Investment Flows by Different Categories

(US $ Mllion)

	1991-92	*1994-95*	*1997-98*
A. Direct Investment	129	1314	3197
(a). RBI automatic route	-	171	202
(b). SIA/IPB route	66	701	2754
(c). NRI (40% & 100%)	63	442	241
B. Portfolio Investment	4	3824	1828
(a). FIIs #	-	1503	979
(b). Euro equities @	-	2082	645
(c). Offshore funds & others	4	239	204
Total (A+B)	133	5138	5025

Source : RBI.

\# *Provisional*

@ *Figures represent GDR amounts raised abroad by the Indian Corporates.*

International developments continue to affect capital flows into India in 1998-99 as well. The provisional estimate of total foreign investment at U.S. $ 880 million during April-December, 1998 was sharply lower compared to the inflow of U.S.$ 4253 million during the corresponding period in the previous year. Although FDI flows were weaker, this overall decline in capital flows was mainly attributable to a net outflow in portfolio investment of U.S.$ 682 million during April-December 1998 as against an inflow of U.SA.$ 1742 million during the same period in 1997. Trends in approvals and actual inflows of foreign direct investment are shown in Table-5.

Table-5

Foreign Direct Investment : Actual Flows vs. Approvals

	1991	*1993*	*1995*	*1997*
Approvals				
Rs Crore	739	11189	37489	57149
US $ million	325	3559	11245	15752
Actual Inflows				
Rs Crore	351	1786	6720	12085
US $ million	155	574	2100	3330
Actual Inflows as % of Approvals (In US $ terms)	47.7	16.1	18.7	21.1

Source *RBI.*

Note *The approval and actual Inflows figures include NRI direct investments approved by RBI.*

Mauritius, as in the previous two years, was the dominant source of FDI inflows in 1997-98 . U.S.A and S. Korea were, respectively, the second and third largest sources of FDI. The striking feature was that S. Korea increased its flow of investment in India from a meagre U.S. $ 6.3 million in 1996-97 (0.2 per cent of total FDI) to U.S.$ 333.1 million in 1997-98 (10.4 per cent share).On the sectoral side, although the engineering industry witnessed a decline in inflows in 1997-98 , it remained an attractive area for FDI being the second largest recipient after electronics & electrical equipments.

The decline in portfolio investment, from 1997-98 onwards has been contributed by a decline in flows of both foreign institutional investment and GDRs as depicted in Table-5.Fresh inflow of funds by FIIS declined from U.S.$ 1,926 million in 1996-97 to U.S. $ 979 million in 1997-98 . This trend intensified in 1998-99 with an estimated outflow of U.S.$ 752 million during April December, 1998 compared to inflows of U.S.$ 973 million during the corresponding period in the previous year. GDRs raised in 1997-98 was U.S.$ 645 million, which was less than half the amount of U.S.$ 1,366 million raised in 1996-97 . The declining trend has continued during the first nine months of 1998-99 with only U.S.$ 15 million raised compared to U.S.$ 612 million during the same period in 1997-98 . The poor performance of portfolio investment is a consequence of both enhanced emerging market risk perception , and the depressed condition of the domestic capital market.

Policies on Foreign Investment

Several measures to boost FDI have been announced in 1998-99 . Projects for electricity generation, transmission and distribution as also roads and highways, ports and harbours, and vehicular tunnels and bridges have been permitted foreign equity participation up to 100 per cent under the automatic route, provided foreign equity does not exceed Rs. 1500 crore. FDI permissible under Non-Banking Financial Services now includes "Credit CArd Business " and "Money Changing Business". Regarding equity participation in private sector banks, multilateral financial institutions have been allowed to contribute equity to the extent of the shortfall in NRI holdings within the overall permissible limit of 40 per cent. The Governmnent has also decided to permit FDI up to 49 per cent of the total equity, subject to license, in companies providing Glopbal Mobile Personal Communication by Satellite (GMPCS) services. Also, minimum capitalisatin norms earlier required for pure financial consultancy services have been relaxed.

GDR/ADR guidelines have been further liberalised in 1998-99 . Unlisted companies are now permitted to float Euro issues under certain conditions. All end-use restrictions on GDR/ADR issue proceeds have been removed, except the prevailing restrictions on investment in stock markets and real estate. The 90 day validity period for final approvals of GDR/ADR issues has been withdrawn and final approval will continue to be valid, thereby imparting greater flexibility to issuing companies regarding the timing of issues. Indian companies are now permitted to issue GDRs/ADRs in the case of Bonus or Rights issue of shares, or on genuing business reorganisations duly approved by the High Court. The companies however, in all such cases, will be required to get approval from the Department of Economic Affairs for the issue of GDRs/ADRs.

Portfolio Investments - NRIs

A number of liberalisation measures have been taken in 1998-99 to promote portfolio foreign investment, In order to avoid NRIs being crowded out by FIIs. the aggregate ceiling for investment in a company by all NRIs /PIOs/OCBs through stock exchanges has been made separate and exclusive of the investment ceilling available for FIIs. In addition, the aggregate investment ceiling for NRIs/PIOs./OCBs has been raised from 5 per cent to 10 per cent of the paid up capital of a company, In the case of listed Indian companies, the ceiling can be raised to 24 per cent of the paid up capital under a General Body Resolution. Also, the investment limit by a single NRI.PIUO/OCB has been enhanced from 1 per cent to 5 per cent of the paid up capital. Policy pertaining to investment in unlisted companies has also been liberlised . NRIs/PIOs/OCBs are now permitted to invest in unlisted companies. However, while investing in unlisted companies, the same norms and approval procedures applicable to portfolio investments in listed companies will apply, and it will be subject to the same investment ceiling as in the listed comapnies.

Portfolio Investments - FIIs

FIIs can purchase and sell Government Securities and Treasury Bills within overall aproved debt ceilings. To facilitate better risk management by investors, authorised dealers have been permitted to provide forward cover to FIIs in respect of their fresh equity investments in India. Moreover, transactions among FIIs with respect to Indian stocks will no longer require post-facto confirmation from the RBI. Also 100 per cent FII debt funds have been permitted to invest in unlisted debt securities of Indian companies.

External Commercial Borrowings (FCBs)

The higher net inflows of U.S. $ 3,999 million of FCBs in 1997-98 compared to U.S.$ 2,848 million in 1996-97 reflected lower amortisation. Disbursements in 1997-98 stood at U.S. $ 7,371 million, which was marginally lower than U.S.$ 7,571 million recorded in 1996-97 have been placed at U.S.$ 8,712 million , which is slightly higher than the level in 1996-97 . Regarding sectoral allocation power accounted for the highest approvals of U.S.$ 3 billion followed by telecom with U.S. $ 1.5 billion as pointed out in Table-6. In 1998-99 up to 23.12.98, approvals have been placed at U.S.$ 3,804 million. The reduced attractiveness of ECB of the corporate sector has been underscored by a very steep decline in actual disburesements to U.S.$ 1.6 billion (excluding U.S.$ 4.2 billion on account of RIBs) in the first quarters of 1998-99 compared to U.S.$ 4.3 billion in the same period last year. Increase in cost of ECB funds has come about due to a general increase in the risk premium for emerging market borrowers, downgrades by international credit rating agencies and the rise in forward premia. After several years of unchanged or slightly improving ratings, major rating agencies started to reexamine our ratings in early 1997 Table. Both the deteriorating external environment and persistent large fiscal deficits have been cited as the main reasons for downgrading.

Table-6
Status of ECB Approvals

(US $ Mllion)

Sector	*1996-97*	*1997-98*	*1998-99**
Power	1874	3014	2733
Telecom	289	1492	75
Shipping	146	210	36
Civil Aviation	45	373	0
Petroleum & Natural Gas	783	230	40
Railways	144	179	15
Financial Institutions	1502	795	50
Ports, Roads , etc.	0	61	0
Others (including exporters)	3797	2358	855
Total	*8580*	*8712*	*3804*

* *as on 23.12.98*

Source : *ECB Division, Ministry of Finance , Government of India.*

ECB is approved by the Government within an annual ceiling that is consistent with produnt debt management, keeping in view the balanced of payments position. The existing ECB policy was reviewed in 1998-99 in light of the financial needs of various sectors and the impact on international markets of both the East Asian crisis and economic sanctions. Regarding the sectoral requirements, infrastructure and exports continu to be accorded hih priority in ECB allocation. The changes in the ECB guidelines are summarised in Box.

NRI Investment

The Indian Capital Market provides significant opportunities to NRIs for investment in corporate securities. But though the flow of NRI investment has beens steadily increasing over the years, the NRI s have shown greater interest in Foreign Currency non-Resident Accounts (FCNRA) of bank deposits than in the stock market investments. The inflow of capital from Chinese living abroad has helped the accelerated growth rate of the Chinese economy in recent years. But such a response from NRIs in investing corporate securities has yet to come. However, due to the present liberalisation move of the government , investments worth Rs. 512 Crore has been pledged by the NRIs till January 31, 1993 for setting worth Rs. 512 crore has been pledged by the NRI till January 31,1993 for setting up of industries in various fields like engineering automobiles, Chemicals and Electricals.

The Resurgent India Bond (RIB) scheme, launched in the current financial year, was open to both NRIs/OCBs and the banks acting in fiduciary capacity on behalf of them. The scheme, that opened on August 5,1998 and closed on August 24,1998, mobilised U.S.$ 4.2 billion. The interest rates on these five year bonds were 7.75 per cent for U.S. dollar 8 per cent for Pound Sterling, and 6.25 per cent for Deutsche Mark. Other features of RIBs include joint holding with Indian residents, allowing them to be gifted to Indian residents, easy transferability, loanability, premature encashment facility, and tax benefits.

Net inflows under non-resident deposits declined from U.S.$ 3,314 million in 1996-97 to U.S.$ 1,119 million in 1997-98 as depicted in Table-7. The outflow under FCNRA continued due to redemption payment. Also, the relative rates of return and the perceived risk premium on emerging market debt has influenced the flows into these accounts . Some of the domestic policy related factores which seem to have contributed towards subdued net flows include imposition of incremental cash reserve ratio of 10 per cent on non-resident deposits and the linking of interest rates under FCNR(B) with LIBOR, which had the effect of lowering interest rates offered under this scheme, and thereby reducing its attractiveness. In order to encourage mobilisation of long-term deposits, and concomitantly to discourage short-term deposits, the interest rate ceiling on FCNR(B) deposits of one year and above was raised and the ceiling on such deposits below one year was reduced in April 1998.

Table-7

Outstanding Balances and Net Flows under various Non-Resident Deposit Schemes

(US $ Million)

A. Outstnading Balance under Different Schemes *

Schemes	*March94*	*March95*	*March96 (Revised)*	*March98 (Revised)*
FCNR(A)	9300	7051	4255	1
FCNR(B)	1108	3063	5720	8467
NR(E)RA	3523	4556	3916	5627
NR(NR)RD	1754	2486	3542	6262
FC(B&O)D	533	-	-	-
TOTAL	*16218*	*17156*	*17433*	*20367*

B. Net Inflows under Non-Resident Deposits*

Schemes	*1993-94*	*1996-97*	*1997-98*
Foreign Currency Non-Resident (Accounts)(FCNR(A))	-1317	-1949	-2305
Foreign Currency Non-Resident (Banks) (FCNR(B))	1075	1773	971
Non-Resident External Rupee Accounts (NR)(E) RA)	728	1244	1197
Non-Resident (NonRepatriable) Rupee Deposits (NR(NR)RD)	1187	2246	1256
Foreign Currency (Banks & Others) Deposits (FC(B &O)D)	-576	-	-
Total	*1097*	*3314*	*1119*

* All figures are inclusive of accured interest.

Source : RBI.

As at the end of March 1998 outstanding balances under various non-resident deposit schemes stood at U.S.$ 20,367 million. Comparison of estimated net flows under non-resident deposits during April-November 1997 shows a compositional shft in favour of Rupee denominated accounts in response to policy initiatives undertaken in 1997-98 . Net inflows under non-residents deposits, (excluding redemption payments under FCNRA which had since been discontinued) at US $ 367 million during April-Novewmber, 1998 were substantially lower than those of US $ 2266 million in the same period of 1997. Positive flows have been recorded only in the NR(E) RA and NR(NR)RD schemes. The initiatives in terms of freeing of interest rates and removal of incremental CRR, may have acted as incentives to attract deposits in these accounts.

Criticisms against Foreign Capital

Doubts have, however , been expressed about the benefits accuring to the country by the inflow of foreign capital. *Prof. B.R. Shenoy* has developed a thesis that "during the First Plan period the bulk of foreign aid financed gold smuggling; the much larger foreign aid during the first three years of the Second Plan was used up principally for hoarding foodgrains, partly to finance smuggling and a small part for purchasing Indian assets owned by foreigners. " He has concluded that foreign capital had not augmented capital formation due to its misdirection. The various grounds of objection against the import of foreign capital in India may be summarised as follows :

1. *Exploitation.* It has been deduced from *Sir George Paish's* estimates of foreign capital in India that 97 per cent of the foreign capital before the war of 1914 was devised for purposes of Government transport, plantations, and finance, i.e. for purposes auxiliary to the commercial penetration of India and her exploitation as source of raw materials and market for British goods and in no way connected with industrial development. The natural result was a 'colonial ' investment pattern open to familiar criticisms that it tends to promote lop-sided rather than ' balanced' growth and that it makes for instability due to high dependence on foreign demand for one or two staple products.

(2).*Attitude of Discrimination* - In twenties and thirties of the present century foreign business units adopted a policy of racial and political discrimination in the matter of credit insurance and transport. Moreover, there was discrimination against Indians in the employment of personnel, particularly on high-salaried offices. The foreign entrepreneurs rarely offered posts of responsibility to the nationals who were mostly appointed on clerical jobs.

(3) *Competition with internal enterprise* - the entry of foreign capital is opposed because of its better comjpetitive efficiency. The hom industrialisats lack in the technique, traditions and organisatin of the industrially advanced countries " What brought foreign business in for criticism was not its fault but its virtues. Foreign firms were resented by domestic industrialists because they were more efficient and could stand up better in hard times ".

(4) *Higher Return*. The cost of foreign private capital is too high. An idea can be had from the weighted average of the return on capital invested by U.S.A. and Canada, in India according to the Reserve Bank's Census of Foreign Assets and Liabilities. In case of investments made by U.S.A. it was 19.2 per cent and on Canadian investments it was 33.3 per cent. The return on U.K. investment in India was reasonable, being 6.5 per cent. Thus American capital is very costly and its inflow would mean a great drain on our limited resources. The average rate of return on U.S. foreign investments in 1955 was about 13 per cent compared with about 10-12 per cent on U.S. domestic investments.

(5)*Uncertain Source* - Foreign capital is an uncertain source of finance. It is a fair weather friend only. During last years the quantum of foreign aid obtained every year has been quite uncertain. Moreover with the development of the industrial base in the country, it was necessary to shift emphasis from project to non-project aid. The circumstances indicated the need of progressing as much in the direction of reducing dependence on foreign aid as possible.

(6)*Selected Froms and Felds* - The recent trend in private foreign investment connotes that it is taking place in undertakings which are effectively controlled in the capital exporting countries. It is represenmted mostly in the form of subsidiaries or branches of firms already established in capital exporting countries. Moreover, the major part of it is going to petroleum and very little foreign investment is occurring in other spheres. Looking at the industry wise breakdown of the foreing business investments between 1948 and 1990 , it may be marked that petroleum and manufacturing groups showed the largest increases since 1948 . The two groups together accounted for about 75 per cent of the net increase in investment during this period.

(7)*Uncertainty of its Stay.*- The recent withdrawals and repatritions have indicated the dangers of reliance on foreign capital. The canons of sound strategy also emphasis the fact that basic and key industries should not be permitted to have foreign capital . Particularly during the period of hostilities it is undiplomatic to trust foreign capitalists. They cannot be confided even in peace times. The Union Minister for Commerce and Industry expressed his fear about the withdrawal of the British from tea industry while addressing the Export Trade Advisory Council meeting in November , 1955. In their parting mood the British management neglected replanation and their Indian successors could not incur replanation outlay, once they had paid fantasticdally high price for the garden acquisition.

(8) *Political Strings Attached* - The persons at the helm of affairs have become quite conscious of this new development . In spite of so much preaching of the precept of "expanding world economy" and passing high sounding resolutions to amellorate the living standards in the under-developed regions and pleading in unequivocal terms the international movement of capital the results are scanty and disappointing. The United States was the first, among the industrially advanced nations, to realise the importance of economic aid designed to rehabilitate the undeveloped countries . But such assistance has been given as a bulwark against Russian expansion. The struggle of Iran, Egypt , Malaya and Indo China today is a singular warning of how foreign aid grew into shackles of bondage so hard to shake off.

(9) *Greater Strain on Foreign Exchange* - Comparison of the direct benefits and costs of foreign investments are made by relating the amount of capital inflow "excluding re-invested profts" to the foreing exchange outgo on account of Capital and profit remittances. The excess of payments over receipts should however,be taken to indicate that fresh capital receipts were too little compared to the recurrent costs incurred on servicing the older investments.

Foreign capital in India has a long history- a record glowing with pioneering efforts, great achievements and wonderful farsightedness juxtaposed with the hateful record of rutheless exploitation, economic dominatin and political subjugation. The conspicuous opening of new fields in jute, coal , tea and coffee planations, and laudable services of managing agencies establishment and management of exchange banks insurance companies and shipping compan in India all go to the credit of foreign capital and management. Whatever might have been the role of foreign capital in the past, it has an important and vital role to play in our of foreign capital in the past, it has an important and vital role to play in our planned economic development. There is a wide gap between our resources and requirements. Internal resources are inadequate to achieve the cherished goal of self-sufficiency and rapid economic development. We lack not only in capital goods but also in the technique, skill and traditions associated with the foreign business firms. Domestic savings have got to be supplemented by foreign assistance, otherwise the programmes of investment will have to be curtailed or the period of the Plan increased or people asked to make more sacrifices in the form of payment of higher taxes or higher prices for the articles of consumption because of inflationary conditions caused by deficit financing.

(10) *Risks of Inconvertibility* - The availability of foreign exchange for the foreign investors to remit dividends interest and capital when they desire is a crucial consideration. 'It has rightly been observed that if an under-developed country were to assure convertibility for the funds, of foreign investors, this would commit to a series of policies which, on the whole it might consider detrimental to its welfare.

In India foreign exchange has been under control since 1939 and the present control is based on the Foreign Exchange Regulations Act 1973 . The problems of balance of payments and mobilisation of capital resources which gave rise to exchange controls may be expected to continue in the immediate future in view of India's industrialisation plans and the world situation. The main purpose of such control has been to aid the government in acquiring and conserving the foreign exchange needed for purchasing necessary imports. But India is committed to the gradual elimination of exchange controls by its membership of the International Monetary Fund and participation in other international agreements which call for eventual lifting of all restrictions on international trade . The extent to which such controls are actually reduced in India depends upon the future effectiveness of these organisations and agreements . But these difficultties have been removed recently. FERA has been relaxed under the policy of liberalisation. Foreign firms have generally been permitted to remit profits earned from their operation in India without difficulty . Indian rupee has been made fully convertible and so on .

(11) *Expropriation of Property* - The expropriation of property without adequate and prompt compensation is another great risk. It is argued that so long as uncertainty exists as to the eventual scope of the nationalisation programmes in various countries this will constitute considerable brade upon the zest of potential investors.

The Government of India has already declared its attitude towards this particular issue. Capital owned by residents of sterlling area, Norway, Sweden and Denmark is freely granted repartriation . Capital owned by residents of other countries if invested after January 1, 1950 , in a project approved by the Indian Government , would also be granted repatriation at any time up to the extent of the original investment and subsequent investments which were approved by the Government . On March 3,1953 , the assurance of the right to repatriate investment at any time was extended to apply to capital gains on such investments. The U.S.A. Investment Guarantee Programme has been considered by the Government of India. This programme provides, by means of inter-government agreements, insurance protection to U.S. foreign investors against the risks of inconvertibility of foreign currency receipts and loss through expropriation or confiscation.

(12) *Limited Return* - Comparative data on profitability ratio and on assets formation show that the performance of the foreign controlled rupee companies was better than the Indian controlled companies. Foreign controlled companies has a better recdord of dividend payment also, compared to their Indian counterparts. Gross assets formation took place at the rate of 12.0 per cent in the case of foreign controlled companies compared to 9.2 per cent for Indian controlled companies.

Further , compared with the rate of return on investment in their respective home countries, the return to the foreign companies in India is greater. According to the U.S. Department of Commerce the earning ratio in respect of U.S . investment in the manufacturing sector of India worked out to 14.9 per cent in 1964 as against 10.8 per cent on world wide basis.

(13)*Heavy Taxation* - It is argued that the high level of taxation in under-developed countries is a great hindrance for the inflow of foreign capital. The double taxation of incomes derived from foreign investment also is generally recognised as an obstacle to the international flow of capital . The authorities invarious capital exporting countries levy and collect a tax on the world total income of individuals and companies resident in their territories. At the same time the authorities in capital importing countries extend their tax jurisdiction over foreign companies operating within their territory. This overlapping of tax jurisdictions tends to discourage both investment and trade. Some progress was made in solving the problem of international double taxation in the inter-war period when a considerable number of bilateral treaties were concluded. However, much remained to be done.

Towards Better Investment Climate :

Since the Indian Government is commited to the concept of globalisation , as it seems and the liberalisation package is being kept enalarged every month, hopefully, it may be able to attract more and more foreign investment including NRI investment in the years to come. But then, to woo the foreing investors, probably a better investment climate could be created and the perceived bottlenecks in the path may be removed. today China became the second largest receipient of inflows among all developing countries in Asia , exceeded only by Mexico. the principle attributable reason being better investment climate which includes low cost large domestic market rising per capita income, development of sufficient industrial infra-structure and above all perfect industrial relations. The following points need thorough examination which may help create better invesment climate in India and lure the foreing investors to come forward.

(a) The existing policy of the government is not clear, Lack of Healthy industrial relations and consequent trabulent industrial environment has discouraged foreing investors to come. The most important task before the government is to come out with a clear cut and bolder policy regarding rationalisation of workforce with a view to ensuring healthy and perfect industrial relations.

(b) One of the major handicaps in attracting foreing investors to India is the poor and inade quate industrial infrastructure, which should be taken care of . Many foreign investors have turned their faces for lack of adequate infra-structure. Recently Japan has agreed to invest in India on the condition that, first, it should be allowed to develop infra structure in the form of setting up " industrial cities" of its own.

(c) Another important area which needs immediate attention of the government is to guard against the inefficiency and indiscipline in financial sector of the economy and strengthen and the financial system as a whole. It should ensure that events like the recent stock exchange scam is not repeated.

(d) Any foreign investor is found obviously interested in a stable political government where he wants to invest. Political stability has a far reaching implication for the industrial development of a nation and simultaneously it creates a sense of safety and security in the mind of the ivnestor. India need feel concern about it, if it is really interest in economic development through foreing investment.

Flow of foreing invesmtnet into India for its economic development in the process of globalisation is a welcome measure. But it needs selectivelty. We must selectively attract investment in priority areas like oil exploration, petroleum refining and petrochemicals, power generation , telecommunication and tourism. Hopefully, such a step may help bridging the huge trade deficit, since investment in these industries will reduce bulk imports and earn foreign exchange. No doubt, foreign investment has a crucial role in export growth and technology upgradation, but the government should watch and guard against the MNCs entering soft areas, transferring out-dated technology and exploiting domestic market instead of helping boost the country's foreing exchange earnings.

****

15

Multinational Corporations

The emergence of multinational corporations on the world scene signifies the beginning of a new international situation with multiple ramifications. Their economic command over economic resources and their enviable possession of managerial skill and technology have provided them with a unique opportunity to influence not only the process of socio-economic development in host countries but all to impregnate indelible the pattern of international relationship. Any institution endowed with such oligopolistic power and influence is apt to become ambitious, it may surpass the frontiers of its immediate economic goal when opportunity arises, if may flout all norms of ethics and fair play in quest of settling permanently in the saddle of politico-economic power. As a matter of fact multinationals have become a vital economic reality of the new economic order of modern economic development.

The Concept of Multinational Corporations

U.N.O. defines aMultinational Corporation as follows:

Multinational Corporations are enterprises which own or control production or service facilities outside the country in which they are based. "

According to W.H.Mareland, "Multinational Corporations or companies are those enterprises whole management, ownership and controls are spread in more than one foreign country."

The United Nations, in one of its reports, have termed them as a transitional corporations. Thus MNCs are concerned about their activities world wide. They have direct investment in several countries, derive profits from foreign investments and operations. International Business Machines (IBM) of USA; Philips, Unilever Ltd. Du Pont, Siemeans, Imperial Chemical Industries are a few promiment names of multinational corporations.

Type of Multinational Corporations

The multinational corporations may be divided into seven categories depending upon their activities . They may be colonial companies, resource based companies, public utilities companies, manufacturing companies service institutions, licensing and turnkey projects. Their brief description is as follows :

1. **Colonial Companies.** Colonial Companies are those companies which are established to procure raw materials for the parental office at native country. They monopolise the purchasing of raw materials. They have rights to operate in different countries. East India Company's name can be cited i n this respect.

2. **Resource Based Companies**. It is the second category of multinationals. These companies purchase raw resources from several countries. They do not believe in exploitation and purchasing of mineral resources. Many developed and developing countries have propagated such types of companies.

3. Public Utility Companies. The public utility companies are established to help the people of the country. The companies enjoy the position of natural monopoly. The multinational in public utility concerns do not remain longer because of nationalism.

4. Manufacturing Companies. The manufacturing companies are engaged in several manufacturing processes. They produce qualitative and quantiative goods in a huge quantity. They invest adequate capital in foreign countries to get higher rate of return. Whenever multinationals or MNCs are referred they indicate to manufacturing companies.

5. Service Institutions. They know the service technology and provide suitable and sufficient services to the people of the countries where they are established . Banking, Insurance, Hotels , Airways, etc. are the several examples of such companies.

6. Licensing. The multinationals grant licenses to some domestic companies to use their trademarks and technical know-how. The license is granted to exploit potential market in the host countries who pay license fees annually to the multinationals to use their know-how for a fixed period. The licence fee may be in lump sum to purchase the know-how.

7. Turnkey Project. Turnkey project is taken up by the multinationals to complete a specific job within a fixed period. The contract for a turnkey project is made on open tender or on the basis of cost plus fee for the services. There may be limit on the total cost. If the multinational exceeds the cost, it has to bear the excess cost.

Advantages of Multinational Corporations (Good Effects)

The multinational corporations have been helpful in transferring foreign investment from one country to another. The liberal trade and investment policy have facilitated multinationals to invest in developing countries. The economic growth of the host country is feasible by the investment . South East Asia, Brazil, South Korea have developed on account of the multinationals The multinationals have helped several countries, domestic industries traders, technological development, low cost of production, employment opportunities, balance of trade, avoidance of market barriers and other benefits.

1. **Development of Countries.** The socio economic development of several countries have been witnessed as a result of foreign investment. The developing countries have low level of saving and investments. The shortage of the multinationals because they bring capital and technology to the developing countries. The untapped natural resources are exploited by them. The production of the country is increased . Market is expanded and the economy is ultimately benefited. The action and interaction of the multinationals bring cultural change to the domestic businessmen who learn something from the multinationals . They develop enterpreneurial skills getting some insights from the multinationals and also develop collaboration with the multinational corporations. Thus, the domestic business men and entrepreneurs get an opportunity to learn some new business skills from them. The domestic entrepreneurs develop their businesses and the country is developed consequently. More investment helps increased production which gives more opportunities to save and invest i n the same country. The virtuous circle of development is accelerated by the funds brought by the multinational corporations.

2. **Domestic Industries.** The domestic industries have been benefited by the collaborations of the multinationals and are individually getting more profits because of the multinationals. They are dynamic and provide growth opportunities to the domestic companies. The high degree of marketability, competitive spirits, help private companies

enter in the international markets by way of providing international market expertise, exchange, and financial arrangements and easing problems of communication. The individuals do not face any problems relating to international markets because the multinationals come to their rescue. The collaboration helps understand mutual problems and finds suitable solutions there of. The potential markets which would have been unexploited without collaboration have been easily peneterated by the mutual efforts of the multinationals and domestic industries . Both of them harness the untapped resources which would have been unutilised in absence of colaboration.

3. **Traders.** The multinationals have brought several international traders together. The domestic traders as well as foreign traders know each other for their respective requirements. Mutual understanding and exchange have been the key factors to help international trade. They gain themselves by the trade as well as other allied persons who are also benefitted by the multinationals. The taxes are earned by the governments on the trade and profits are also taxed which are sources of revenue to the governments. The total investments by multinationas in world trade has been increasing from time to time. Investment in developed countries and also in developing countries has also increased significantly. Manufacturing and service industries have been benefitted by the increasing investment of multinationals. They have owned about one fourth of the fixed assets of world economy. Aluminium, tobacco, cocoa, pharmaceuticals, chemicals etc, are owned mainly by multinationals. They have increased the operational efficiency of these industries. Economy of scale has been experienced by them.

4. **Technological Development.** The multinational corporations have provided adequate technology to the developing countries. Technological development in many

countries is the outcome of these corporations. Organisational, technological and managerial developments have undergone changes in these years in all the countries. Only domestic technology cannot contribute significantly to the development of the country. No country can sustain its growth unless supported by modern technology. The domestic and international technology are essential for expanding international marketing which provides adequate opportunities of development of the countries. Production and markets, the two pillars of development,. have always experienced innovation. Marketing of traditional pattern cannot last longer and it requires modernisation. The multinationals with their wide experiences of several countries can contribute significantly for the technological development. The technological developments in the areas of production and market have benefitted the multinational as well as the host countries.

5. Lower Cost of Production. The lower cost of production is an important consequences of the economy of scale which is possible by multinational production and marketing. The multinationals have gained the benefits of world wide production and marketing. The developing countries have specially benefitted by such activities. Developed countries are benefited by higher profitability of the multinationals. The great seven countries viz. United States, West Germany, Japan, France, Britain, Canada and Italy have larger number of multinationals. they have contributed maximisation of production in different countries while extracting considerable amount of profits. Recently some countries have also entered in this field. The lower cost of production has benefitted the developing countries. the purchase of raw materials at lower cost use of sphisticated production technique and innovative markets have contributed to higher profitability.

6. Employment Opportunities. The multinational corporations provide employment opportunities to the people of host countries in their production and marketing activities. Apart from the direct opportunities of employment, several persons are invited to allied activities. Production enhances the purchasing capacities of the people giving them push to increase their standard of living. The from the traditional purchases to the modern purchases. People are satisfied with new products. Employment in other countries is also increased by way of expanded markets in foreign countries.

7. Balance of Trade. Export and import of host countries rise as per the multinational activities. Inter regional and infra regional trade increased in many developing countries. Export of the multinationals has given an opportunity to rectify the unfavourable balance of trade.

8. Trade Barriers. Multinationals by way of production in different countries avoid trade barriers. The trade regulations are followed by the host countries. They follows the regulations of pricing promotion, product liability and personal practices.

9. Other Benefits. Many multinationas get the benefits of more profits. The domestic shareholders are also benefitted by the higher rate of dividend. The capital market of the host country is improved by such activities and people at large are benefitted. The qualitative improvements are also witnessed with the expansion of multinationals in the country . For example, Indian soft drink in foreign countries has no market on account of low quality whereas the Indian soft drink in collaboration with Pepsi-cola got adequate market in foreign countries because of improved quality.

Disadvantage of Multinationals (Bad Effects)

The multinationa corporations have some negative effect also on the national economy, capital market , trade, consumers and political dominance. They are as follows :

1. Economy . The multinationals are mainly interested in making profit and least care about the economic development of the host country. Labour raw materials and foreign exchanges are used for their self-benefits. Labour being cheap in developing countries are exploited to the maximum by the multinational corporations. Had these corporations traded in their respective countries, they would have paid more wages to their labour because labour is costlier in their respective countries being developed economy. The labour in developing countries are cheaper and multinationals pay lesser amount to them. Thus, the cost of production is minimised. The raw materials are purchased at cheaper rate. The producers of raw materials do not get adequate return on their produce . Therefore, the cost of production is lower. The multinational develops the shape and form of monopoly and is benefitted by the activities of this nature. Lower taxes are generally paid by the multinationals because of encouragement of the government. The multinationals remit foreign exchange to their families in their respective countries. As a result, it reduces the foreing reserves and a shortage of foreing exchange is greater problem to the developing countries. The remittance of the foreign exchange to other countries add another problem. Therefore, it is considered that multinationals add problems to the economy.

The multinationals do not care for the development of local research and technology of host countries because they are afraid that the local development may create competition. They may come to the rescue of the local industries only when they are compelled to do this. They put some undersirable logic not to dilute the technology to the local industries. Employment is not increased as per anticipation. Sometimes they appoint foreig n nationals. The local employment is rare and only at the lower level. Only a part of the production process is made by themultinationals. The production is lagging behind in host countries.

2. Capital Market. The multinationals do not bring much of the capital from their countries to the host country . In many of the cases , they use the local capital for their industrial development. They borrow the local capital instead of inviting local shares. This helps them trading on equity and they earn adequate amount of dividend. This requires sending of dividend in the form of foreing exchange to their countries. Foreign exchange is drained out whereas none or very little foreign capital flows in by the foreign nationals.

Rapid change in production technology, stimulated economic activities and a large influx of capital lead to inflations in the host country. The economy does not move up with the money in supply and inflation creates unique problems. Less market, more production, inflatin and maladjustment of the economy are the various symbols of the rigid markets. The local government has to plan to contain the inflation, otherwise the distorted capital market may stumble the economy. Payment on account of dividends, royalties , interest, managerial and technical fees etc. decrease the foreign exchange.

3. Trade. The multinationals create sometimes artificial problems in trade. They overprice the import and underinvoice the export. It helps them to contain the payment in foreign countries. The excess of import and the short price of export are taken by their holding companies. They send a larger amount of profit to their countries and avoid taxes. Multinationals have increased world competition. They operate their work in specified areas. Trade is localised. The host country has unbalanced market development. The balance of trade becomes unfavourable. The competition from multinational corporations affects the local industries, negatively. Since the local industries are not developed fully, they do not stand with their competition. For example, indigenous soft drinks in India do not stand with the Pepsi cola soft drink.

The small and medium industries suffer from the competition with the multinationals. The small and medium industries cannot purchase adequate amount of raw materials at a time, cannot employ modern technology, cannot pay higher wages to their labour, cannot work in cooperation with other industries and cannot find adequate markets in the country because the multinationals defeat them at every front of trade. They enjoy international market, capital, technology and expertise. They enjoy international market, capital, technology and expertise. They can defeat any industries in the host country. Thus, the local trade is adversely affected by the multinational corporations. Balance of payments becomes unfavourable more on account of foreing debt and outflows of profits to shareholders in foreign countries.

4. **Consumers.** The consumers interests have not been much protected by the multinationas because of their profit motives. The multinational corporations ignore the consumers' rights consumers' interests, health and protection. The multinationals are monopolistics and exploit the markets for their benefits. Multinationals concentrate economic power and use it for their self benefits. They are reluctant to lower prices. On the other hand, they use strong marketing and promotion techniques, product differenctiation and so many other techniques to capture the market. They are in a position to increase prices and exploit the market. The consumers are suppressed with the higher prices and inflationary trend created by the multinationals. They adversely affect exchange rate and push up import prices.

The multinational corporations produce goods mainly for rich markets for maximising profits where consumer needs are sold under higher pressure salesmanship and sales promotions whereas the host countries have poor consumers and cannot afford to purchase such goods. The consumption patterns in developing countries are upset by luxurious production of multinationals. In the developing countries the gap between poor and rich increases , the latter purchase the produce of multinationals whereas the poor have no capacity to purchase them. Middle income group people are suppressed with the demonstration effect. The society experiences dissatisfaction and distortion. The structure power and operation of multinationals are of exploitation nature. They exploit consumers at every front from their self-benefits.

5. **Political Dominance** . The political dominance of multinational corporations begins with the economic concentration. They monopolise the power politics with alliance to the ruling parties. The Indian history is a glaring example of political dominance of the East India Company.

The multinational corporations from their structure to maximise their profits and minimise costs. They try to maximise the profits by operating performance, management expertise, technical know-how, financial assets and market intelligence. The multinationals have inadequate knowledge of the local market and so they try to coordinate with the activities of the local industries to gain the benefits of local markets. The production as well as marketing interdependence has facilitated multinationals to acquire adequate quantity of raw materials and dispose of in markets. The marketing activities are complementary for the different products made by different manufacturers. Standardised advertisement and promotion activities are uniform in their marketing activities. The organisatin structure of multinational corporations can be of five forms; centralised organisation, regional organisation, product organisation, functional organisation and combined structure of organisation.

1. **Centralised Organisation.** The centralised organisation keeps the rights of formulating policy, capital expenditure and appointment of key employees with the head office. The attributes of internationalism are adopted by

centralisations by adopting a uniform policy, adequate control and direction of growing international activities which are the main advantages of this structure. The international marketing with sectoral divisions can be effective form of centralisation. It means there should be ultimate control of the head office while the routine activities are performed by the regional offices. The international centralised organisation may be used in product as well as functional organisation. The complete centralised organisation suffers from less motivation , non-effective communication, less expert services , delays in carrying out the decision and other drawbacks of centralisation.

2. **Regional Organisation.** Regional organisation gives authority and power to the regional offices . Since the regional offices are well aware of the local, economic, social, geographical and political conditions, they can have effective management philosophies and procedures. They can exploit local raw materials , labour and marketing effectively by maneuvering the environmental conditions. The heterogeneous markets are approached differently . The advantages of regional organisation more than offset their disadvantages. Area-wise management with ultimate control by the head office is the effective method of management.

3. **Product Organisation.** The product organisation deals with product divisions. The product divisions may be organised on centralised or decentralised basis. These divisions are useful when different products are offered by the corporations. Therefore, they can form separate organisation for each product although the ultimate authority is vested to the organisation of the head office. Pure product organisation without assistance of the central office may lead to confusions of different products and their markets. They lack international marketing and expertise.

4. Functional Organisation. The functional organisation is based on the divisions of organisation as per activity. If there is more than one function in a multinational , the organisation can be divided into the different functions as per the nature of the functions. The functions if separated and identified differently can give a good organisation structure. Since the multinationals are not based on functional variations in many cases, such organisation is rare in multinational corporation. Functional competence in the areas of finances, production, personnel and marketing can be the basis of world wide as well as regional organisation.

5. Combined Structure. The Organisation, structure of multinationals can be combination of regional and international, product and functional, and any other combinations depending upon the need and structures of the multinational corporations. Regional and functional organisation, regional and product organisation, international and functional organisation, and international and product organisation may be the combined forms of organisation structure.

Multinational corporations in India have contributed significantly in the economic development of the country. To-day no country can afford to develop without multinationals. The role of multinational corporations in India's economic growth can be analysed under contributions to capital technological development, entrepreneurship, export performance, foreign exchange and economic development.

1. Capital: Multinational corporations bring capital with them to invest in the host countries . In India , too the multinational corporations have brought capital in the form of the direct investment and other capital which amounted to Rs. 59.0 crores in 1973-74 . The equity capital was to the extent of Rs. 3.3 crores and loans were Rs. 23.2 crores in 1973-74.

The number of branches of foreign nationals corporation was 358 in 1978-79 and the number of subsidiaries was 125. Their assets have increased significantly.

Many of the branches of multinationals in India are from the United Kingdom. The USA , Japan, West Germany and Switzerland, They have established their businesses in the areas of manufacturing , processing and chemicals.

The invitation to multinational corporations was given to ensure continuous inflow of capital and technology. The government decides whether foreign collaborations, foreign capital, technical collaboration or combination of these facilities are desirable in a particular sector. The government may impose restrictions in inflow of foreign capital because it has adverse effects on the foreign exchange and technological development in India.

Equity participation. The Government of India has allowed selective participation in the equity capital. The important criteria are priority of the industry, the nature of technology, export potential, transfer of technology, etc. The recent rules and regulations of equity participation are that the foreign nationals cannot participate more than 40 per cent of the equity of the company being established in India by foreigners. However, foreign investment to the level of 100 per cent is permitted in the 100 per cent export oriented units. The investment from OPEC does not require transfer of technology. They can invest in hotels and hospitals. Foreign capital is brought with the prior conditions that they will bring their technology in India and will dilute the technology in India for her development.

2. Technological Development. The technological development of India has witnessed the contribution of multinational corporations . The technology should be adapted to India's needs and requirements. They have contributed to the research and development of India. The Government of India have inducted advanced technology and have permitted creation of capacity large enough to meet the competitive requirements of world markets. The multinationals have helped development, absorb, adapt and disseminate modern technology for the economic development of India. The efficiency and effectiveness of industrial production have increased with their technical collaboration . India will not permit import of those technologies which compete with the Indian technology and create unemployment problem. Where foreign collaboration, financial or technical, is not essential, the government has not permitted their import by the multinational corporations or renewal of agreements. The renewal of collaboration agreements is done after careful scrutiny on merits. It is done for promotion in export, to absorb the sophisticated know-how and to manufacture essential items.

Purchase of technology is also permitted by the Indian Government. The best available technology is out rightly purchased by the government. Sometimes, the technology is used for a temporary period on payment of royalty. The rate of royalty depends upon the nature of technology but it does not ordinarily exceed 5 per cent on ex factory selling price. Royalty payment is subject to taxation laws in India. The multinationals which dilute the know how are welcome in India provided they do not compete with the Indian technology. It has been observed that Japan has contributed more in Indian technology than those of other countries. The U.S.a. , U.K., France , Germany and Italy have contributed considerably in the development of product quality, design, sales, services and promotion. The multinational corporations of Switzerland and Sweden have emerged recently as powerful international marketers to have product differentiations and have contributed in the industrial development of India. They have greater ability to deal with the labour problems, competitors and government. The multinationals in India have proved that labour and technical progress can move up with their help.

3. **Entrepreneurship.** The multinational corporations have made significant contribution to the development of entrepreneurship in India. they have helped the Indian companies to increase production and profit. The entrepreneurship in India is lagging behind. Many Indian companies developed as per availability of inculcated the spirit of risk taking and challenging activities. Agreements between Indian entrepreneurs and foreign investors have provided adequate training and experiences to the Indian industrialists.

The government of India has listed some industries where foreign collaborations or foreign investment is not permitted because they will provide competition to the indigenous industries. Oil, insurance, steel, coal, etc. are the industries where multinational corporations are not allowed to operate in India.

4. **Export Performance.** The export performance of multinationals in India has been satisfactory. Eight per cent of Indian exports have been effected by the multinational corporations. The Government of India has provided several incentives and subsidies to enhance the exports of multinationals from India; without government assistance, it would not have been possible to increase their exports. If multinational corporations take interest in export , India can lead the exports performance to a higher lavel because of its high potentials in the areas of technology, finance, marketing and personnel . The Government of India can find ways and means for export enhancement. The unit to unit agreement for export may encourage them to expand the markets of Indian goods in foreign countries.

The export performance of multinational corporations has revealed that it has increased from Rs. 309 crores in 1977-78 to Rs. 513 crores in 1980-81 whereas the production increased from Rs. 5331 crores in 1977-78 to Rs. 8740 crores in 1980-81. The import payments in their connection increased from Rs. 285 crores in 1977-78 to Rs. 625 crores in 1980-81 . It should be kept in mind that multinationals in India came with the objectives of exploiting the existing resources for their benefits and not for maximisation of export which was secondary objective to them. They have gone for exports, because of export-incentives, availability of import licenses for replenishment to exporters, special relations with the socialist blocks and export obligations put by India Government. The exports of multinational corporations have also increased on account of their business repute in foreign markets. However, it is clear that the multinational corporations in India do not take active part in export unless they are compelled to do that by Government.

5. **Foreign exchange**. It is expected that multinational corporations in India will conserve adequate amount of foreign exchange. They can export their goods and services to earn adequate amount of foreign exchange . Since they have a foreign base, their efforts to expand international marketing will be a success. They possess adequate infrastructural facilities such as worldwide network , adequate sources of information, product image and complete knowledge of world-market. They have approaches to the parent company , subsidiaries and sister concerns and other importers. They can appoint agents and representatives to have effective distribution channels. The parent company and sister companies may buy the product of the subsidiaries to reduce cost of production. The subsidiaries help the host countries to frame the international marketing programmes. They mutually help each other to design adequate product , fix prices and adopt promotional media.

The potential of multinational corporations to earn maximum foreign exchange has not been utilised by them. They generally exploit the local markets and do not like to compete in foreign markets unless they are compelled to do that. The result of foreign collaboration in India has been very discouraging . The value of net outflow of foreign exchange was Rs. 42 crores in 1977-78 which increased to Rs. 184 crores in 1980-81. The total foreign exchange payment was Rs. 352 crores and Rs. 697 crores respectively in the corresponsding years whereas total foreign exchange earning by the foreign collaborations was merely Rs. 310 crores and Rs. 513 crores in the respective years, It shows that the foreign exchange position in India deteriorated on account of multinational corporations.

6. Economic Development. The multinational corporation provided foreign capital, techniques, managerial skills develop the India's economy. The foreign investment in India after independence has made a rapid economic development of the country. Britain contributed 85 per cent of total foreign private investment in India, the U.S.A. contributed merely 9 per cent of total foreign private investment in India. The total technical contribution by multinational corporations in India was to the extent of Rs. 57.85 crores in 1985 which was merely Rs. 245 crores in 1970 and Rs. 80.92 crores in 1980. On the other hand, the direct investment in India was Rs. 913.4 crores in 1974 and other capital investment was Rs. 1029.6 crores in 1974. This shows that the multinationals have contributed in the India'sdevelopment . The multinational corporations have helped development of textile, pharmaceutical, chemical , vehicles and rubber industries in India.

****

16

Rail Transport in India

Railway are the principal carriers of men and material and have a major role to play in improving the economy of the nation. Besides , Railways, truly inculcate among the people the spirit and bonds of national integration. It is the main source of supply of essential commodities by transport through the length and breadth of the country and also the main force to bring economic well being for all citizens of the country. Ever since the invention of steam engines. Railways have played an important role in industrialisation and development of any nation. All developed and developing countries in the initial stages of their development and industrialisation had heavily relied on Railways for movement of goods and the pace would not have been that rapid if the Railway had not provided basic infrastructure needed for it. In short, railways have played a catalytic role in economic development of advanced countries and in a developing country like India , the contribution has been really great having its network covering very remote areas in the country.

Advantage of Railways

Following are the important advantage of Rail transport:

1. *Capacity to Carry Large Quantity of Goods:*-Among all the different means of transport, railway can carry at a time largest quantity of goods in the inland transport, Although the ships in water transport can carry many railway trains as such.

2. *Fast Speed* -Out of any other means of inland transport, railways have got the fastest speed . Long distances are covered in lesser time.

3. *No Effect of Weather Changes*- Except the flood situation, the railways are not affected by season.

4. *Expenses Decrease with Increased Traffic* - The Law of Increasing Returns applies to Railways . The more is the traffic the lesser will be per capita operation cost.

5. *Special Facilities of Goods Transport* -Railways provide special categories of containers and wagons for the transportation of specialised categories of goods. Similarly, in foreign trade also, it can carry the goods up to port towns and they bring the imported goods to the workshop of the manufacturers . Railway yards are also provided in the factory premises of selected manufacturers.

6. *Helpful at the Time of Famine* - Food products and foodgrains can be easily transported to the famine affected areas. Similar help can be provided for the other disturbed areas also.

These benefits are being multiplied from time to time by extending many services from the Railways. It is considered more comfortable and beneficial to travel by train, so that the persons can save even the night time.

Drawbacks of Railways

Following are some of the important shortcomings of Railways

1. *Monopoly* -Government has a monopoly on railways and often people are bound to suffer due to lopsided policies of this monopolistic organisatin.

2. *More Capital Investment* - A heavy capital investment in required in railways. It is considered that for one kilometre of railway track the expenses are about 8 times than that of one kilometre of metalled wide road.

3. *Delay in Loading and Unloading* - Much time is wasted in loading and unloading of the goods at the Railway station. Therefore , it is found more time consuming for short distance transportation of goods.

4. *Accidents* - It is a very big organisation and the whole network of the operations of railways depends on the mutual cooperation of all the staff. Accidents often occur due to sheer negligence of one category of staff, which causes heavy losses to life and goods.

Efforts are being made to replace the old lines, the new bridges and double lines are also helping in the smooth operatins of the railways. Electrification of railway routes has further increased the efficiency and speed of the railways, and it is expected that some practical shortcomings of railways will be minimised.

Indian Railways

Indian Railway are the main artery of Nation's inland transport extending over 61,600 route kilometers (in 1984-85) ; of which 6440 route kilometers or about 10 per cent are electrified. With an investment of more than Rs. 9,500 crores and regular staff strength of 1.7 million the Indian Railways are Asia's largest and World's second largest State owned Railways System under a single management.

Development During Plans -

Since 1950-51 , Indian Railways have implemented Eighth Five Year Development Plans apart from Annual Plans and are now in the second year of Ninth Five Year Plan (1997-2002) . The aims and achievements of Indian Railways during various plan periods have been as under :

First Five Year Plan (1951-56) - It was essentially a rehabilitation, modernisation plan. This had become necessary as the Second World War had run down the system badly and there were heavy arrears of overaged assets which needed to be replaced. In this programme a little more than half of the total outlay was on Railway in order to equip the railways with the minimum equipment and installations necessary to carry the additional load to be placed on it as a result of development in other sector of the economy. The First Five Year Plan provided for an outlay of Rs. 217 crores for Railways.

Second Five Year Plan (1956-61) - The rehabilitation and modernisation of Railway assets, both mobile and immobile , were to be continued during the Second Plan so as to reduce the proportion of over-aged stock retained in service and to facilitate the removal of speed restrictions in force over obsolete portions of the track. Also the increases in line capacity and rolling stock had to be planned to meet the greater demand for rail transport. 'The railway plan had also to take into account the effective coordination of all forms of transport in their appropriate functions to avoid wasteful duplication. The Second Five Year Plan provided for an outlay of Rs,. 723 crores for Railways.

Third Five Year Plan (1961-66) - The main objective of the Third Five Year Plan was to keep rail transport policy ahead of demand. A beginning was made towards modernisation of tradition with dieselisation and electrification. The plan provided for an outlay of Rs,. 1326 crores for Railways. The programme for Railways was formulated on the basis of originating freight traffic reaching a figure of about 245 million tonnes in one year, 1965-66 *i.e.* the last year of the third plan. The volume of traffic was thus expected to increase over that in 1960-61 by 91 million tonnes *i.e.* by about 59 per cent. It provided for an increase of 3 per cent per annum in the non-suburban traffic and the increase of a substantially high order was to be in the suburban traffic.

Annual Plans (1966-69)- In Annual Plans (1966-69) emphasis shifted to completion of quick result yielding ongoing schemes. Optimum utilisation of capacity already created was another aim.

Fourth Five Year Plan (1960-74) -The Fourth Five Year Plan the Railway development programme provided for anticipated increase in freight and passenger traffic. Equipment and operations were to be modernised to improve the efficiency of the system and reduce costs. The pace of conversion from meter gauge to broad gauge was accelerated in areas of rapid economic development and high traffic potential. The plan provided for an outlay of Rs. 100 crores for this programme excluding an expenditure of Rs. 525 crores to be met by the Railways from the Depreciation Reserve Fund. In addition , there was a provision of Rs. 20 crores for metropolitan transport.

Fifth Five Year Plan (1974-78) - By 1978-79 the railways were to be equipped to carry an estimated originating freight traffic of 250 to 260 million tonnes, the largest single commodity being 98 million tonnes of coal. The Fifth Five Year Plan provided for an outlay of Rs. 1523 crores for Railways which included the outlay financed from Depreciation Reserve Fund. Full provision was made for completion of ongoing traffic and project oriented lines. Emphasis was on achieving financial viability through improvement in efficiency, reduction in costs and better utilisation of existing assets. To tackle the problem of commuter traffic, a beginning was made on provision of rapid transit system in the metropolitan cities.

Sixth Five Year Plan (1980-85) - In the Sixth Plan , against an outlay of Rs. 5100 crores the expenditure was around Rs. 6573 crores. The performance during the years 1981-82 and 1982-83 was creditable and set pace for future development. With the wagon fleet unchanged in numbers, 47 million tonnes of additional freight traffic was carried. Fares and freight rates were rationalised and brought more or less in line with costs. Contribution to Depreciation Reserve Fund was substantially steped up from Rs. 125 crores per year in the Fifth Plan to Rs. 850 crores in the later years of the Sixth Plan.

Seventh Five Year Plan (1985-90) -A provision of Rs. 12334 crores has been made in the Seventh Plan for the Railways.

Eighth Five Year Plan (1992-97) - For the Eighth Plan, the approved outlay for Railway development is Rs. 27,202 crore. The strategy and broad objectives of railway development are as follows :

(1) To complete the process of rehabilitation, replacement and renewal of overaged assets; (2) To improve maintenance in order to increase productivity and efficiency of assets; (3) to augment line, terminal and rolling stock capacities and convert on a selective basis metre gauge to broad gauge; (4) To achieve technological upgradation, reduce operation costs and to increase productivity of labour and capital; (5) To conserve energy particularly through electrification; (6) To increase line capacity on saturated routes through alternative routess and construct new lines for industrial development of the areas; and (7) To continue system approach to reduce costs of operation and to achieve balance between capital and labour inputs. It is hoped that the aforesaid measure would promote railway development in the Eighth Plan.

It is proposed to acquire 96000 wagons, 6970 passenger coaches, 950 electrical multiple units and 1235 diesel/electric locomotives during this plan period. Also 19000-21000 km. of track renewal is to be undertaken with priority accorded to renewal works on high density corridors. 3400 kms of track would be electrified with priority being given to high density routes. Apart from this, the capacity for the manufacture of passenger coaches, EMUs (electric multiple units) and electric locomotives would be increased communication network would be upgraded and computer based freight information system will be brought into operation.

OPERATIONS OF INDIA RAILWAYS

	1950-51	1960-61	1970-71	1980-81	1990-91	1995-96	1996-97	1997-98
1	2	3	4	5	6	7	8	9
1..Route Kilometers (Thousand) :								
Electrified	0.4	0.8	3.7	5.4	10.0	12.3	12.7	--
Total	53.6	56.3	59.8	61.2	62.4	62.9	62.8	--
2..Originating Traffic (million tonnes)	73.2	119.8	167.9	195.9	318.4	390.7	409.0	--
Revenue Earning	93.0	156.2	196.5	220.0	341.4	405.5	423.4	--
Total traffic								
3. Goods Carried (billion	37.6	72.3	110.7	147.7	235.8	270.5	277.6	--
tonne-km.):Revenue Earning Total Traffic	44.1	87.7	127.4	158.5	242.7	273.5	280.0	--
4.Earnings from Goods Carried (Rs,. crore)	139.3	280.5	600.7	1550.9	8247.0	15290.4	16669.2	-
5. AverageLead : all goods Traffic (Km.)	470.0	561.0	648.0	720.0	711.0	675.0	661.0	-

6.Average Rate Per Tonne-Killometer (paise)	3.2	3.9	5.4	10.5	35.0	55.4	58.9	
7.Passenger Originating (million)	1284.0	1594.0	2431.0	3613.0	3858.0	4018.0	4153.0	
8. Passenger Kilometers (billion)	66.5	77.7	118.1	208.6	295.6	341.9	357.0	
9. Passenger Earnings (Rs. crore)	98.2	131.6	295.5	827.5	3144.7	6124.5	6633.2	--
10. Average Lead :Passenger Traffic (km.)	51.8	48.7	48.6	57.7	76.6	85.1	86.0	--
11. Average Rate Per Passenger-Kilometer(paise)	1.5	1.7	2.5	4.0	10.6	17.9	18.5	--

* Provisional.

Source : Ministry of Railways.

OPERATION OF INDIAN RAILWAYS

The Indian Railways consists of an extensive network spread over 62,495 km, Comprising Broad Gauge (43,083km.) Metre Gauge (15,804 km.) and Narrow Gauge (3,608 km.) .Electrified networks with a length of 13,962 km. account for 22.3 per cent of the total route kilometre.

Revenue earning freight tariff moved by Railway has increased from mere 73.2 million tonne in 1950-51 to over 429.4 million tonnes in 1997-98.

A positive growth rate has been witnessed in iron ore for export, fertilizers, POL and balance (other goods). All other items including coal, raw materials for steel plants, iron * steel cement and foodgrains showed a decline in carriage . The slowdown in industrial production and economic activity in general have adversely affected freight traffic.

The Railways employ about 16 lakh persons, the largest for any undertaking in the country. Manpower planning systems in the Railways have resulted in staff reduction, in absolute numbers, despite a higher level of activity and traffic growth. This has been made possible by enhanced staff productivity . The manpower decision/making process has been strengthened through computerised analysis of manpower data and productivity-related benchmarking exercises. A number of initiative have been taken to improve the learning environment in the railways by putting in place a framework for management of the training function.

Problem of Railways

The following are important problems that the railways have to face in India :

(1)*Travel without Tickets.*- In India large number of passengers travel in railways without purchasing tickets. It has been estimated that railways suffer a huge loss every year because of ticketless travellers.

(2)*Railways Accidents* - As compared to other developed countries, the incidence of railways accidents in India is greater. Now and then we come across news of railway accidents. Most of the accidents take place because of the errors and negligence of the railway employees.

(3)*Attack on Railways.*- A very typical feature in India is that if disturbances erupt in any part of the country due to any reason, whatsoever , the railways have to bear the brunt of the collective resentment of the people. The Indian railways have to suffer loss of crores of rupees during political disturbances in different parts of the country.

(4)*Expansion of Railway Lines.*- The expansion of railway lines is also a very important problem in India. Keeping in view the rising population and development schemes of the country, substantial expansion of railway lines is necessary to cope with the increasing number of passengers and transport of goods.

(5)*Problem of Replacement*- In India , the problem of replacement of old and outdated railway engines, wagons and other equipment is also quite important.

(6)*Problem of Fuel.*- There is a lack of high quality coal in India. The rate of electrification of railways has also been very slow because sufficient quantity of electric power is not available. Diesel traction has also proved problematic because there is a great shortage of diesel in India.

(7)*Problem of Gauge.*-More than fifty per cent of railway lines in India are of metre and narrow gauge . There is an urgent need for converting some of them into broad gauge. But the rate of conversion of metre and narrow gauge into broad gauge has been very slow. However, it has increased rapidly in recent years.

(8)*Operation of Un-remunerative Lines* -In view of the need to discharge the responsibility of a public utility service and operate as a commercial undertaking , the Railways have to incur expenditure on the operation of unremunerative lines and on the provision of services below cost.

(9)*Problem of Laying Double Lines.*-In India most of the railway lines are on single track. Great inconvenience is being experiienced because of these single lines. They involve a lot of wastage of time and other inconveniences to the railway organisation as well as to the passengers. Efforts have been made to construct double lines on the existing single lines under the Five Year Plan but the rate of expansion has been very slow.

(9)*Lack of Financial Resources for Railway Development.* There is a lack of financial resources for the development of Indian railways. Recently borrowings from the market have been started through the sale of railway bonds.

(11)*Financial Position of Railways.*- In the Railway Budget for 1995-96 there has been an increase of 10% in the fares of upper class a nominal hike in suburbanmonthly season ticket charges and a 7% increase in the freight rates for all commodities, except foodgrains for PDS sugar and chemical manures. This will help in mobilising Rs. 750 crore required to bridge the resource gap for Railway Plan for 1995-96 . This modest mobilisatin is the lowest in five years. The excess in the Railway Budget for 1995-96 comes to Rs. 1,305 crore after meeting the requirements of Depreciation Reserve fund Pension Fund and Dividents and making other adjustments.

****

17

Road Transport in India

Road transport is one of the most promising and potent means for rapid industrial and agricultural advancement. It plays an important role in the economy of the country and is particularly suitable for short and medium distances. It provides the basic infrastructure for bringing the majority of the people who are living in far off villages into the mainstream of life by connecting them with the rest of the country. While railways occupy the predominant position in the transport net work in the country, the role of road transport has steadily been increasing. With the spread of green revolution in the country and industrial growth and opening up of new areas , the road transport has assumed greater importance as the growing demands for supply of inputs like fertilizers , seeds etc. as well as the transport of agricultural produce to markets have to be met largely by road transport.

Importance or Advantages of Road

Road transport offers a number of advantages such as flexibility, reliability, speed and door to door service. Other transport modes too function more effectively when linked to road. Road transport has also a vital role to play in the development and opening up of backward and interior remote areas of the country. It has also been an important source of employment for skilled and semi skilled labour. The automobile, which is essentially a product of 20th century, in a very short time has come to prominence and today occupies an important place in the transportation system of every industrially advanced country. It has shown admirable and quick response to transport requirements of the civilised world unparalleled by railway industry.

Following are the main advantages of Roads :

(1)*Less Capital* :-Roads need less capital than the railways. The construction of railway lines for connecting all the villages in the remote areas of the country is not possible, as it will involve heavy incestment. Countries facing shortage of capital have added importance of road development.

(2)*Flexibility* :- It is a most flexible means of transport. The great advantage of road transport is that it can render rapid, flexible and more individual types of services. Motor vehicles can run not only between two places but also from one door to the other. '

(3)*Saving of Time and Cost* :-Goods in small quantity can be transported daily through quick means of road transport whereas, railway department waits till they book full wagon load of goods.

(4)*Small Units* :-As against railways, road transport service is performed through small units, like trucks, tempo etc. Not much capital is needed to buy these vcehicles.

(5)*Personal Service* :- Personal service is another special feature of road transport which is made possible because of small units. Apart from this, for short distances, specially, motor transport is superior to railway transport. Its safety, regularity, mobility, frequency and cheapness, motor transport has a decisive advantage over railway and other modes of roads of transport.

(6)*Multi Purpose Tendency* :-Roads are not built for specitic vehicles. Different type of vehicles can be pressed into service. Roads can be used by bullock cart, tongas, rickshaws, cycles, motors etc. whereas rail tracks are meant only for railway trains. Similarly, water and air transports are also meant for special type of vehicles.

(7)*Development of Agriculture* :-There are many areas in the country lacking efficient means of transport. But these are fit for growing all types of crops including cash crops. The development of road transport is indispensable for liking up the agricultural areas with the important trade centres and Railways Junction. They would also bring improvement in agricultural marketing. According to "Indian Road and Transport Development Institute " by extending roads to the rural of area, it is possible to increase cultivable area by 25 per cent.

(8)*Production of Perishable Goods* :- According to Road Re-organization Committee;s Report , road-system encourages the sale of such perishable goods as vegetable, fruits, milk, butter , etc. in the wide markets wherefrom the farmer returns with the knowledge of fertilizers , implements and improved methods of agriculture production.

(9)*Advantage of Industries* :- Industries are also benefitted from the development of roads . It is through roads that raw materials reach the factories and finished products to the consumers.

(10)Employment :-Road transport is a significant employment generating sector. Road transport provides employment to large number of people . Expansion in road transport will provide considerable additional employment. According to Road Transport Development Committee , an outlay of Rs. 3,500 crore on roads can generate employment for 170 lakh persons.

Classification of Roads

Indian Roads are classified into five categories for administrative purposes, namely

(1) National Highways

(2) State Highways

(3) District Roads

(4) Villages Road and

(5) Unclassified Village Roads.

National Highways -Are the principal arterial routes connecting the Union capital with the State capitals, major ports and various highways and meet the strategic needs of the defence of the country.

State Highways - Connect State capitals with district headquarters and important cities and towns within the State, the National Highway and the highway of the adjacent States and meet the needs of the traffic to and from the districts.

District Roads take the traffic the main roads to the interior of each district and rural area and to smaller units. They connect the areas of production and markets with each other as well as with the other highways and railways. They are sub-classified into Major District Roads which are metalloid roads and have a higher standard and specification and other District Roads which are of relatively lower specification and design.

Classified Village Roads connect villages or groups of villages with each other and the nearest district roads and other main highways , railway stations and river ghats. These roads form the basic infrastructure in the matter of linkages to villages and rural areas.

Unclassified Village Roads are mostly earthen roads and are of much lower standard and would in most cases be tracks in the rural areas.

Development of Roads and Road Transport during various Plan period.

Since the inception of planning the road network expanded from 4 lakh kms. in 1950-51 to 17.7 lakh kms. According to NTPC (National Transport Policy Committee) about four lakh villages are not connected by Fair Weather Roads. Therefore, in order to improve transport facilities, it is necessary to have sufficient Rural Link Roads. In many such village people are prevented from selling there produce because as soon as the monsoon sets in, the village is cut off and communication to the village becomes difficult . So, Rural Link Roads should be treated as a measure for Rural Reconstruction.

First Plan :-The total provision in the First Five year Plan for road development was about 100 crores of which about a quarter was to be spent on development of national highway and the rest mainly on State Roads.

Second Plan :-During the Second Plan the general policy for the development of road transport was to favour the setting up of Corporations under the Road Transport Corporation Act, 1950 and a provision of Rs. 10 crores was made in the railway plan which enabled the Railways to participate in these Corporation . Such Corporations lead to the coordination of rail transport with road transport so as to secure integrated operations in teh best interest of the country. A programme of about Rs. 3 crores was approved for Delhi Transport Service making the total invesment to be made on nationalised road transport about Rs. 17 crores.

Third Plan :- The road development programme for the Third Plan was formulated in accordance with the broad objectives laid down in the twenty year Road Development

Plan for the period of 1961-81 . The cost of this programme in the Third Plan was about Rs. 324 crores covering National Highways and roads of interestate and economic importance. During this plan the expansion programme of the nationalised road transport undertakings in the State were estimated to cost Rs. 26 crores.

Fourth Plan : In the Fourth Plan a provision of Rs. 418 crores was made for development programme in the Central Sector to bring about improvements in the existing network of national highways. Special emphasis was given on the development of rural roads and maintenance of existing roads. The total goods traffic by road transport was expected to increase form about 40,000 million tonne kilometres in 1968-69 to 84 TMTK (Thousant Million Tonne Kilometres) in 1973-74 . A provision of Rs. 89 crores was proposed for augmenting the services of the nationalised transport undertakings of the States. A large part of the expansion of road transport was expected to be in the private sector.

Fifth Plan :- During the Fifth Plan period the main emphasis was on completion of spill over works of the 4th plan, including a number of missing bridges and road links. Besides, there was also provision for certain new schemes of essential character particularly relating to the safety of traffic.

Sixth Plan : - In the Sixth Plan 2,687 kms., of roads were upgraded as National Highways and 5.77 lkah kms. of different types of roads were added to the road grid. About 16000 villages were connected with roads under minimum Need Programme as against the target of 20,000 . The work on upgradation of National Highways, which was continued, comprised construction of 166 kms. of missin glings, 4224 kms. widening to two lanes, 90 kms. of four laning 50 by-passes, 7 missing major bridges and 467 minor bridges. An outlay of Rs,. 830 crores was provided in Sixth Plan under the Central Sector roads programme. The expenditure however was about Rs., 760 crores the shortfall occurring largely as a result of cutbacks in allocations.

Seventh Plan :- Many broad objectives have been planned in the Seventh Plan period for the development of roads and Road Transport. Outlay for road development under the Seventh Plan for Central sector was Rs. 1,019.75 crore, for state sector Rs. 3,666.98 crore and for union territories Rs. 513.31 crore. During the Seventh Plan, Rs. 6,179.75 crore was spent on road development.

Eighth Plan:-The following will be Thrust Areas and Strategy with regard to development of Road Transport for Eithth Plan.

(1)The existing deficiencies in national highways (NH) will be removed by the construction of missing links, four-laning and two -laning of various sections, construction of bridges and by-passes, etc.The first priority will be for completing the ongoing works.

(2)For state highwayss, consolidation of existing network should receive high priority. The pavement structure would be widened to minimise vehicle operating costs and maintenance expenditure. A number of bridge would be constructed.

(3)Rural roads would receive attention on the following lines :

(i)Linking all villages with a population of 1,000 and above on the basis of 1981 census.

(ii)Backward regions and tribal areas will receive greater attention.

Rural road construction under Minimum Needs Programme (MNP) and local area development planning would be integrated more closely for better results in this regard.

For the Eighth Five Year Plan, an outlay of Rs. 2,600 crore and Rs. 10,610 crore has been approved for Central sector roads and state sector roads respectively. During the Eighth Plan, Rs. 3,200 crore was spent on Central sector roads and Rs. 12,622 crore spent on state sector roads.

OPERATION OF ROAD TRANSPORT

		1950-51	1960-61	1970-71	1980-81	1990-91	1993-94*	1994-95*
1	**2**	**3**	**4**	**5**	**6**	**7**	**8**	**9**
1.Length of roads	**(Thousand**							
Total	**km)**	**400.0**	**524.0**	**918.0**	**1419.0**	**2037.0**	**2779.2**	**2884.0**
Surfaced		**157.0**	**263.0**	**398.0**	**684.0**	**1001.0**	**NA**	**NA**
2.Length of National Highways	**(Thousand**							
Total	**km)**	**22.0**	**24.0**	**24.0**	**32.0**	**33.7**	**34.1**	**34.1**
Surfaced		**22.0**	**21.0**	**23.0**	**32.0**	**33.7**	**34.1**	**34.1**
3.Length of State Highways								
Total	**(Thousand)**	**NA**	**NA**	**57.0**	**94.0**	**127.0**	**133.0**	**135.3**
Surfaced		**NA**	**NA**	**52.0**	**90.0**	**122.0**	**NA**	**NA**
4. Number of Registered Vehicles	**(Thousand)**	**306.0**	**665.0**	**1865.0**	**5336.0**	**21310.0**	**27660.0**	**30287.0**
All vehicles		**82.0**	**343.0**	**343.0**	**542.0**	**1411.0**	**1691.0**	**1796.0**
Goods vehicles		**34.0**	**57.0**	**94.0**	**159.0**	**333.0**	**392.0**	**425.0**
Buses								
5. Revenue from Road Transport								
Central	**(Rs. Crores)**	**35.0**	**112.0**	**452.0**	**1423.0**	**4596.0**	**5377.2**	**6918.2**
States		**13.0**	**55.0**	**231.0**	**750.0**	**3035.0**	**3993.3**	**4424.7**

* Provisional

PRESENT OPERATIONS

India has one of the largest road network in the world. The country's total road length was 30,15,229 km in 1994-95 . Eighth plan laid emphasis on a coordinated and balanced development of road network in the country under (i) primary road system covering state highways; (ii) secondary and feeder road system covering state highways and major district roads ; and (iii) rural roads including villages roads and other district roads. Substantial outlays were proposed for road development in the rural and tribal areas.

(i) *National Highways* -National Highways are the prime arterial routes spanning about 49,600 km throughout the country and cater to about 40 per cent of the total road transport demand. According to a study (carried out by the sub-group for the 9th Five Year Plan on the road sector), a sum of Rs. 74500 crore (at the 1996 price level) would be needed to address the deficiencies of the existing national highway network. According to another study, there is a further need to have 15766 km of expressway network by the year 2020 of which a length of 4885 km needs to be added by 2005 , on a priority basis.

(ii) *Enhanced Allocation* -While there has been a decline in the allocation of funds over various plan periods in terms of the percentage of total plan outlay, the Government has now enhanced the allocation for 1998-99 by about 42 per cent over the preceding year.

(iii) *National HIghway Authority of India (NHAI)* -National Highways Authority of India (NHAI) , established as an implementing agency of the central Government, has already undertaken several projects. Adequate funds have been provided to the NHAI for its capital base and to enable it to leverage funds from the market. An additional tax at the rate of Rupee 1 per litre of petrol has been levied in the Union Budget, 1998-99 and the likely accrual of Rs. 790 crore is proposed to be allocated to the NHAI.

(iv) *Private Sector Investment* -The government has taken further initiatives to attract private sector investment in the road sector. The provisions relating to foreign investment have been further liberalised. Automatic approval will be accorded for foreign equity participation upto 100 per cent in the construction of roads and bridges, provided the total foreign equity in any such project does not exceed Rs. 1500 crore. A model concession agreement for Build Operate-Transfer (BOT) projects is being finalised. The initial response of the private sector has been statisfactory and as many as 17 projects , involving a sum of Rs. 835.5 crore, are in various stages of implementation . Several projects have been awarded on a BOT basis .

(v) *National Integration of Highway Projects* - It may also be be stated that as a matter of priority, the National Integrated Highway Project merging the golden quadrilateral connecting Delhi, Mumbai , Chennai and Calcutta with the East-West (Silchar to Saurashtra) and North-South (Kashmir to Kanya Kumari) corridors has been launched. The total length to be covered in this projects is 13000 km. Work on four laning of the golden quardrilateral connecting Delhi, Mumbai, Chennai and Calcutta is already in progress.

PROBLEM OF ROAD TRANSPORT AND SUGGESTIONS.

Main problems of Road Development in India are as follows;-

(1)*Costly* :- Road transport is a costly affair so far as long distance journey is concerned. This is happening mainly because increasing price of accessories, fuel and alike. This has caused growth in the number of commercial vehicles on the roads.

(2)*Irregular Means* :- It is an irregular means of transport and so is undependable.

(3)*Inadequate Roads* :- Roads are bad and inadequate in India. There are 34 kms. long roads per 100 sq. kms. are in India while in Japan 270 kms. and in West Germany 167 kms. roads are there Government should spend more on the development roads.

(4)*Heavy Taxes* :- There is heavy tax burden on motor transport in India. The cost of operating vehicles in high due to taxation, less and other duties.

(5)*No proper Maintenance* :- Roads are not maintained properly in India . Less than 0.1 per cent of the national income is spent on the maintenance of roads in India while in Japan, it is 3 percent of the national income. Due to bad roads running cost of motor vehicles is increased. It is therefore, essential that more money be spent on the upkeep of the roads.

(6)*Effect of Rainy Season* :- Most of the roads in India are kacha and are of little use during monsoon.,

(7)*Lack of Co-ordination*:- There is little co-operation and co-ordination among different states with regard to motor transport. As such , motor transport faces lot of difficulties. The states should pursue a co-ordinated policy in this matter.

To ensure coordination between them and operation of the different modes of transport, the Government of India has set up a Transport Development Council. the Inter-State Transport Commission is responsible for the development, coordination and regulation of road transport services on inter-state routes. An association of State Road Transport undertakings set up in 1963, coordinates the activities of 58 State undertakings, and helps, to secure procedural uniformity , higher standards of services and economy in operation.

(8) *Lack of Centeral-State Relation* – The development of roads in India has suffered because of Central-State relations. The state always looked upon centre to develop the roads, whereas the centre depended upon states to develop such facilities.

(9) *Less Roads in Rural Areas:-* Sixty percent of villages are without roads in India. It adversely affects our agriculture and rural economy. Government should develop roads speedily in rural areas.

(10)*Lack of Guest Houses:* There is lack of guest houses and motels along the roadside in India. More guest houses , should be built along the road sides, so that people may undertake long road journeys easily.

****

18

Air Transport in India

In a country of the size of India where major industrial and commercial centres are far apart and transport services must contend with a variety of terrain and climatic conditions, air transport has a significant role to play. It offers savings in time that cannot be matched by surface transport over long distances. Air transport helps optimise technological, managerial and administrative skills in a resource scarce economy.

Advantages of Air Transport

Main advantages of Air Transport are :

(1)*High speed:-* It is high speed means of transport . Passengers and goods can be transported speedily from one place to the other.

(2)*Transport of Costly and Light Goods* :- It is convenient to send costly, light and perishable goods through air transport.

(3)*Minimum Cost* :- Unlike railways and road transport there is no need to spend any money on the construction of any track or road. One has only to construct air -ports.

(4)*Free from Geographical Constraints* :- Mountains ,occans and rivers create no obstruction to air transport. This means of transport is therefore, free from geographical constraints.

(5)*Useful for Agriculture* :- Aeroplanes are used to make aerial spray of pesticides and insecticides in the wate of the spread of plant diseases.

(6)*Strategic Importanct* :- Iit has great strategic significance. Soldiers arms and ammunitions can be airlifted to the troubled spot in no time.

(7)*Useful during Sateral Calamities* :- Relief can be sent easily and quickly to flood hit and drought stricken areas by air-transport.

Disadvantages of Air Transport

Main disadvantages of air transport are as under:

(1)*Expensive* :- It is most expensive means of transport . Masses cannot avail of it.

(2)*Accodents*:- It is most accident prone means of transport.

(3)*Irregular*:- It is an irregular means of transport because inclement weather conditions like fog, dust-storm , hailstorms etc. obstruct its operation.

(4)*Limitd Capacity*:- It has limited capacity to carry passengers and cargo . Its services are restricted to big cities only.

STRUCTURE OF AIR SERVICES IN INDIA

There are a number of agencies which are involved in providing civil aviation services in the country. While Air India, Indian Airlines and Vayudoot provide air services. International Airports Authority (IAAI) and Directorate General , Civil Aviation (DGCA) , provide infrastructural facilities.

The activities of Civil Aviation fall under three broad categories - operational , infrastructural and regulatory -cum -developmental.

Indian Airlines - Domestic air services in the country are provided by Indian Airlines Ltd. After incurring continuous losses for 8 years, the company has made a net profit of Rs. 47.3 crore during the year 1997-98 . A net profit of Rs. 50 crore is expected for the financial year 1998-99.

Private Airlines - Private airlines also (Secheduled and non-scheduled) provides domestic air services. These private airlines providing regular domestic air services along with Indian Airlines .

Air India and Indian Airlines Limited - International services are provided by Air India Ltd. and Indian Airlines Limited. Air India Ltd. reported a loss of Rs. 181 crore in 1997-98 which was lower than the loss of Rs. 296 crore i n 1996-97 . The losses can be ascribed to factors like reduction in yield due to increased competition and increse in operational costs; the incidence of depreciation and interest on new aircraft; the increase in the wage bill and other staff costs; and the depreciation of the Rupee.

Pawan Hans. - Pawan Hans Helicopters Ltd. provides helicopter services for the petroleum sector and remote areas of North-Eastern region of the country.

Air Taxi - There are air taxi operators in Civil-aviation providing airtaxi /non-scheduled air transport services.

PRESENT POSITION

In India the activities of Civil Aviation are being provided Indian Airlines Ltd., Air India Ltd., Pawan Hans Hellecopters Ltd. and private airlines. 2 . Scheduled private airlines are providing regular domestic air services alongwith

Indian Airlines . There are also 31- air-taxi operators providing air-taxi /non-scheduled air transport services and nearly 37 per cent of the domestic air traffic is being presently carried to by private operators. Despite the entry of private airlines and air-taxi operators, Indian Airline has retained its position as the major player in domestic air transport services.

PRIVATE SECTOR ENTRY

The Air Corporation Act 1953 repealed on March 1, 1994 ended the monopoly of Indian Airlines, Air India and Vayudoot over scheduled air transport services. Six private operators,who were hitherto operating as air taxis, have since been granted scheduled airlines status. In addition 19 air taxi operators have been initially given permition for charter/non-scheduled air transport services.

The number of passengers availing of private air services has increased from 15,000 in 1990 to 42.6 lakh in 1997.

A new policy for private investment in the domestic air transport service sector was announced in April 1997 allowing for 100 per cent NRI/OCB equiting and 40 per cent foreign equity participation in domestic airlines directly or indirectly , has not been permitted.

STRUCTURE OF CIVIL AVIATION IN INDIA

Directorate General of Civil Aviation

The Department is headed by the Director General, Civil Aviation with headquarters at New Delhi. The organisation of the Directorate General of Civil Aviation is responsible for the regulatory functions in the fields of civil aviation for safe air travel.

National Airports Authority

The National Airports Authority has been set up by the Government on the 21st of May ,1986 and has become operational on the 1st of June ,1986. The National Airport's

Authority is responsible for providing infrastructure for civil transport operations in India. The following are its main functions :

(i) To manage the aerodromes, the civil enclaves and the aeronautical communication stations efficiently :

(ii) To provide air traffic service and air transport service at any aerodrome and civil enclave :

(iii) Inter-alia the Authority may -

(a)plan, develop, construct and maintain runways taxiways, aprons and terminals and ancillary buildings at the aerodromes and civil enclaves:

(b)plan ,procure, instal and maintain navigational aids, communication equipment , beacon and ground aids at the aerodromes and at such locations as may be considered necessary for safe navigation and operation of aircraft ;

(c)provide air safety services and search and rescue facilities in co-ordination with other agencies ;

(d) establish schools or institutions or centre for the training of its officers and employees in regard to any matter connected with the purpose of this Act (The National Airports Authority Act 1985).

(e)construct residential buildings for its employees;

(f)establish and maintain hotels , restaurants and restrooms at or near the aerodromes;

(g)establish warehouses and cargo complexes at the aerodromes for the storage or processing of goods ;

(h)arrange for postal , money exchange , insurance and telephone facilities for the use of passengers and other persons at the aerodromes and civil enclaves ;

(i)make appropriate arrangements for watch and ward at the aerodromes and civil enclaves ;

(j)regulate and control the plying of vehicles and the entry and exit of passengers and visitors, in the aerodromes and civil enclaves with due regard to the security and protocol functions of the Govt. of India;

(k)develop and provide consultancy services in India and abroad in relation to planning and development of airports, air-navigation services, ground aid and safety services or any facilities thereat;

(l)establish and manage heliports;

(m)provide such transport facility as are in the opinion of the Authority , necessary to the passengers travelling by air;

(n)form one or more companies under the Companies Act, 1956 or under any other law relating to companies to further the efficient discharge of the functions imposed on it by this Act;

(o)take all such steps as may be necessary or convenient for, or may be incidental to, the exercise of any power or the discharge of any function conferred or imposed on it by this Act; and

(p)perform any other function considered necessary or desirable by the Central Government for ensuring the safe and efficient operation of aircraft to, from and across the air space of India.

The Airports Authority of India (AAI) earned a net profit of Rs. 196.1 crore in 1997-98 as comapared to Rs. 132.1 crores in 1996-97 . The higher profit is mainly attributed to increase in Airport charges andPassenger Services Fee etc.

International Airports Authority of India

The International Airports Authority of India, which was set up in 1972, is responsible for providing efficient air transport services at the four international airports viz. Bombay, Calcutta, Delhi and Madras except provision of Air

Navigational services which continue to be the responsibility of the Department of Civil Aviation . Within the short span of its existence, the International Airports Authority of India has acquired commendable expertise in the field of airport consultancy and construction, in India as well as abroad.

PLAN -WISE DEVELOPMENT OF CIVIL AVIATION

First Plan -(1951-56) - In the last few years, the Airline Industry has witnessed a global recession. Both the domestic and international carriers found it increasingly difficult to meet the high operational costs. Notwithstanding this situation, Air India and Indian Airlines have been among the very few carriers in the world who had earned profits in the year 1983-84 . They made net profits aggregating to Rs. 57.39 crores and Rs. 45.85 crores respectively.

PLAN -WISE DEVELOPMENT OF CIVIL AVIATION

First Plan -(1951-56) -At the time of the drafting of the first Five Year Plan, Civil Aviation was a new line of development. To ensure that the existing airports worked on an economic basis, integration of existing airlines was decided upon and a State Corporation was proposed to be set up for the purpose. The plan provided a sum of Rs. 9.5 crores for the purchase of 13 aircraft , three of which were to be of the type required for long distance international air services and for payment of compensation to the then existing air companies. During the period of this plan, progress on schemes relating to education and training had been relatively slow. Efficient Air Services demanded high standards of training and equipment.

Second Plan (1956-61) - During this plan a sum of 30.50 crores was provided to spent for development of Air -Transport in India out of which 14.50 crores was fixed for Air India and Rs. 16 crores for Indian Airlines . However the actual expenditure was tune to Rs. 15.9 crores only. To look into this matter , a committee was appointed by the Government and in pursuance of the recommendations made by this committee , it was decided to centralise training at Allahabad and to raise training standards for commercial pilots. This project was undertaken during the Second Five Year Plan.

Third Plan (1961-66)-Third Plan provided for Rs. 25.5 crores (Rs. 2550 lakh) on Civil Aviation distributed among various categories as follows :-

Work at aerodromes	Rs. 1850 lakh
Aeronautical Telecommunication	
Equipment	Rs. 500 lakh
Air routes & aerodromes	Rs. 100 lakh
Training & Education equipment	Rs. 84 lakh
Research & Development equipment	Rs. 16 lakh
Total	Rs. 2550 lakh

Fourth Plan (1969-74) -In the Fourth Plan, the aircraft of much bigger size and with greater speed were expected to be introduced. This plan envisaged improvements of runway, terminal and communicatin facilities at the four International Airports at Bombay, Calcutta, Delhi and Madras to make them suitable for operation of heavier and larger capacity aircraft like Boeing 747 (Jumbo) Jets. The plan also provided for the development of various airports for domestic air services.

Fifth Plan (1974-78) -The Fifth Plan had a provision of Rs. 65.15 crores which *inter alia* included outlays on aeronautical communicatin services and works at aerodromes. Under aeronautical communication services, provisions had been made for augmentation of calibration facilities and for improving the aeronautical fixed and mobile telecommunication net-work in order to improve the safety of aircraft operation.

GROWTH OF CIVIL AVIATION

		1960-61	1970-71	1980-81	1990-91	1995-96	1996-97	1997-98
1	2	3	4	5	6	7	8	9
1. Total fleet strength								
(i) Air India		13	10	17	24	26	28	--
(ii) Indian Airlines		88	73	49	56#	59	54	--
2. Revenue tonnes-kilometers	(Rs. Crores)							
(i) Air India		7.56	27.52	98.01	138.10	161.90	149.95	--
(ii) Indian Airlines		10.00	20.00	40.03#	71.91#	72.27	76.52	--
3. Number of passengers carried	(Lakh)							
(i) Air India		1.25	4.87	14.18	21.61	28.53	29.51	--
(ii) Indian Airlines		7.90	21.30	54.29#	84.19#	77.40	81.70	--
4. Passengers handled at IAAI Airports	(Lakh)	NA	NA	107.38	177.23	256.40	364.90	--
5. Cargo handled at IAAI Airports	(Thousand tonnes)	NA	NA	178.70*	377.33	561.58	680.04	--

* Provisional

\# Includes Vayudoot.

NA: Not Available.

Source: Ministry of Civil Aviation.

Sixth Plan (1980-85) -In the Sixth Plan emphasis was placed on the provision of safety oriented equipment, so as to make air operation more safe and reliable . Under the programme of Civil Works at aerodrames, the policy of generally developing the existing airports rather than construction of new ones was to be continued , the main programme under this head being upgrading of the existing airports so as to facilitate the safer operations of jet aircraft . In total an outlay of Rs. 859.10 crores was provided for the Civil Aviation Sector . The actual expenditure however was Rs. 931.03 crores.

Seventh Plan (1985-90) -Due to resource constraints, an amount of Rs. 2015.5 crores has been provided in the Seventh Plan which was thought suffice to meet the expenditure on ongoing schemes and a few new starts. While sanctioning programmes, priority has been accorded ,to the development of support, Civil Aviation activities include flying clubs and development of air strips, for which an amount of Rs. 27.63 crores has been provided.

Integration of various functional services to improve productivity and service efficiency, streamlining of facilitation procedures at airports, development of selected domestic airports to serve as satellites, relieving pressure on the existing international airports and increase in throughput with the aid of operational and tariff measures designed to even out traffic leaks to the extent possible are some of the measures which have been taken during the seventh plan to enhance the capacity of international airports.

PROBLEM OF AIR TRANSPORT IN INDIA

The following are the import problems of air transport in India :

(1) *Shortage of Aircrafts* -There is a great shortage of aircrafts for civil aviation.

(2) *Dependence on Foreign Countries* -The building of aircrafts for civil aviation is in its experimental stage, and we have to depend mostly on foreign countries for the produrement of aircrafts.

(3) *Inadequate For Military Purpose* - The urgency of increasing the number of aircrafts for military purposes has been seriously felt because of the nafarious designs of Pakistan.

(4) *High Cost* - The cost of air service is high because of the high cost of fuel.

(5) *Competition* - It has to face competition from foreign companies.

(6) *Lack of Training Facilities* - So far, sufficient facilities for training able and efficient pilots are lacking; and this is the reason why the desired numbers of good pilots are not available. *Pawan hans Ltd. was incorporated in October 1985* to provide helicopter based air transport services for the petroleum sector. *Indira Gandhi Rashtriya Uran Adakemi was set up at Fursateganj in district Rai Bareilly in U.P. in 1986 for training pilots (also helicopter piolots)*

(7) *Accidents* - The problem of accidents is also a serious factor in air transport . The incidence of accidents in air transport in India is comparatively greater than in other countries. To remove this problem, surveys of airways should be conducted.

(8) *Shortage of Finance* - There is a great shortage of finance in the country which is providing to be an obstacle in the way of technical development of civil aviation. Necessary finance should be made available for the purpose.

(9) *Liberalisation* - In recent years under the policy of liberalisation and privateisation followed in the country, several private sector companies have started providing air services in India. This has increased the quality of services and instilled a spirit of competition and modernisation in this sector.

From the above analysis , it can be concluded that we have achieved a lot of progress in air transport after independence, yet we are still lagging behind. We have to tackle a number of problem to improve air transport in the country.

****

19

Water Transport in India

Water transport is a very ancient mode of transport was found in India. In ancient time shipping was quite popular in India. History, is evident of this that water transport was very popular in trading activities among different nations. India has got about 14,500 kms of navigable waterways which comprises of rivers, canals, backwaters , Greeks etc. The inland water transport is most popular in India as it is known to be a fuil efficient and environmentally least hazardous mode and is basically rural employment oriented.

Advantage or Importance of Water Transport

Importance of water transport is evident from the following:-

(1)*Important for Foreign Trade* :- Expansion of foreign trade has taken place mainly due to water transport. In ancient time, water transport was only mode of transport to cover long distance. Current volume of India's foreign trade is quite large and it is likely to further expand for the sake of economic development of the country . Keeping in to consideration this fact. importance of water transport cannot be under rated.

(2)*Foreign Exchange* :- Shipping has also enabled the country to save enough of foreign exchange . Foreign exchange is of utmost importance for country's economic development. India has already been facing acute foreign exchange shortage.

(3)*Defence*:- Development of shipping is essential for defence of the country also. It is regarded as second line of defence.

(4)*Cheapest and Slowest of Transport* :- Water transport is the cheapest and slowest means of transport. Water ways are provided by nature. Oceans and rivers are the free gifts of nature. No cost is involved in their construction unlike that of railways and roads. The operational and maintenance cost is very heavy in other mode of transport as large amount of capital expenditure is required to build roads and railway tracks.

(5)*Transport of Heavy Goods*:- Heavy and bulky goods can be transported at little cost through water transport. A boat has a large carrying capacity which can carry goods weighting about six times its own weight. Contary to this the weight of a raiwlay wagon is nearly one half to three foruth of the actual load at carries. Therefore it is cheaper to send bulky goods not requiring quick delivery by water transport.

(6)*Useful during Natural Calamities* :- During natural calamities like floods, heavy downpour etc. when rail or road transport is disrupted, water transport alone is possible.

(7)*Less maintenance Cost* :- Compared to other means of transport maintenance cost of water transport is very little. The operating expenses are very low as conpared to other mode of transport.

Disadvantages of Water Transport

Main disadvantages of water transport are as under :

(1)*Limited Area:* - Area of water transport is restricted. Rivers and oceans are free gifts of nature. Accordingly the operational area remains fixed.

(2)*Slow Speed* :- It is a slow means of transport . Water transport suffers from relatively slow speed as compared to other means of transport. Failure of monsoon results into fall in the water level of rivers making navigation difficult. Due to all these drowbacks it is suitable for sending only those goods which need not require early delivery. Some time circutous routes have to be followed which leads more delay.

(3)*Less Safety* :- As against other means of transport, it is less safe. The loss of ships due to berils of the sea involves considerable loss of life well as goods. There is all possibilities that ships or boats may sink.

(4)*Deterioration of goods* - Sea water is carrusive which may affects the quality and the flovour of goods. The element of pilferage also seems to be very high in water transport. Because of these reasons goods transported by water transport requires special pac king.

Shipping

Coastal Shipping

India has a vast coastline of 5,560 kms. with a number of ports and harbours. there is considerable scope for the utilisation of coastal shipping for the transportation of goods and passengers. Coastal shipping is generally accepted as the most energy efficient and cheapest mode of transport for carriage of bulk traffic over longer distances. Like any other form of water transport it entails no investment in line haul capacity except in navigational aids and terminal facilities. It can play an important role in the integrated transport network of the country.

Coastal trade in India is reserved exclusively for the Indian merchant marine under the Merchant Shipping Act, 1958. The Coastal Shipping traffic increased progressively in the 1950's from 2.59 million tonnes in 1952 it increased to 3.75

million tonnes in 1963. It dropped to 0.94 million tonnes in 1979. there has been slight increase thereafter mainly due to increased quantity of coal transported for Tamil Nadu Electricity Board Power Plant at Tuti- corin.

Coastal Shipping faces several constraints. The overaged vessels are fuel inefficient and involve high maintenance and operating costs. This has led to increase in bunker costs, operating expenses, higher stevedoring charges and uneconomic freight structure which do not compare well with either rail or road. Also, coastal shipping carries low rated bulk commodities like coal, cement, salt for which railway freight rates are lower with consequent consumer preference for rail transport,.

Inordinate delays at ports too have affected competitive advantage of coastal shipping. Apart from cumbersome port and custom procedure, other restrictions like inadequate draft have precluded optimal utilisation of shipping capacity. Directional imbalances in coastal traffic movement are also there.

Development of Shipping during various Plan periods

First Plan :- During the period of the First Five Year Plan the programme for the development of shipping was designed primarily to enable the coastal trade of the country to be reserved for Indian vessels and to ensure their fuller participation in oversea trade.

In begining of first plan, Indian shipping was equapped with ships of 3.91 lakh tonne of weighting capacity but among them half of the ships were old of more then 20 years. During this plan a sum of Rs. 18.7 lakh were spent on development of shipping the Government of India resulted of which weight capacity 4.8 lakh tonnes ships were in working condition and ships of 1.2 lakh tonne. Capacity were under construction. A sum of Rs. 27.6 crore were spent on development of ports and harbours in the public sector during the first plan. In order to encourage ship building, the ownership of Vishakhapatnam Ship Yard was taken over by the Government . A loan sum of Rs. 23.5 crore was also provided on easy terms for purchase of ships to private Indian ships companies. At the end of this plan the weight transporting capacity of Indian ports has gone to 2.6 lakh tonnes.

In begining of first plan, Indian shipping was equpped with ships of 3.91 lakh tonne of weighting capacity but among them half of the ships were old of more then 20 years. During this plan a sum of Rs. 18.7 lakh were spent on development of shipping by the Government of India resulted of which weight capacity 4.8 lakh tonnes ships were in working condition and ships of 1.2 lakh tonne capacity were under construction. A sum of Rs. 27.6 crore were spent on development of ports and harbours in the public sector during the first plan. In order to encourage ship building , the ownership of Vishakhapatnam Shipyard was taken over by the Government . A loan sum of Rs. 23.5 crore was also provided on easy terms for purchase of ships to private Indian ships companies. At the end of this plan the weight transporting capacity of Indian posts has gone to 2.6 lakh tonnes.

Second Pland :- The broad objectives of the second plan in respect of shipping were (i) to cater fully for the needs of coastal trade with due regard to the possibility of diverting some traffic from railways to coastal shipping; (ii) to secure an increasing share of India's overseas trade for Indian Ships and to build up the nucleus of tanker fleet. The schemes which were started in the first plan were to be completed in this period . It was also aimed to modernise and equip the docks to provide for new needs arising from the economic and industrial development of the country.

During this plan a target for spent of Rs. 46.23 crore was fixed for development of ship industry to increase shipping capacity upto 3.9 lakh GRT. However, actual expenditure during the plan was tune to Rs. 55.7 crore and the capacity of Indian shipping was 8.6 lakh GRT. A target for increase the capacity of Hindustan Shipyard, Vishakapatnam up to 4 thousand ships per year was also fixed.

During this plan a target for spent of Rs. 46.23 crore was fixed for development of ship industry to increase shipping capacity upto 3.9 lakh GRT. However, actual expenditure during the plan was tune to Rs. 55.7 crore and the capacity of Indian shipping was 8.6 lakh GRT. A target for increase the capacity of Hindustan Shipyard, Vishakapatnam up to 4 thousand ships per year was also fixed.

Third Plan :-A provision of Rs. 55 crores had been made for shipping in the Third Plan. The expansion of shipping had the high priority to enable savings to be effected in foreign exchange expenditure which was being incurred o n the carriage of the country's overseas trade.

Fourth Plan :- During the Fourth Plan period , ships with a capacity of 0.62 million GRT (Gross Registered Tonnage) were to be delivered on order. A provision of Rs. 135 crores was made for acquisition of ships to reach about 3.5 million GRT of Shipping Tonnage by the end of the Fourth Plan.

Fifth Plan :- The Fifth Plan provided an outlay of Rs. 308 crores for major ports, including about Rs. 200 crores for spill over schemes. The total outlay finally envisaged was Rs. 521.46 crores including Rs. 363.55 crores for spill over schemes.

Sixth Plan :- During the Sixth Plan , the target was to increase the coastal tonnage from 0.254 MGRT to 0.5 MGRT (Million Gross Registered Tonnage) in 1984-85 . The actual addition however, was only 0.10 MGRT , thus taking the total coastal fleet to about 0.35 MGRT by the end of the pland period. Coastal vessels carred 5.5 million tonnes of traffic in 1984-85 . Over the years, dry cargo volume mainly salt and general cargo, has declined while the wet cargo volume has gone up.

Seventh Plan (1985-90) :- It was planned to spent a sum of Rs. 827 crores for the development of shipping. It was sheduled to re-established more than 25 lakh GRT old shipping capacity . A target to achieve 75 lakh tonne GRT shipping capacity but achievement was only 59.8 lakh GRT capacity .

Eighth Plan (1992-97) - In this plan a sum of Rs. 3668.9 proposed to spent for development of shipping whereas there was planned for additional expenditure of Rs. 3592 crore for development of port and light houses. In this plan alongwith modernisation of Indian shipping a target was also fixed for re-establishment of 10 lakh GRT capacity and creation of 10 lakh GRT capity . Hence a target to achieve 70 lakh GRT shipping capacity was fixed to achieve by the end of eighth plan.

Table-1

Development of Shipping During Planns (1950-98)

At the End of Plan	*Expenditure on Development (Rs. in Crores)*	*No. of Ships*	*Shipping capacity (Lakh GRT)**
1950-51	-	80	3.9
First Plan	18.7	126	6.0
Second Plan	55.7	172	8.6
Third Plan	93.0	221	15.9
Fourth Plan	165.0	274	30.9
Fifth Plan	450.0	375	53.6
Sixth Plan	433.0	450	64.0
Seventh Plan	827.0	408	59.8
1990-92	140.0	430	62.8
Eighth Plan	3669.0	460	70.0

* *GRT denotes Gross Re gistered Tonnes*

Development of Shipping during Seventh Plan Period

(a)*Coastal Shipping*

Growth of coastal shipping on a sound financial basis calls for a clear and firm policy statement by Government on its future role in the country's transport system. It is necessary for Government to allot an assured quantity of traffic to coastal trade on a long term basis taking into account the comparative advantage , so that it may programme for operating an adequate number of ships between designated ports on a regular basis.

Under the present operating conditions costs of coastal movement are generally uneconomical and there is little hope for coastal shipping to survive on its own unless it receives Government financial support. There is a distinct possibility for coastal shipping to become financially viable only when there is a potential for closed circuit project oriented movement of coastal traffic in large buil. Such potential needs to be explored while locating new industries along the coast.

(b)*Shipping*

Though sizable Indian shipping tonnage still does not compare favourably with that of several maritime countries. Indian shipping accounts at present for only one per cent of the total world fleet. From a modest 0.39 MGRT in 1950-51 the country has acquired a diversified fleet of 6.32 MGRT , the maximum increase of 3.73 MGRT taking place in the seventies.

The Shipping industry has been experiencing prolonged recession since the close of 1974 except for a brief revival during 1980-81 . Conference operators are facing keen competition from non-conference operators lines in general cargo movements in almost all trades. Conscious of these factors, India is trying to keep pace with the changed situation in shipping.

Adverse Features in regard to Indian Shipping

Indian shipping benefits from advantages like lower labour costs and a vast meritime boundry and strong state support. Nevertheless, it has been affected by several adverse features, including its own structural weakness.

First, the fleet is overaged, resulting in high operating costs,

Second , India's geographical position is such that a number of foreign vessels are able to use Indian ports as wayside ports, when returning from Gulf or sailing towards the Far East. Their task is made easier in the absence of proper protectionist measures. *Third,* while the world is moving rapidly towares containerisation, the Indian container fleet is almost negligible. *Fourth,* Indian shipping suffers from inadequate infrastructure support like ship repair facilities , dry docking and cargo handling.

Shipping Corporation of India Limited.

The Shipping Corporation of India is operating services on all important sea trade routes of the world. Besides regular cargo liner service, it also operates passenger cum-cargo services, overseas and coastal tanker services, dry bulk cargo services, overseas bulk carrier services and overseas tramp services.

The recession in the international shipping industry is continuing . SCI has taken several steps to improve their performance. These included:-

(a) revision of tariff on liner services wherever possible.

(b) rationalisation of port of calls,

(c) development of way port trade,

(d) restructuring of container services,

(e) use of modern fuel efficient engines in the new ships being acquired,

(f) monitoring the consumption of bunkers and taking corrective measures to optimise the same,

(g) sale/scrap of old vessles which are uneconomical ,

(h) aggressive marketing efforts etc.

SCI has taken measure to cope with the requirements of marketing and agency services at the Inland Container Depots (ICDs) . With a view to provide smooth and efficient movement of containers and bring about customer satisfaction in terms of services agency arrangements of ICDs have been linked to the concerned gateway port. Shipping Corporation of India Limited has an authorised capital of Rs. 100 crores and paid up capital of Rs. 70 crores.

The SCI continues to maintain clost relationships with the partners of various belateral shipping agreements. Bilateral shipping services between India and USSR/Poland /GDR/Egypt have been functioning satisfactorily.

The Mogul Line Limited , another Public Sector Shipping Company, has been merged with the Shipping Corporation of India Limited w.e.f. 30-6-86 . With this merger the total fleet strength of the company at p resent is 146 vessles of 32.26 lakh GRT and 53.73 lakh DWT. In addition is 24 vessles of 10.89 lakh DWT are on order in various Shipyards in India and abroad.

Chartering Wing - Transchart

The Chartering Wing is a service organisation responsible for making shipping arrangements on behalf of all the Ministries, Deptt. of Govt. of India, State Governments, Public Sector Undertakings and Projects . The activities of "TRANSCHART' are aimed at utilising Indian tonnage to the maximum extent possible for shipment of Govt.

owned/controlled cargoes so as to ensure best possible utilisation of Indian tonnage (thus saving foreign exchange to the country on freight payments) and finalising, where necessary, foreign ships at competitive and economical rate. This Wing also advises the indenting Departments /Projects on shipping matters and shipment problems.

The Chartering Wing (TRANSCHART) was set-up in 1960 and as the centralised body for arranging shipment of Govt. owned/ controlled cargoes has now developed into one of the biggest chartering agency in the world. The development of Indian tonnage received a big fillip with the setting up of transchart and the cargo support that is provided to Indian shipping. Transchart has developed expertise in chartering of all types of vessels including specialised vessels.

Inland Water Transport

Inland Water Transport (IWT) is the cheapest mode for certain kinds of traffic , both over long and short hauls provided the points of origin and destination are located in water front and no transhipment of goods is involved . It is also one of the most efficient modes of transport from the point of view of energy consumption. Besides, this mode has other inherent advantages as well. It can provide immediate access wherever navigable waters exist without requiring investment in line haul capacities as in other modes of transport. Inland Water Transport is a labour intensive mode and generates more employment per rupee of investment than any other mode and so particularly benefits weaker sections of the community.

The share of inland waterways in country's transport system is one per cent, and the density is 0.44 km. per 100 sq. kms. The navigable inland waterways extend nearly to 14500 kms. comprising a variety of river systems, canals bad waters, creeks and tidal inlets out of which only 5,200 kms. of major rivers and 485 kms. of canaks are suitable for operation of mechansed crafts . The present level of waterway traffic is negligible which reveals gross underutilisation of a major transport assets,

Inland waterways are the ways found in the inner parts of a country. Inland water transport includes natural modes such as navigable rivers and *artificial* modes such as canals. These waterways are the cheapest means of transport within the country .The inland waterways have played an important role in the Indian transport system since ancient times. These have proved helpful in carrying the heavy and spacious goods from one place to another. However, in recent times the importance of this mode of transport has declined considerably with the expansion of road and rail transport. In addition, diversion of river waters for irrigation has also reduced the importance of inland transport. The decline is also due to deforestation of hill ranges leading to erosion, accumulation of silt in rivers and failure to modernise the fleet to suit local conditions. India's navigable inland waterways extend nearly 14,500 kms. comprising a variety of river systems, canals , backwaters , creeks and tidal inlets. In India, the rivers like Ganga and Brajamputra , serve the purpose of inland water transportation.

The operations of inland waterways are dominated by country boats and mechanised operations are confined to a few specific locations. The transportation of goods in an organised form is confined to West Bengal , Assam , parts of north eastern region and Goa.

1.*Rivers.* Rivers are an excellent means of transport of goods by small boats and steamers. Important nevigable rivers in India are: Ganga and Brahmaputra and their tributaries, Godavari, Krishna, Mahanadi, marmada and Tapti and their canals. Bukingham canals in Andhra Pradesh and Tamil Nadu, the backwaters and canals of Kerala, and Mandovi and Zuari rivers in Goa. The river transport system is of considerable importance in the states of Assam. West Bengal and Bihar.

River transport accounts for half the trafic between Assam and Calcutta . In Kerala, rivers and backwaters are used for transporting goods and people. However rivers of Sourthern India are unfit for navigation purposes as most of them flow on rocky and uneven land. In summers they go dry. As against this, rivers of Northern India are perennial. Snow melts on Himalayan tops in sumers and ensures regular flow of water to these rivers.

2.*Canals* . Canals are the artificial waterways which have been constructed both for navigation and irrigation purpose. In India the two most important canals for navigation purposes are the Ganges canal running from Hardwar to Kanpur and Buckingham canal running parallel to the east coast in Madras.

Developments during plans

The Development of Inland water ways has bodly suffered in India during planning because major emphasis in the country placed on railways and the diversion of river for irrigation purpose. Inland Water Transport (IWT) during the successive Five Year Planned and till the seventh plan received only low priority as explanned in the following description .

First Plan :- No major emphasis was given for the develont of water transport during first plan. As a taken efforts of development only *Ganga-Bramputra water-Transportation Board* was constituted jointly by government of Uttar Pracesh, West Bengal , lBihar and Assam to develop water transport in the river Ganga , Brahamputra and its associate rivers. The board was entrusted with the responsibility to establish co-ordination between developmented work and arrangement of modern ship.

Second Plan. During the first two plans less than Rs. 1 crores were spent on development of inland water ways. In 1958 Water Transport Corporation was established

Third Plan- During third plans a sum of Rs. 7.5 crores were spent on inland water transport. Beside State Government arranged for a sum of Rs. 1.4 crores for the development. However, anctual expenditure during the plan was only Rs. 4 crore.

Three Annual Plans During these three annual plans for the development of water transport in the country, the central Inland water transport corporation was set in May 1967 with its authorised capital of Rs. 4 crores. It is a Government of India undertaking with its head quarters at Calcutta. The Central Inland Water Transport Corporation (CIWTC) is engaged in transportation of goods by Inland waterways in Ganga -Hooghly-Bhagirathi, Sunderbans and the Brahaputira rivers.

The Corporation is operating regular cargo services between Calcutta and Pandu (near Guwahati) , between Calcutta and Korimganj (Assam), Calcutta -Bangladesh and between Haldia and Patna.

Fourth Plan (1964-65) - The Fourth Plan expenditure on inland water ways was about Rs. 11 crores as against the outlay of Rs. 12 crores. A sum of Rs. 9 crores were spent for complition of incomplite works of third plan. During this plan project of development of Jogigopa and Pandu ports and modernization of Calcutta and Rajbagan doc yard was complited.

Fifth Plan (1974-75) - The revised fifth plan has proposed on outlay of Rs. 25 crores for the development of inland water transport. The developmental work of Forroka Project was accorded priority during the plan. In this plan reforms were undertaken on *Hugli* and river *Ganga* services *Chompkara* and *Nindkara* river and *Bankidom river* in Andhra Pradesh.

Sixth Plan (1980-85) - By accepting the importance of development of inland water transport in the country, a sum of Rs. 72 crores was proposed tobe spent on the development of inland water transport . The anticipated expenditure is estimated at Rs. 70.33 crores. The development programme under the plan includes capital repairs of vessels, acquisition of additional vessels and creation of infrastructure facilities for the smooth flow of vessels etc.

Seventh Plan (1985-90) - The Seventh Five Year Plan had laid emphasis on development of those area where IWT had already been in existence and called for the technological improvements considered necessory in modernisation of fleets and terminals. Keeping in to consideration the aforesaid view the plan aims at :

(a) developing inland water transport in the regions where it enjoys natural advantage;

(b) maodenising vessels and country crafts to suit local conditions and ;

(c) improving productivity of assets.

A provision of Rs. 225.73 crores had been made for the development of IWT in the seventh Five Year Plan. This included Rs. 155 crore in the central sector and Rs. 70.73 crores in the state sector. In the Central sector on expenditure of Rs. 131.81 crore has been incurred on the development of IWT during this plan as against the total outlay of Rs. 155 crore.

Eighth Plan (1992-97) - During this plan for the development of inland water transport a sum of Rs. 240 crores and 107.63 crores was proposed to be spent by the Central and State Government respectively.

In our country the task of formulating policy for the development of inland water transport has been conferred on the Central Inland Water Transport Board, New Delhi. The

Central Inland Water Transport Corporation set up in 1976 at Calcutta operates various river services carrying goods between Assam and Calcutta and also performs other activities like ship building , ship repairing, clearing and dredging, etc.

The CentralInland Water Transport Board, New Delhi Formulates policy for the development of Inland water transport in the country. The Inland Water Transport Directorate of the Union Ministry of Shipping and Transport gives technical advice to the States, which are responsible for the development of inland water ways.

The states of Andhra Pradesh , Assam, Karnatak, Kerala, Madhya Pradesh, Maharashtra, Uttar Pradesh, and West Bengal and the Union territory of Goa, Daman and Diu have set up inland water transport organisations to formulate and implement schemes.

National Waterways

The need for introduction of concept of national waterways in conformity with objectives of national highwaysin India has been suggested by various State Government. Due to financial stringency and poor plan outlays State Governments have not been able to take adquate measures for river and canal conservancy. Consequently, navigation has become hazardous and some waterways have fallen into disuse.

The issue of national waterways has been examined by various committees, the consensus being that important waterways be declared as national waterways. For declaring a particular waterway as national waterway, the following principles are taken into consideration.

(a)It should possess capability of navigation by mechanically propelled vessels of a reasonable size.

(b) It should have about 45 metre wide channel and minimum 1.5 metre depth.

(c) It should be a continuous stretch of 50 kms. , the only exception to be made to waterway length is for urban conglomerations and intraport traffic.

(d) (i) It should pass through and serve the interest of more than one State , or

(ii) It should connect a vast and prosperous hinterland and major ports, or

(iii) It should pass through a strategic region where development of navigation is considered necessary to provide logistic support for national security, or

(iv) It should connect places not served by any other mode of transport.

Inland Waterways Authority of India

Several committees set up by the Government of India recommended declaration of important navigable waterways as national waterways and acceleration of their development for promotion of inland water transport in view of its low cost and for securing certain other advantages such as energy efficiency , generation of employment among weaker sections of community and less pollution. The national Transportation Policy Committee also observed that the existing set up of Inland Water Transport Directorate in the Ministry of Shipping and Transport was not geared to undertake and discharge the responsibility for proper development of National Waterways as this was merely an advisory body without any powers to allocate funds for development schemes and their execution. To overcome this difficulty the committee recommended setting up of an independent authority for the development, maintenance and regulation of

National Waterways. The government accordingly introduced a Bill ' The Inland Waterways Authority of India Bill 1985 in Lok Sabha on 28th August 1985 . The Bill was passed by Lok Sabha on 25th November , 1985 and Rajya Sabha on 18th December, 1985 . It was assented to by the President on 30th December , 1985. It proposes to set up an Inland Waterways Authority of India which would be an independent authority for the development, maintenancxe and regulation of National Waterways for shipping and navigation and also to organise studies and investigation on waterways under consideration for declaration as national waterways.

Central Inland Water Transport Corporation

Central Inland Water Transport Corporation was incorporated as a Company on 22nd February, 1967 with an authorised capital of Rs. 4 crores and took over the assets and a few liabilities of the River Steam Navigation Company, PLC (a Sterling Company incorporated under UK Act) under the scheme of Arrangements approved by the High Court of Calcutta on 3rd May, 1967. The Company's authorised capital was Rs. 20 crores with a paid up capital of Rs., 18.90 crores as on 30.9.84.

The activities of the Company are divided into three major Divisions. The River Services Division of the Company carries cargo on Inland Waters of the North Eastern REgion of the country through Bengladesh. The main InlandWater routes operated are (i) Calcutta -Calcutta (ii) Calcutta Karimganj- Calcutta (iii) Calcutta - Gauhati- Haldia- Budge Budge- Calcutta (iv) Haldia-Farakka. Makjor bulk cargoes carried on North Eastern Region are cement, foodgrains like rice and wheat edible oil, jute, tea, bamboo, On Haldia - Calcutta -Farakka route major bulk cargoes carried are oil containers , jute, pulses, stone, chips, fertilizers etc. The Rajabagan Dock-yard undertakes major repairs of Inland vessels, construction of new vessels, and general engineering .

The Deep Sea Ship Repair Division with its units at Calcutta and Port Blair undertakes repairs of sea going vessels and bus body buildings.

In addition to above major works , the Comapny undertakes dredging of river Bhargirathi for Calcutta Port Trust, maintenance of Pandu and Jogighopa Ports. It has recently undertaken development of National Waterways Phase. I, in the Haldia -Farakka stretch of the Ganga -Bhagirathi-Hooghly river system.

With a view to improving the working of the Company, the Dutt Committee and an Inter-Ministerial Study Team for an Indepth Study of CIWTC were constituted by the Government of India during 1982-83 . Based on the recommendations of the Dutt Committee, Division -wise Costs and Profit Centres have been set up with decentralisation of operational, financial and administrative powers.

An Assessment of Inland Waterways

As stated earlier, water transport is a conveninent mode for carrying heavy and bulky goods like coasl timber, brick, etc. The cost of operation is also considerably lower as compared to other means of transport. If planned properly, it can be used to relieve congestion on the Indian railways. The sparesely populated and fragmented areas of this vast country can also be unified through canal and river nevigation.

However, inland waterways suffer a number of disadvantage . Because of their very nature, they can cater to only those cities and towns that lie along their banks. They cannot connect areas where there are no rivers or canals. In Sourthern states where rivers go dry in summers, inland waterways cannot be operated during those days. In addition this mode of transport is extremely slow. Therefore it takes longer time to transport goods from one place to another by inland waterways as compared to other means of transport.

Problems of Water Transport

Main problems of water transport are as follows:

(1)*High cost*-Operating cost of water transport is quite high. Ship building industry in India is not doing well at a desired pace. Therefore, cost of production of Indian ship is quite high.

(2)*Foreign Competition*- Indian shipping companies have to face lot of competition of foreign shipping companies. This problem mainly arised because government (during British period) did not made any effort for the development of Indian shipping, therefore, it could not develop capacity of facing foreign competition.

(3)*Shortage of Ships* - Indian shipping find a great shortage of passenger ships and for the transportation of oil. The ships which are being used for transporting goods have become very old and outdated. These ships urgently need to be replaced.

(4)*Shortage of Foreign Exchange*- On account of shortage of foreign exchange, growth of shipping is facing difficulties. Development of shipping is very much dependent on the availability of foreing exchange.

(5)*Competition* - Rail -Road Transportation creates sufficient competition for the costal transport.

(6)*Labour Problem* - Indian shipping companies have to suffer huse lusses because of frequent strikes of the duck workers.

(7)Shortage of Ports - In India there is great shortage of all types of ports -small , medium and big.

(8)*Skilled Personnel* - Indian shipping is also victim from shortage of efficient and skilled technical personnel.

(9)*Shortage of Finance* - There is lace of sufficient finance shortage of finance has put serious difficulties in the way of rapid expansion of shipping in India.

(10)*Inadequate Hauling Capacity*- Hauling capacity of Indian shipping is inadequate.

****